FROM BARLEY FIELD TO ACADEME

Robert H. Blackburn

© University of Toronto Library 2014
Printed in the U.S.A.

ISBN 978-0-7727-6095-1 (cloth)

Library and Archives Canada Cataloguing in Publication

Blackburn, Robert, 1919–, author
From barley field to academe / Robert H. Blackburn.

Includes bibliographical references.
ISBN 978-0-7727-6095-1 (bound)

1. Blackburn, Robert, 1919–.   2. Academic librarians – Canada – Biography.
3. University of Toronto. Library – Biography.   I. Title.

Z720.B63A3 2014   020.92   C2013-908551-3

Except where otherwise noted, all photographs are courtesy of the author.

Contents

Preface v

Acknowledgments vii

1 Two Sheaves of Oats and a Field of Barley: A Sort of Introduction 3

2 Hard Sledding 9

3 Radio and Other Events 20

4 Victory School 27

5 The Last Six Grades in Four Schools 39

6 Coming through the Barley to University 55

7 California, Here I Thumb 75

8 The English Department 85

9 Preparation for a Career 100

10 Enlistment, Military and Marital 109

11 Navigation Instructor, Portage la Prairie 125

12 Calgary Public Library, and Hail Columbia 143

13 Beginning at the University of Toronto Library 155

iv   Contents

14 Abraham Flexner and His Gift of Travel   165

15 Working with Wallace   182

16 Staffing the Library   192

17 Promoting the Library in the University   204

18 Catalogues and Computers   216

19 Fireworks, 1959 to 1969   230

20 A Sabbatical Year   251

21 Retirement   261

22 Gardens and Fields   280

Works by Robert H. Blackburn   289

Preface

The story of my life is centred around my thirty-four-year career as a librarian at the University of Toronto. My experiences during the twenty-eight years before that, varied as they were and haphazard as they seemed to be, all counted as useful preparation. In the three decades since my official retirement, my life has continued to be enlarged and enriched by those middle years.

Though the story covers three periods, it is not a neat narrative that keeps within those periods, or even within the individual chapters of this book. It is a yarn with many strands, some short and some long enough to reappear from time to time after being entwined with other strands.

My Norwegian grandmother had a knack for stretching a skein of yarn between her two outstretched feet while she whirled her hands, one over the other, winding the skein into a neat round ball before she began knitting anything with it. I did not inherit that talent. This book is knitted directly from a loose skein of memories. I have never kept a diary, except of travels during my one sabbatical year. For a few dates and other details I have referred to previous publications that are listed in my personal list of writings at the end of this book, or to my father's two books, *The Blackburn Story* (1967) and *Land of Promise* (1970). Apart from those bits, I have had to select from a headful of memories – events, names, places, dates – that kept calling to me, wanting to be included.

I have been blessed throughout my life to have had a dear family and good friends, and in the middle years to have been allowed to take part in a period of exciting changes in the size, services and management of university libraries. Blessings are meant to be shared.

Acknowledgments

This book is the result of my former colleague Merrill Distad having suggested, even insisted, that it should be written. I am grateful for his encouragement and advice.

Special thanks must go to my wife Verna, not only for her encouragement, suggestions, and guidance along the way, but mainly for taking upon herself nearly all the chores of housekeeping and gardening during more than two years, to give me a clear window of time for writing and rewriting; otherwise it could not have been done. The book is her doing as much as mine.

Thanks are due also to those who, besides Verna, read through the earliest draft; our friends Gladys Douglas and Victor Shepherd, and my son Rob. And to my son Harry, daughter-in-law Trudy, and stepdaughter Susan who helped at various times, when my computer balked, to get it up and working again.

I am grateful also for the corrections and improvements suggested by two patient editors, first Linda Distad, who went through the text shortly before she died, and then Matthew Kudelka, who went through it again.

Pictures, except those of me and my family, were provided by Linda Sword Cripton, Ilze Bregzis, Joan Esplin, the University of Alberta Archives, and the University of Toronto Archives.

And finally I must thank Larry Alford, my third successor at the University of Toronto Library, for sponsoring this publication, and his assistant Karen Turko for bringing the project to completion.

FROM BARLEY FIELD TO ACADEME

Robert H. Blackburn

1 Two Sheaves of Oats and a Field of Barley: A Sort of Introduction

"You better get that boy all the education he can hold – he'll never make a farmer." So spake my grandfather, an expert horseman, to my father, when he saw me throw down two bundles of oats beside my wagon, as food for my team, and then hurry away to lunch without taking their bridles off so that my horses could eat. It was an important mistake. I was sixteen, and having my first chance to drive one of the bundle-wagons at threshing time. I was about to enter my last year of high school; until then there had been no real thought of my going on to university.

There was one other person who helped, without knowing it, to turn my footsteps toward higher education. She sat across the aisle from me in my last year at Vegreville High, and she had lovely eyes. My parents did not like her nearly as well as I did, but I thought they misjudged her entirely. She was really a very nice girl. And if she seemed lonely it was quite understandable, because the fellow to whom she was engaged was away that year, doing time at the penitentiary.

By the end of that winter my parents had become really anxious to send me away to university, but university was a very faint possibility in Alberta in the dry summer of 1936, in the middle of the Great Depression. I guess it would not have been possible, except for another mistake. One of my jobs that summer was to walk through our fields carrying a scythe and weed poison to be applied to the Canada thistle and sow thistle that were beginning to come in from Ontario, along with foreclosure notices. We had about six hundred acres in crop that year, mostly wheat and oats, but down at the south end of the place we had sown a hundred acres of barley. Barley was supposed to do well in a dry year, but when my thistle patrol took me down to that part of the farm I could find barely any barley at all. There was only a short spear here and there, hidden down among the pigweed and stinkweed.

When I told my father about it he decided to plough that hundred acres under as summer fallow, but we were busy at other things and by mistake let it go until the weeds had gone to seed and it was really too late for ploughing. By then the barley had begun to ripen and there was a bit more of it than I had seen earlier, possibly enough to make it worth harvesting. We debated what to do and arrived at a compromise: Father would buy the parts and binder twine if I would repair an old retired Massey-Harris binder and do the harvesting.

As it turned out, that field yielded one thousand bushels, and barley was worth 24.5 cents a bushel. In those days, $245 was quite a lot of money, but we didn't suppose it would be enough to pay for even one year at university. Then the grain buyer phoned to say that our barley had been tested and found suitable for malting. By some miracle the dry season had given it a special quality that doubled the price. Did we want to sell it as malting barley for 49 cents a bushel? $490! Well, that question posed a moral problem for us. Malting was used in making beer, and beer was a bad word in our house. If we accepted the premium price we would be contributing to the manufacture of beer, but I might be able to go to university. If we stuck to our principles and refused, then I had no hope of going. But then it occurred to me that the grain buyer was a young fellow who was known to like drink, and if we did not collect the premium price he would certainly do so himself, and maybe spend it all on booze that could be his ruination. So out of concern for him we compromised, accepted the premium price, and I went up to Edmonton to university.

The only university graduates we knew were doctors or lawyers, and I registered in what amounted to a pre-medical course. In residence I made the mistake of sitting at a table with several senior medical students. One of them offered to take me through the anatomy lab one day right after lunch; in half an hour he managed to destroy any ambition I had to become a doctor. The next year I switched to an honour course in English literature, which in those days was somewhat less anatomical.

After graduating in English a couple of times (BA and MA), I decided to enlist in the Royal Canadian Air Force. This was another compromise for me, because during the first part of the Second World War I had thought of myself as a conscientious objector. When I finally decided to join up I did not know that Canada would have a rehabilitation scheme after the war to help those who survived, so I thought I should provide my own rehabilitation scheme in advance, in case I survived and needed it. One of my professors had encouraged me to think I might have a future as a writer of fiction, and because authors could not support themselves merely by writing, he advised me to find some easy job with short hours and light work, to leave me plenty of time and energy for writing. I supposed he was talking about university teaching, but not so. It turned out he was thinking of either the permanent army or library work. Given that choice, I chose library work. Neither of us understood that nearly all the writing I would do, for several decades as a librarian, would be done evenings and weekends, and would consist of budgets, annual reports, briefs and proposals of various kinds, budgets, building programs, soft answers to hard letters, budgets, and hardly any fiction. His advice and my acceptance of it were based on what might be called a forty-year misunderstanding. He thought there was a good professional one-year course in librarianship at McGill University, but I found there was one also at Toronto, $50 cheaper, so I compromised and went to Toronto. Being short of money, I was very glad to be given a part-job at the university library.

The Library School in those days was mainly a preparation for public libraries, because many university libraries, including Toronto, seemed to train their own people on the job. So in 1945, after three years as a navigation instructor in the RCAF, I began my library career at the public library in Calgary. The annual salary of $1,300 was not really enough for a man with wife and child, as I was by then, so we ate into our small savings that year. Then my wife Patricia, a librarian who was always a great help and encouragement to me and who knew about the advice my grandfather had given, encouraged me to spend the last bit of our savings on more education. So I registered for the master's course at the Library School at Columbia University.

Refused a US visa unless we could show we had a place to live in New York, we managed to buy an old car and a second-hand house trailer. On the way to Columbia we made a wide detour to make prospecting calls at the public libraries in London and Toronto. In Toronto I made a crucial mistake, one in navigation. Having never driven in that city before, I got mixed up in the traffic around Queen's Park, and late in the afternoon found myself in the circle around the university campus. Since it was probably too late in the day to find Mr Sanderson in his office at the Public Library, I compromised and called on Mr Wallace at the University Library instead. That is how Wallace happened to know that I was still alive and on my way to Columbia, where he wrote to me that December, offering to pay my way to Toronto for an interview. The university had established a new policy requiring every senior officer to have an understudy, so he was obliged to appoint an assistant librarian. Would I be interested? By that time I was looking forward to a career in public libraries, and I had received an offer from London Public at $1,900, but Wallace's offer of $3,500 forced a compromise. I accepted the Toronto offer, thinking to try university work for one year. Later on, when Wallace got to know me better, he told me there had been other compromises besides mine. The university would really have preferred to find an assistant professor for the job, but professorial staff were hard to find just then, so it settled for a librarian instead.

Hugh Langton, former Registrar of the University of Toronto, became Librarian at the beginning of 1892, when the university opened its first separate library building, with a new collection after the great fire of 1890. He was succeeded by a former history professor, Stewart Wallace, in 1923. I succeeded Wallace in 1954, after being his understudy for seven years. When I retired at the end of 1981, the three of us, one after the other, had occupied that office for ninety years to the day. Whatever else the University of Toronto Library may have had, it did have continuity of direction. In this, as far as I know, it may hold the record for North America, maybe for the world.

The events leading up to my appointment as Chief Librarian were deplorably incorrect, probably illegal by today's standards. The position was not advertised, and there was no search committee, nor were there any applications or interviews. President Sidney Smith merely called me one day and offered me the position; I accepted after ascertaining the title and salary. The university now has rather elaborate procedures to be sure that no such mistake will ever be made again. If I had been invited at the time to state my qualifications, the first on my list would have been my seven years of experience as understudy.

If I were to be asked now to say how it was that I was able to remain in office, I would begin by saying I am not more thygmotactic than most other academic administrators. Thygmotactic is not a household word for people who have never had occasion to study the habits of cockroaches or silverfish. It is a word used by biologists to describe creatures that like to be pressed from above and below and thereby squeeze themselves into tight places and stay for long periods; it is a word to be pondered by all administrators. I do not think I am more thygmotactic than most people, but I had a tradition to uphold, and I had the advantage of a rather wide and useful variety of other experiences.

For example, before coming to the library in 1947 I had made my living for a few years as a navigator in the RCAF. We did quite a lot of night flying, without benefit of radar or other fancy electronic aids. We navigated by map reading, which by night was either difficult or impossible. Sometimes we managed by taking bearings on radio stations, though these were notoriously skittish and subject to distortion. Of course we had the timeless stars, moon, and sun to steer by, when we could see them, but we observed them from a very shaky platform. In fact, by the time we had taken three sextant readings and plotted them on a chart, the most we could hope for was to find out approximately where we had been a hundred miles ago. Under those circumstances a navigator learned to make important decisions and alter course with whatever information was at hand, without knowing exactly where he was or precisely which way the wind was blowing, or how the wind might change to blow him off course again. It was excellent training for an academic administrator.

Before that, in my student days, I had some summer jobs that were also quite helpful. One summer I ran a passenger elevator in the Banff Springs Hotel, before the days of self-operated elevators, and the following summer I drove a sightseeing car in the Rocky Mountains. Both these jobs involved taking people up to where they wanted to go and bringing them down again as gently as possible, useful practice for anybody who was to be in charge of a university division in the 1950s and up through the 1960s, and down through the 1970s into the 1980s.

An unexpectedly useful part of my preparation, I now realize, was the summer I worked underground in a copper mine on the West Coast. This was long before the Ham Report on mine safety. Again I was working in the dark, and there is no place darker than two or three thousand feet underground. Each man carried a small carbide lamp on his hard hat, and by its flame had his own dim view of the surroundings, but otherwise we were in the dark. Each miner had a helper, and for several weeks I was helper to a miner who was known simply as the Big Finn. It was said that the Big Finn was known in mines all up and down the coast, from Mexico to Alaska, for his size, strength, and a sort of perpetual rage. He had little English except for a supply of swear words that he used for about eight hours a shift, directed against the world in general and his helper in particular. Whenever anything happened to displease him greatly, which was often, he was given to flinging things around rather indiscriminately; wrenches or shovels or fifty-pound boxes of dynamite would be thrown down and kicked or stamped on. There is a scar on my cheek where he knocked me down one time, accidentally, with the end of a four-foot drill-steel. Whoever worked with the Big Finn soon learned to keep his eyes open and be ready to duck. Whenever I think of him it is with a feeling of gratitude, for he gave me the sort of conditioning and seasoning no academic librarian should be without. After working with the Big Finn, it has seemed comparatively pleasant, most of the time, to work with students, library staff, professors, deans, principals, vice-presidents, and even presidents.

Of course there were stressful times for university presidents and their librarians, especially during the late 1960s and early 1970s when many students across the continent were in revolt and public support for universities was dwindling. In 1971–72 alone, at the eleven largest libraries in the United States, seven directors lost their posts, only one by normal retirement. In 1973 a survey found that half of the largest academic libraries on the continent had changed directors during the previous three years, four of them twice. Before the report could be published, the surveyor himself died. Of the people who represented their universities at the Ontario Council of University Librarians in 1968, nine had resigned before 1978, one had retired, and three were about to do so, leaving only me.

Between 1850, when it was founded, and 1981, when I retired, the University of Toronto had only twelve presidents. It was my privilege to be Chief Librarian under six of those twelve. My time in that position was an important part of my life, given to me by a long string of mistakes, misunderstandings, and miracles that began with two sheaves of oats and a field of barley.

2 Hard Sledding

My mother's parents, the Olsons, were married in the great Nideros medieval cathedral in Trondheim, Norway, in 1878, just before setting sail for America on their honeymoon. They pioneered in Minnesota (sod hut) and South Dakota (prosperous farm) and then in orchard country in the State of Washington. In 1905, when their two sons were close to twenty years old and ready to think about having farms of their own, the family finally settled comfortably on two farms close together in a Scandinavian district near Ryley, Alberta. My mother, Palma, then seventeen, was the youngest of four surviving children.

My father John Blackburn's family moved to a farm in the same district in 1911 from Chicago, where my grandfather's business had failed. In 1917 my father volunteered for military service but was rejected. That summer, at age twenty-two, he became engaged to Palma Olson. He also bought a farm of 640 acres, south of Lavoy, about fourteen miles from Vegreville, and moved there in October with a large herd of cattle.

In December he hired a man to tend the cattle while he took the train to Edmonton, to meet Palma there and to be married. A few days later the hired man met them in Vegreville, where they stocked up on groceries and household supplies. On the way home, bundled up in robes and horse blankets, they passed over a large snowdrift that upset the sleigh, dumping the occupants and their baggage, supplies, and groceries, all to be gathered up out of the deep snow before they could go on. The body of the sleigh would have been an ordinary wagon box, not an easy thing to set right. They got home after dark without further mishap. There is no record of the joyful bride being carried over the threshold of her new home.

By the following spring, Canada's military requirements had changed, and my father received notice to report for duty, an unexpected interruption of the plans they had made. He was allowed a short time to put his affairs in order, and was posted to Toronto for training in the Royal Flying Corps of the British Army, in which the mortality rate for aviators was very high. My mother went home to live with her family during his absence, however long that might be. Fortunately, the war ended in November, and he received a discharge in time for them to be back home together for Christmas on their farm. It was only a few weeks before I was due to enter the world.

At the beginning of February 1919, when my mother felt that I was getting ready to be born, the roads were drifted too deep for safe travel with team and sleigh. The fourteen-mile sleigh ride to the small hospital in Vegreville was mostly cross-country, over stubble fields and open range. My father could not wait with her in Vegreville, on such short notice, because he had about a hundred head of cattle to feed and water.

At that time the telephone line had not yet reached our district, and there was no mail delivery. But Hark Morris, the nearest neighbour, was at the hospital with his wife and newborn first son, awaiting permission for them all to go home; he would carry any news there might be before they left Vegreville. The next day, as my father walked out to the mailbox to look for a message, he saw the Morris sleigh approaching, and received a shouted message that he, too, had a son, and that mother and child were in good health.

Childhood memories are bound to be mixed with and framed in information that is learned later, and edited by the passage of time, but I have a few that are vivid and that reflect a time quite outside the experience of modern readers. One of my earliest is of being praised by my Aunt Nora Olson in her house near Ryley. It was after breakfast. I was in my sleepers, in a high chair at the end of the table, and there were Christmas decorations. I had just finished reciting the story of the Gingerbread Man, who was pursued by a long line of people and animals as he kept calling, "Run, run as fast as you can! You can't catch me, I'm the Gingerbread Man"; but the fox did catch him and ate him up, bit by bit. Aunt Nora praised my performance. But when Grandmother Olson thought there had been enough said, she stood me on a chair beside the heater, took off my sleepers and rubbed my chest with turpentine and goose grease to cure my cold. Her hands were scratchy after years of bare-handed scrubbing.

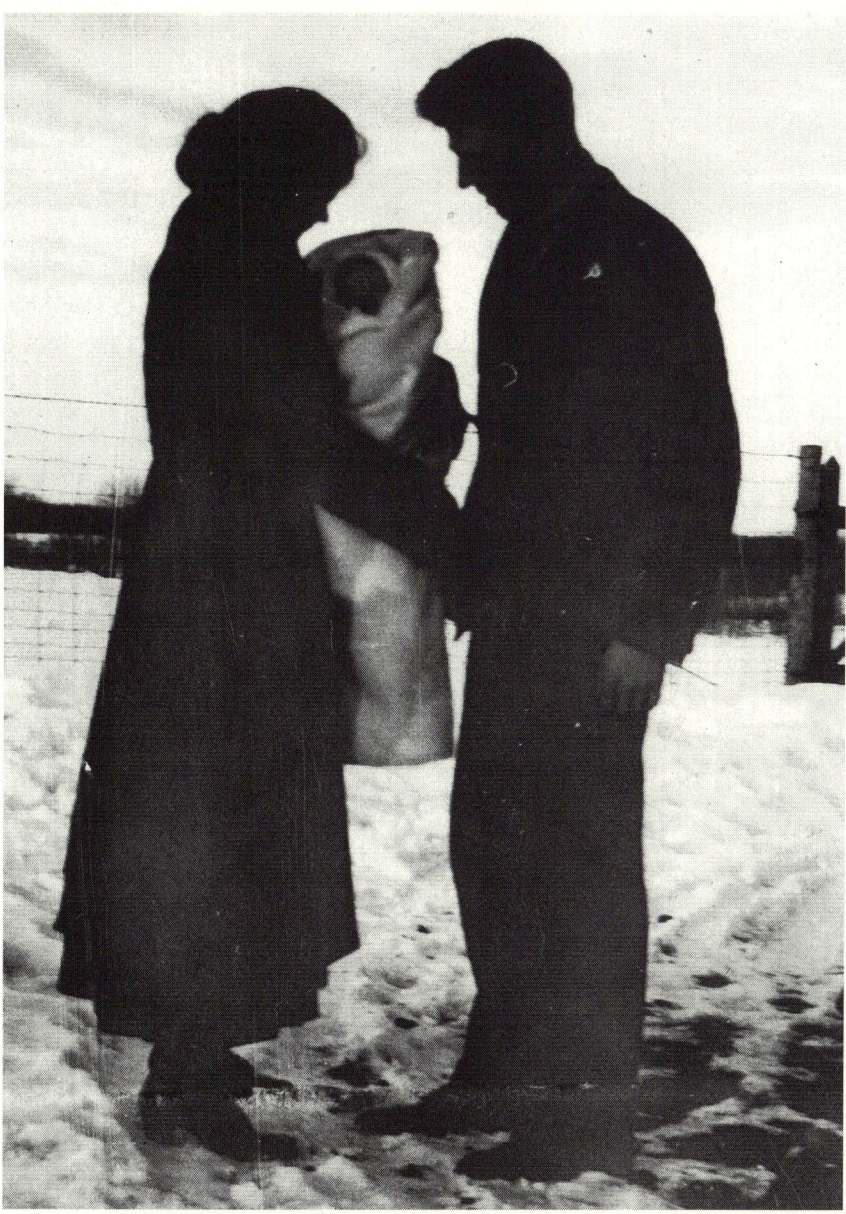

My first picture, a silhouette of my parents bowing over me, evocative of parenthood and place, taken by a novice who failed to adjust the time-setting on the camera.

I remember being on the midnight train with my mother when I was two. We sat close to the window and watched the lights of Edmonton getting closer. I stayed at her sister's big house, and from the upstairs window could look down into the backyard and watch the chickens around a yellow shed. They were grey, not red like ours at home. And my aunt took me to the hospital to see my newborn sister, Marian.

When I was three, Grandmother Olson gave us a Model T Ford so that we could visit her now and then in the summer when the roads were good. By that time we had a party-line telephone, but Ryley was long-distance. Long-distance calls were reserved for emergencies and had to go through the operator, Dr Arthur in Lavoy.

That summer my father had an operation and for a few days after getting home was too sore to do any work. One afternoon he was sitting in our "other room" in a rocking chair with me in his lap. Without warning I vomited on myself and on his striped bathrobe. Mother felt my head, found I had a fever, and put me to bed. Father called Dr Arthur in Lavoy, who came and said I had cholera infantum and that I should drink nothing but distilled water and eat nothing but eight dry cornflakes a day. I remember the flat taste of the water and still shudder at the taste of dry corn flakes. After two or three days, my fever had not abated and I was very weak. My father was alarmed when he saw that I did not bother to brush off a fly that walked across my face. Still very sore himself, he limped out to the car and drove six miles to his father's house, from which he could call Dr Reid in Vegreville without calling through Dr Arthur at the Lavoy exchange.

I remember nothing about my recovery, except that when my permanent teeth came in, the front four had fever dents that were visible until I had them filled fifty years later.

One day while my sister and I were little, Mother kept us strictly in the house because of the roundup. She watched with us as a large herd of red cattle passed within a few feet of our west window. We had been told they were coming and that those with horns might be dangerous.

There must have been two or three riders herding them, but what amazed me was the sight of my great-uncle Oliver Cromwell Blackburn riding past in his city clothes, on our own saddle horse, resting his big belly on the front of our old saddle from which the horn was fortunately missing. We knew that some of the cattle were ours, but most of them belonged to Uncle Ol. Early in the century he had come up from Kansas, rented a team and buckboard in Edmonton, and with his brother

Tom made a wide circuit to the south and east, buying several farms along the way. In fact it was to one of those farms that my grandfather had moved from Chicago. Uncle Ol had brought several Mennonite farmers from Kansas as good renters for most of his farms. He also had about two thousand acres of grassland a few miles to the south of us and used to place a large herd of cattle there to graze in summer, to be rounded up in the fall and driven to the stockyard in Lavoy. On the occasion I remember, he stopped them on the way to market, to be fed, watered, and rested in our corral.

My sister and I were always glad to see Uncle Ol when he stopped at our place in the course of his round of visits to his renters. He usually brought two or three prairie chickens he had shot along the way. He always had a loaded shotgun standing ready in his Model T, and there was a hole in the roof where he had hit a rut that jarred the trigger. Waiting for supper, he would sit in the kitchen with his knees wide, his gold watch chain between the upper pockets of his vest, and a few peppermints for us to find in the lower pockets. He would sometimes play at making faces to frighten us, with his upper teeth turned upside down to show the black false gums.

When I was nearly five we went to the Christmas concert at the Baptist church in Lavoy. My sister must have been left at home with the hired girl. My father's family was Presbyterian, my mother's Lutheran, and this was my first experience of church. It was a long concert interspersed with telephone calls from Santa Claus to the minister who was master of ceremonies. Finally Santa arrived with a jingle of bells and sack of treats "for every good little boy and girl here!" Children were called forward by name, each to receive a small bag of goodies, while I waited more and more anxiously. Through some misunderstanding my name was not called, and Santa trotted out. I was overwhelmed by feelings of disappointment, shame, and guilt, but was comforted by Rosie Bricker, the seven-year-old daughter of our Jewish storekeeper. She leaned over the pew in front of us and insisted that I have her bag.

My first regular childhood chore, when I was about four years old, was to feed the chickens, fill their trough with milk or water, and gather the eggs. The little chicks, still in a small pen with their mothers, received cottage cheese. The rest of the flock received a daily ration of broken grains and weed seeds, waste from the threshing machine and fanning mill. Before scattering it for them I sometimes sat on the old chopping block with a handful, coaxing them (unsuccessfully) to eat out of my hand. Usually I just scattered the feed on the ground and watched for a long time as they picked it up or scratched for it, raising their heads now and then to turn a wary eye in my direction.

When airmail was first begun in Alberta there was a special flight northward, by which my cousin Glenn Olson once sent me a letter from Ryley via Aklavik on the Arctic Ocean. One of the regular mail routes eastward from Edmonton followed the Grand Trunk Railway line, some miles south of us. I would hear the faint hum of the airplane motor and see a black speck moving eastward, one or two degrees above the horizon. The chickens, scattered all over the yard, also heard it and ran to the safety of the chicken house, clucking their alarm at what they must have thought was some kind of hawk. That was more than 85 chicken generations ago; I don't suppose modern birds pay any attention to passing aircraft. That many human generations would take us back to before the days of Julius Caesar.

Farmhouse and Farmyard

The house, when my father bought it, was a small rectangular cottage with three rooms in a row: kitchen on the west, bedroom on the east, and a middle room. About four years later my father, with the help of a neighbour, built an addition that consisted of a large new kitchen and a screened back porch. The porch had a pump in the centre over a newly bored well, a great labour saver. The kitchen had a doorway into the old middle room; on the night it was finished, Father held me up in my nightgown to look through into the new empty room in which the pine floor had been oiled and could not be walked on until next day.

Two or three years later there was a second addition that gave the house its final form: four bedrooms, three clothes closets, kitchen, back porch, and front room opening onto a front porch that had corner posts supporting a porch roof.

The whole building sat on a concrete foundation, but the cellar, reached by way of steps down from a trap door in the kitchen floor, had earth walls and an earth floor. The house walls had no insulation between the board siding and the inside lath-and-plaster. In winter there was some insulation at floor level. Before snowfall a three-foot width of tarpaper was wrapped around the siding at ground level, tacked with lath at the top. Then loads of fresh barnyard manure were banked against the tarpaper. This was more than a shield against the cold, as composting of the manure was a source of slow heat.

My Grandmother Olson knitting on our new front porch.

At an auction sale, Father had bought a large kitchen stove and large round heater. During the second round of construction the heater was moved from the front room to the cellar and encased in a tin-and-asbestos jacket topped with a deep heat-reservoir of sand. Pipes led from there to hot-air registers and cold-air returns in every room of the house except the old bedroom and the kitchen. The kitchen had its own heat from the cookstove and a wide L of stovepipe wired up beneath the ceiling.

The kitchen was the biggest room, but quite unlike a modern kitchen. Being without electricity or plumbing, it had no sink, no refrigerator. The cookstove had six round iron lids with different heats, the two over the firebox being hottest. On one side was a hot-water reservoir, and above was a warming oven big enough to hold half a dozen loaves of bread-dough to rise overnight. There was a woodbox, a coal scuttle, and a box for overshoes under a row of coat hooks. There was a washstand with a water pail, washbasin, and slop buckets. There was a hand-cranked cream separator, a cream can, a round wooden churn, and a large wooden bowl that my Grandfather Olson had carved, the bowl in which butter was separated from buttermilk. There was a three-shelf dumb waiter that could be pulled up from the cool cellar. There was a blackboard on which the children learned their letters and numbers and played games. The Winnipeg couch was for a short rest, a sick child, or a bed for a guest. Two large cabinets had zinc counters for work space, and the one that my father made had a tip-out bin that held a hundred pounds of flour. There was a foot-pedal sewing machine; Mother was an expert seamstress, and some of the clothes she made there are in the Clothing Museum at the University of Alberta.

In the middle of the kitchen was a round pedestal table that could be extended with boards to seat ten people at harvest time or for other special occasions. Over the centre of the table hung our principal light, first a kerosene mantel lamp, later a gasoline one, far brighter than the kerosene wick lamps that we carried into the other rooms. Thus the table was the centre of family life, from after chores until bedtime. This was before electricity in nearly every house, with its lights and other manifestations in every room, exerted a centrifugal force on family life, scattering family members all through the house except perhaps at mealtimes.

Of course the kitchen, the only source of warm water, was also the room in which baths were taken. Baths were usually on Saturday night so that we were clean for Sunday's day of rest. Bathing was done in a tin laundry tub set on a rug near the stove, with soap and towel nearby on a chair. Even with water limited to a few inches in the tub, there was not enough warm water for everybody to have fresh water; there had to be some sharing. We had heard about a British Order of the Bath, but the prairies order of the bath was said to be "first Ma, then Pa, then the kids and then the hired girl."

The front room was much smaller than the kitchen but had space for the piano and for a large oak writing table at which my father often sat on stormy days in winter, figuring accounts or writing letters. He sometimes acted as a scribe for neighbours who needed help in filling out forms or replying to notices. He once composed a marriage proposal for a young fellow who could neither write nor think of the right words; some time later he received a letter of thanks from the bride, who wrote with very uncertain hand and signed her letter with OXOXO for hugs and kisses. And one winter he sat at that table writing a series of airplane stories that he hoped to sell to *Saturday Evening Post*, for which he had been a delivery boy in Chicago. The front room had space also for a pair of oak armchairs with leather seats, and a three-shelf bookcase with retractable glass doors. After the round heater was moved to the cellar there was room for three or four tables of bridge. Quite a changed house since the night my mother came to it as a bride!

All our rooms, walls and ceilings, were coated with cream coloured kalsomine. The front room had a varnished picture rail. At the same level the kitchen had a narrow floral border, painted with the aid of a pasteboard stencil made by my mother, just for pretty. She had painted the outside walls of the house a pale yellow, with white trim. All the outbuildings except the barn were dark red. When Father balked at the cost of paint for the barn, Grandmother Olson gave him her Norwegian recipe – buttermilk and red ochre – that turned out to be a good match. Much later, when I was old enough to help, the cedar shingles on all the roofs were stained with lampblack and crankcase oil.

Our farmyard was a square area fenced with barbed wire, eight or ten acres halfway along the north side of our 640-acre section. The barbed-wire gate, near the middle of the north side, opened to a lane that passed the house, toward the barnyard. Along the west side of the lane was a clump of poplars, trembling aspen, where I learned to climb trees. Eventually I built a rustic chair and hammock there, so rough that Mother refused even to try them. In the early days the east side of the lane had a short growth of bush, mostly diamond willow and silver willow. Later the bush was cleared to make way for a small field between house and road, seeded to brome grass for the horses. The brome field sloped down toward the corner by the road into a dip that became a slough when snow melted. One spring, when the slough was more than a foot deep, cold weather returned and froze the surface deep enough for me to skate on it for a week or two. The ice had not a ripple or crack, and I spent part of my time on my knees, looking down at the movement of the underwater life, beetles and tadpoles, and mosquito wigglers swimming up end-over-end for a sip of air just under the ice.

Our house faced north, about a hundred yards from the road. Other buildings were not placed close to it, or to each other, perhaps as a precaution against fire. The chicken house, west of our house and near the west fence, was a low, floorless, two-room shack with a wide cloth window that was covered in winter with a solid shutter that hinged upward. The first room had a roosting rack that hinged upward to allow for cleaning. The back room was for feeding and nesting, and there was a small feed bin attached to the far end. South of the chicken house was the granary with a large bin at each end, each with a trap door at wagon-top height. Between the end bins was a narrower one with a door facing the house; when it was empty in the fall, men hired for the harvest made their beds there with straw and horse blankets.

South of the house, past the woodpile, was a workshop with bench, tools, and racks of harness and other things waiting to be repaired on rainy days. At the far end of the workshop was a small granary, the usual bedroom for a single hired man when it had no grain in it. Beyond that building was the horse barn with a gable roof over the hayloft. It had a central aisle between the mangers, with three double stalls on each side and a ladder to the hole through which hay could be thrown down. Just outside the door to this aisle was a lean-to bin for chopped oats.

Along the south wall of the horse barn was the cow barn that my father had built with the help of a Ukrainian hired man. The walls were rows of upright poplar poles, with sticks nailed across them, and thoroughly plastered with a mixture of straw, cow dung, and white clay from a sticky patch of gumbo in the pasture. The roof, too, was of poplar poles, covered with a thick layer of straw that was not entirely waterproof. It was a very rough structure with mangers and a half-floor also of poplar poles, but the cows did not seem to mind.

The barn formed the northwest corner of the corral. At the southwest corner was the forty-foot steel windmill to pump water into the round wooden water tank, about twelve feet in diameter, the wooden sides about two feet high. The tank was half within the corral, half within the feedlot, so that several animals could drink at the same time. Father had rigged a wooden float in it, fixed to a lever that would turn the windmill off when the tank was full and turn it on when the water got low. There was a drilled well that never went dry.

The rectangular corral enclosing the barnyard was big enough to hold more than a hundred cattle. It was built of poplar rails nailed horizontally to tamarack posts, which were resistant to rot. The top rail was at least five feet from the ground and strong enough to be steady when I was old enough to walk distances along it, between the long wooden gates. There was one gate beside the barn, facing the house, one beside the windmill opening to the fields on the west half-section, and one beside the water tank, opening the way through the feedlot and pasture to the east half. West of the barn, by the end of summer, there would be two long haystacks and at least one of "green feed," that is, bundles of oats cut before ripening from the sloughs and potholes that had been too wet for planting when the regular crops were sown.

Just outside the corral fence, on the east side, was a small enclosure that led into the branding chute. It was a narrow, box-like passage just wide enough for one animal to enter and then be immobilized, pressed tightly against a side that was hinged at the bottom. The animal's head protruded through the front end of the contraption and was held steady there. In that position yearling cattle, one at a time while others waited, were marked with our brand (J upright and J upside down) with a red-hot branding iron. Then the animal was dehorned with a large two-handled cleaver. And then the males were castrated. The whole operation took ten minutes or less. When it was over and the chute opened, the poor critter would stumble out, stunned and bleeding. Years later I used to be reminded of this scenario as I sat among dignitaries on the platform of Convocation Hall at the University of Toronto, watching the line of graduating students come forward, one at a time, having the hood looped over the head, kneeling on the stool, holding hands in a steeple to be touched by the Chancellor as he repeated the four magic words in Latin, then rising from the stool and stepping away rather unsteadily with a rather bewildered look, newly branded.

3 Radio and Other Events

In 1920 my father played a part in having the provincial telephone authority install a rural party line in our district around Lavoy. I was only one year old then and so cannot remember a time when there was not a phone mounted on the front wall of our "other room." The phone was an oblong oak box, its long face having two round bells for eyes, a long black nose to speak into, a wide pencil shelf for a mouth, and ears represented by the crank on one side and the black bell-shaped receiver hanging on the other. It served as company and convenience at ordinary times and as help in any kind of emergency. Our road had its row of telephone poles connected by two wires hung on glass insulators that were forbidden but tempting targets for boys with slingshots. Our ring was one long and three shorts, and we heard it fairly often. At that time our district knew nothing of radio.

When I was five years old my Uncle Ralph phoned from Ryley to say he was coming for Christmas and would bring his radio. We were excited. Mother spread the news over the party line. Our neighbour Fanny Morris, on hearing it, asked what a radio was. Mother said she didn't know exactly, but thought it was something like a telephone without wires. And Fanny replied, "Well, I guess that means we'll have to be careful what we say around the house!"

Uncle Ralph's radio was a wonder. It was half the size of an apple box, with a row of large bulbous glass tubes at the back and at least three knobs in front, two for tuning and one for volume. It had to be connected to a car battery and there was a long copper wire as aerial to string around the room. Two rather heavy headsets, adjustable for size, plugged into it for listening. Each headset had two rather large earphones snapped into it, but they could also be snapped out so that each set could be shared by two people sitting close together.

For several evenings in Christmas week, neighbouring families were invited in to listen and be amazed. As master of ceremonies, tuning from one station to another, my father needed one headset while the visitors took turns, moving up toward the radio and sharing the other headset. The listeners were suitably impressed, all except old Mrs Slack, who declared that "nobody will ever get one of them halters over my head." Before the end of the week, Father got the idea of placing the earphones in a large chinaware pitcher, part of an old bedroom set, and turning up the volume to maximum. The pitcher could sit in the middle of the room, and everybody could hear programs well enough without any halters.

Within the next month or so we got our own radio, and took it along with us when we visited cousins the next Christmas. We went by sleigh, of course, because the car was not much use in winter even if the roads were passable; the radiator had to be drained and battery kept in the kitchen to prevent it from freezing. Starting a car became quite a chore: the radiator had to be filled carefully with warm water, but not too hot or it would cause a crack. The battery had to be taken outside and installed, and the engine cranked by hand. If the crank did not do the job, then a team of horses had to be harnessed and hitched on to the car and driven in a wide circle around the yard until the motor started. And while the car was out, it had to be cranked and started every couple of hours to keep the motor warm. It was much easier just to hitch a team to the sleigh, in which there was plenty of room for blankets with a charcoal foot warmer underneath, and maybe one or two warm rocks.

Father was keeping a list of the radio stations he could reach, besides CJCA and the university station in Edmonton. I remember standing with him on the sidewalk in Lavoy, in the rain, waiting for him to finish comparing his list with a neighbour's list. Salt Lake City, Denver, Cincinnati, and Oakland were standard fare, but there were others more remote. At Bricker's general store we heard a new satiric phonograph record called *Tuning In*; it alternated snippets of different imaginary programs with the usual screeches and howls of the tuning process. The part I remember was a mock story for children, ending with "so the powerful elephant dashed the roaring lion to the ground, and there was bloo-oo-ood for blocks around. Good night kiddies, pleasant dreams!"

To improve reception, Dad strung a long aerial from our house to the workshop, each end held up by a sixteen-foot plank anchored to each building, with a long pole bolted to it for additional height. We watched fearfully as he leaned the extension ladder against the pole and climbed up to the top to fasten the wire to insulators, but he was determined to do it. The radio had quickly become an important member of the family, with programs of music, news, drama, and comedy. My sister and I listened regularly to the friendly voice of "The Farmer," who played catchy songs and read stories, letters, and birthday greetings to children, including us.

We traded that first radio for a larger cabinet model. It had a walnut case with latticework and silk in front of the loudspeaker. It even had its own storage batteries. And it had three tuning dials that had to be perfectly synchronized for good reception. I used to lie with my head under the radio on Saturday nights, when I was allowed to stay up past nine o'clock to listen to *Hockey Night in Canada*. Even at my grandfather's house there soon was a radio, and Father's long-standing custom of reading aloud to us there on Sunday afternoons had to be modified to accommodate *Amos and Andy*, *Eddie Cantor*, and *Fibber McGee and Molly*. And we heard some of Aunt Lila's favourite music programs: the Boston Pops, Galli-Curci, Menuhin, and Paderewski.

In those days, and for many years, the federal government collected an annual fee for each receiving set to help support the new national broadcasting system. Nobody that I knew had more than one radio in the house. Only gradually have various kinds of radios multiplied and proliferated until they are everywhere: in almost any room of the house, in cars, in farm tractors, in alarm clocks, in our pockets, in outer space, and in surveillance devices. It has almost reached the stage imagined by our neighbour Fanny Morris, when we must be careful what we say around the house.

The year of our first radio, 1925, was memorable in many ways. Threshing had been interrupted by rain and early snow the previous fall, but the sheaves had dried under the snow and were now pulled out for winter threshing. Most of our horses and some cattle were wintered in the fields, around the straw stacks, and they would eat into the stacks. Sometimes a stack, after too much of this, would topple and cover a beast. We had lost a few cattle that way, and that winter we also lost a clumsy young horse we called Sparkplug, after Barney Google's horse in the funny papers. We were sorry to lose him, but his large black hide, properly tanned, served us well on many winter trips.

In March my father had a carpenter/neighbour help him build a tenant house, because single hired men were floaters who could leave whenever they got tired of living in a granary. The house was two rooms, one above the other. My father's book says they were twelve by fourteen feet, and the construction costs, apart from his own work, were $160 for lumber and hardware, $40 for the carpenter. The first tenants were Harry Pilgrim and his wife. Just as they were moving in, Uncle Ol surprised us by driving up in a shiny new green Essex, with glass windows and what were called "balloon tires." There were already scratches along the sides of the car, from chasing cattle through the bush.

One afternoon in May, Marian and I were sent across the road and along a path through a pasture to play with the Morris children, who were just our ages. As we left our house the hired girl was hanging a sheet high up in the windmill, as a signal for my father to come in from his work in the field. We had supper with the Morrises, with bread and black currant sauce for dessert. When Father came to take us home he said that Dr Reid had come out from Vegreville and that we had a baby brother, named Harold. Mother wrote to our Aunt Lila, who was spending the year in California for her health, that delivery at home was so much easier than in hospital. Mrs Pilgrim, the red-haired wife in our tenant house, was a nurse, and there was also a hired girl to help with the housework.

Our mile-square farm had a foot-deep layer of good black earth. My parents had expected to pay off the mortgage in three or four years but had lost the first three crops to hail, drought, and frost. The next four years had been more hopeful; the yield had been fairly good, and new land had been broken, raising the total to nearly 600 acres under cultivation.

In the spring of 1925 the crops looked very promising. The wheat, knee-high, was in the shot blade, preparing to make heads. Then, on the afternoon of 18 June, there was a heavy hailstorm. Mother was working in the garden, with the children, when she saw it coming. She sent me to turn off the windmill and chain open the corral gate that led to the pasture. Father and the hired man were out on the east half with the wagon, mending fence. Watching from the back porch, we saw them racing the team through the pasture, trying to get in before the storm hit. They were almost in time. The horses squeezed through the barn door with the neck-yoke still between them, the men following close behind. Hailstones the size of pullet eggs were bouncing helter-skelter and soon covered the ground. When the storm had passed, there were broken windows. And as the hail melted, we saw that the fields were black mud, the wheat broken off and pounded into it. After we had walked out into the field for a look, Father said for me to get a couple of milk pails and help him gather enough hailstones, along the side of the barn, to make ice cream. As it turned out, the storm was followed by hot weather that brought new growth up from the roots, and there was something after all for a late harvest.

That spring my father had bought a new tractor. He built a drive shed for it, high enough for the threshing machine and long enough to hold the fanning mill in which seed grain was cleaned, the large circular saw with which poplar poles were cut into firewood, and the grinder in which oats became chop for the horses and in which wheat was ground for our porridge and for Mother's bread making.

That July Father helped dig the basement for a community hall in Lavoy. His part of the work was with a team of horses hitched to a "slip," a large scoop that could take a large bite of earth, haul it out, and then dump it when a handle was lifted at the back of the scoop. When the hall was finished it became a place for Friday night dances, concerts, and events of all sorts. It served also as a place for services of the newly organized United Church congregation, which moved later into its own building – another project in which Father played a prominent part.

In the summer of 1925, Mother and the children spent a couple of weeks with our relatives near Ryley. Grandmother Olson had been to California and had brought home with her a thing for her rheumatism. It was a shining oak box, about ten inches each way, with a dial on top, two covered wires plugged into it, and a black handle on each wire. She let us play with it. One of us would turn the dial up slowly while the others sat in a circle, holding hands, the child at each end holding a black handle. As the dial was turned, those in the circle felt the tingle of electricity increase until somebody could stand it no longer and broke the circle. That child dropped out and the test repeated until only one child was left, the winner!

One afternoon Aunt Nora took Mother to Tofield for some shopping and they came home with their hair bobbed. We hardly recognized them without the braids and buns that we had always known, and I wept. By letter, Mother compared hairdos with Aunt Lila in California. Apparently hairdo liberation was sweeping the continent, maybe the world.

That same summer we attended some parts of the week-long Chautauqua program under a big tent in Vegreville. We saw a magician, a play, and Vilhjalmar Stefansson showing his magic lantern slides of his travels by dog team in the Arctic. There was also a lecture on liquid air, with demonstrations. First, a small amount of liquid air was poured

My mother with my brother Harold and sister Marian and me, and the Model T.

from a flask into a goldfish bowl; the fish froze solid but gradually came to life again. Next, a lump of frozen air was dropped into a small empty tea kettle, the kettle placed on a block of ice, and white vapour streamed out of the spout. A somewhat observant old farmer sitting behind us objected that "his water was boiling before he put it on the ice!"

It had been arranged that we would meet my Blackburn grandparents at the Chautauqua and that I would go home with them for a week's visit. But the visit was cut short after I cut into a watermelon without permission, and played a joke on Grandmother by locking her in the unlighted cellar for a short while.

The radio, the new tenant house, the baby brother, the new tractor, bobbed hair, balloon tires, the community hall, and other events of 1925 were capped, for me, by the fact that in September I started school.

4 Victory School

Somewhere there is a snapshot of me setting off to school for the first time, in September 1925. There I stand at age six-and-a-half, in my long stockings, knee pants, new jacket and cloth cap, pencil box, new scribbler, and lunch pail in hand, squinting into the morning sun beside my little sister, with the dog and cat that Mother had summoned for the occasion. There is the chicken house in the background, and nothing to suggest that this was the beginning of more than eighteen years of school for me.

I suppose that Victory School, the one-room schoolhouse in which I took my first ten grades, was typical of most of the schools on the Canadian prairies in the 1920s, but it was certainly different from the schools that my children and grandchildren and great-grandchildren have attended. It was set in the middle of a schoolyard about two hundred yards square, across a road allowance from the teacher's two-room "residence." The main building was twenty-six feet long and nineteen-and-a-half wide, inside measurements that were confirmed once every year when a certain class reached that part of its arithmetic lessons. Stuck out like ears on each side, at the back, farthest from the road, were the vestibules, one for the boys and one for the girls, with three or four steps leading up to them. Out in the yard, a pump with a long wooden handle was the source of our water supply. Behind the school was a shed for wood and coal, its door askew for some years because one of the lady teachers was an amateur driver. Up the slope at the back fence, far apart, were the two outhouses. And in one of the back corners of the yard was the barn, big enough for six or eight horses, because some of the children had to come more than three miles.

In the schoolroom, light was provided by a row of large windows along the east wall. The teacher's desk was at the front in the left-hand corner, beside the windows. In the right-hand corner was the bookcase, the shelves occupied by supplies of chalk, erasers, ink, and some textbooks, as well as a much-used bird book, an atlas, a dictionary, a row of donated red-bound volumes of *Makers of Canada*, unused, and a portable globe on which the pink of the British Empire was much in evidence. Above the blackboards, across the front and along the wall facing the window, were a Union Jack and several roll-up maps. At the back was a large round convection heater surrounded by a black metal jacket about five feet high and four feet across, beside the woodbox and coal scuttles. The tan ceiling above it had a big patch of blue in memory of a large ink bottle that had blown its cork after being set to thaw on the screen above the stove.

The four or five rows of desks were all single, each top with its pencil groove and inkwell, a shelf for a scribbler underneath, and the seat with a drawer under it. They were graduated in size, the smallest at the front for the little children. To the space in front of the desks, between the teacher's desk and the bookcase, each junior class would be called up about twice a day to stand in a row and have its lesson in reading, writing, arithmetic, or memory work. There were always poems to be memorized, all the way from nursery rhymes up to Browning and a Psalm or two; after hearing them recited year after year for eight or ten years, we had them pretty well welded into our heads forever.

My father had been secretary of the small committee that had arranged for the school to be built in 1919, the year I was born. Our house was the closest one to the school. It was only half a mile west of our gate, and at age four or five I used to wait at the gate in the afternoon for all the eastbound kids to come past on their way home. There would be maybe a dozen of them, all ages, a noisy, slow-moving group, bickering, laughing, and on the lookout for fun, sometimes stopping to fill their lunch pails from the ditch, then pouring a deluge down a gopher hole and waiting in a ring, waiting for the gopher to come up and be clubbed. One very muddy spring day, when they stopped at our gate, some of the big guys skidded their shoes in the muddy road to show how slippery it was, and said they needed me to get them some nails for grips. Being eager to please them, I ran up to our workshop and ran back with a handful of shingle nails. They told me those were too small, they needed really big nails. So I ran back and got a handful of spikes, and ran out again to be met with shouts of "April fool!" Back at the house, Mother laughed and explained what they had done to me.

On the first day of school, after she had assigned the older children to their tasks, the teacher called the three of us who were in grade one up to the front. After inviting us to say our names, and to print them if we could, she had us count our buttons, to see who had the most. The winner was the boy who included his belly button in the count. And so the process of schooling began.

We soon learned the routine. Each day began with a good-morning song:

Good morning to you! Good morning to you!
We're all in our places with sunshiny faces
For this is the way to start a new day!

Then there was the Lord's Prayer in unison, and the roll call, before work could begin. Higher grades would be assigned their own work, a section of textbook to study or a set of problems waiting for them on the blackboard; their work would be gone over with the teacher later in the day after the lower classes had been called to the front, in turn, and sent back to their seats with tasks to do.

The system put a very heavy load on the teacher, but it worked well in those days for those of us who could learn to study by ourselves, and while the whole school had an English-speaking background. It presented problems, later, when some children arrived with little or no English. In the fourteen families represented in the school in those early days, none of the parents had been born in Alberta. Three of the families had come from Ontario, one from British Columbia, one from England, and all the rest, I think, from the United States as my own parents had. The children were all first-generation Albertans, and most of us first-generation Canadians. Four families were of German background, one Swedish, one Norwegian, but all had English. About 1930 the first Ukrainian family arrived with three boys of school age, the youngest with no English at all. By the time my younger sister Betty started school there in 1936, she was one of only two or three non-Ukrainian pupils in the school.

Eventually, when school districts were consolidated, Victory School was closed and the building bought by one of my former classmates, who hauled it away to use as a granary. In its day the building and its grounds had served not only as a school but also as a community centre for meetings, dances, card parties, and picnics; now the school site, like the site of our own farm buildings, is only a small undifferentiated part of a large grain field, farmed by the heavy machinery of a Hutterite settlement that has all its buildings in a village some miles to the south.

But I must go back to my beginning at school, and what school life was in those days. My first teacher was Miss Hill, who lived at home and came to school on horseback, about five miles each way. She must have set out early, in winter, to light the stove and have the room warm enough to begin classes. Or maybe she lived in the teacher's residence across the road allowance during the winter. Then there was Walter Dinwoodie, a nephew of our neighbour Fanny Morris. He was eighteen years old and had been to a summer course at Normal School, to become a teacher. He had black wavy hair and a quick laugh, and came out at noon to play games with us or be the referee. Our favourite game was soccer, with four sticks of firewood set up as goalposts. Our ball had a rubber bladder inside it that sometimes leaked and had to be repaired, and had to be pumped up through its neck, and then the ball relaced. Most of the games we played were very competitive, and sides were chosen each day, including all the boys and girls, big and little. Even the little ones could manage now and then to get a kick at the ball, or a turn at bat, or a swat at the can. The boys sometimes played shinny, a kind of field hockey played with willow sticks and a tin can that had to be replaced when it became too battered and sharp-edged. These games we could play even in winter, in the dry snow that soon became packed.

There were many other running games: prisoner's base, pump-pump-pullaway, run-sheep-run, anti-I-over, hide-and-seek, and sometimes hare-and-hound, where the two hares were given a five-minute start to lay a trail of paper bits through the hilly woodland of poplar and diamond willow trees that extended half a mile to the north and to the west of our schoolyard. There were two other kinds of trees there also: at the north end, near the dry creek bed, was one birch about as thick as a thumb, and one spruce about three feet high. We used to make an occasional pilgrimage to visit them, and were very sad when we found that somebody had taken a fatal strip of bark from the birch, and taken the spruce away one year just before Christmas. One winter noon hour we spotted a weasel (ermine) out in the bush and chased it until the bell rang for us to return. A few of the boys returned late bearing their trophy, the small dead animal, all white except for the black tip on its tail and the red blood at its nose.

On days that were too cold or wet to play outside, we found plenty to do in the schoolroom. At the blackboard we played cat, or noughts and crosses, or some guessing games. Often we played at geography: with the world map rolled down, the leader would pick a place name, the smaller the better, and call it out; then the first to find it on the map became the next to name a place. Another geographic game called for choosing sides; one side announced a place name, the other side had to think of a name that began with the last letter of the first, and so on, back and forth. Or some of us improvised board games, checkers and even chess, to play on a desk before a small gallery of watchers. And before Christmas we could spend several noon hours making paper chains and streamers, and using stencils and coloured chalk to draw holly borders around the blackboards.

At the fifteen-minute recess periods, mid-morning and mid-afternoon, we were not supposed to go outside the fenced schoolyard, but there was time for skipping or hopscotch, or a wrestling match or even a fist fight between boys who had a score to settle. We never played hooky or imagined anybody doing it; there was, of course, nowhere to go. In my nine years there we did have one excursion, when all the pupils climbed up into the back of my father's grain truck on a Friday afternoon and went off fifteen miles to the Vimy Theatre in Vegreville to see the silent movie *Ben Hur*.

There was one other outing. For Canada's Diamond Jubilee celebration in Lavoy, the First of July 1927, our school had the only float in the parade. Nine of us in the lower grades were outfitted in some way to represent the nine provinces, as there were then, and each had learned a few appropriately boastful lines to recite. Our float was a hayrack with decorations that included the Union Jack, the flag from school, and was drawn by a team of decorated horses. Our float, preceded by a big drum and followed by our classmates and other kids who were not on the float, started near the railway station and stopped where the crowd had assembled, at the first intersection, in front of the Palmer House Hotel. There Dr Arthur climbed up onto our hayrack and delivered a patriotic address that seemed to go on forever, while the nine of us representing provinces stood in a row, waiting to say our pieces. I was Nova Scotia, clad in my father's yellow oilskin sou'wester and oilskin raincoat pinned up to fit my size, and as the hot sun beat down on us I nearly roasted. I envied my classmate George Morris who stood next to me as New Brunswick, with his light shirt and shorts and clam-digger's spade and bucket. As usual on public occasions, we began with "O Canada" and ended with "God Save the King."

When all the speeches were over, and we had led in saving the King, our hayrack moved on through town to the picnic ground, followed by our classmates, the pupils from the town school, and then the crowd, maybe two hundred people, more than twice the whole population of Lavoy. After lunch there was a baseball game, and then races and prizes for all age groups, male and female, including three-legged races and a special egg-and-spoon race for the ladies. And then there were various contests, such as a nail-driving contest, a straw-hat-decorating contest, and a pie-eating contest in which the contestants had their hands tied behind them. My father saw me watching the pie eaters as I licked a large ice cream cone on which I had spent five cents of my prize money, and he asked why I had not entered the contest if I was hungry. I told him I did not like raisin pie.

Firecrackers were not allowed at the picnic ground, but the confectionery store near the hotel had an endless supply, so many of us boys were gathered there in the street, later in the afternoon, letting off strings of tiny cracklers, tossing ordinary two-inch crackers to explode in the air, and standing well away from the occasional big banger. We heard shouts in the beer parlour and saw a burly Scottish war veteran come out onto the hotel veranda, holding a small Polish farmer by the scruff of the neck. He gave him a solid punch, then flung him over the railing and across the sidewalk, well out into the gravel street, where he landed with a sickening crunch. The Scotchman and his cronies waited a minute or two to see the poor victim gather himself painfully and make a dazed retreat, before they went back into the beer parlour for further moistening of their patriotism. For us that was a sad ending to a great day, to which our own little Victory School had made a leading contribution.

Back at school the next autumn, the last part of Friday afternoon usually offered some special treat, if our work was all done. The teacher would read us stories, or lead us in a singsong, or there would be a spelling match with sides chosen, or a concert of recitations, riddles, and jokes, or rehearsals for the Christmas concert, always something to send us home happy at the end of the week.

There were a few who would not go home happy. One spring there appeared two ragged teenage brothers and their sister, Rose, around twelve years old. They and their father had taken over an abandoned shack at the edge of the school district. Their mother had died. Their senile grandmother, having left them, tramped into our house in worn-out work boots and stayed until my parents found her a more appropriate refuge. When the teenage brothers spoke of snaring gophers, we gathered that they were using them for meat. One day in hygiene class the teacher asked Rose, as gently as possible, how often she thought people should have a bath; she answered "Once a month in summer, but of course in winter it's too cold." She tried hard to keep up with the other girls, even to the extent of accepting a dare to eat a caterpillar. But one day Rose sat weeping at her desk. She was in pain, bleeding, and thought she must be dying. Miss Burkholder took her out to the girls' cloakroom for a long talk, and sent her home.

Gladys Burkholder was the young lady from town who had bumped the corner of the woodshed with her car. I am sure she was a good teacher, but the thing I remember best about her year was the wildlife. One hot spring afternoon a gopher, probably after exploring the lunch pails in the boys' cloakroom, entered the classroom and announced his presence with a characteristic whistle. Miss Burkholder at her desk replied with a shriek and an order for somebody to put it out and close the door! That spring also brought a great plague of tent caterpillars. We could not walk anywhere without stepping on them, and the poplar trees, as far as we could see, had no leaves left, only white silky nests spun by the invaders. The outside wall on the shady side of the school, for the first six or eight feet above ground, had a solid coating of caterpillars one or two inches deep, waving back and forth as they covered themselves with silky webs. One day the teacher, writing at the blackboard, suddenly squawked and ran to the girls' cloakroom, whence she called one of the big girls to help her remove a caterpillar that had dropped down her neck. Next day some boys brought our garden rakes to school, peeled the caterpillars off the wall into small piles, and mashed them. But Miss Burkholder had us keep all the doors shut for some time after.

Another memorable event was the arrival of the teacher's boyfriend, late one afternoon. He stood at the back of the room for a few minutes before school was out, and then we had plenty of time to inspect his big Reo sedan. On the way home we had fun setting a few nails points upward in the dust of the road, to give him a flat tire, but luckily our childish prank was a failure.

Since we all heard and observed the lessons of all the grades every day, it was fairly easy to skip a grade, and a few of us were shifted forward, somewhere in the early grades. I had an added advantage, as few others did, in that our house had a bookcase. It included a full set of *Book of Knowledge*, a good dictionary, a set of the world's best hundred short stories, and the works of O. Henry and Jack London, as well as other enticing things to read. My two sisters who came behind me had the same advantage, but few of our classmates had any books at home.

For a year we had Joe Stonehawker as teacher, a slim red-haired young man who usually walked the five miles home to Lavoy for the weekends. In spring he walked cross-country and through many clumps of poplar, to climb up and gather crow's eggs. I remember emptying gopher tails out of a pocket in my overalls, onto a paper spread on his desk, and from a small pail counting out my own collection of crow's and magpie's eggs. At the end of the season, the teacher handed out the municipal bounty, at the rate of 1 cent per gopher tail or crow foot, and 2 cents per egg, at a time when my mother was taking chicken eggs to the grocery store in Lavoy for a credit of only 15 cents a dozen.

Joe Stonehawker taught us several rousing Baptist hymns, as well as rounds and other songs, and carols for the Christmas concert that was the primary event of his year with us. As the concert drew near, we spent much time rehearsing the carols, solos, recitations, skits, and drills. Then we produced a version of Dickens's *A Christmas Carol*, with very few stage props except a real log-chain for Marley's ghost, and a card table set with a half-spherical desk bell as the goose for the Cratchit Christmas feast. And there I had a terrible moment, almost too much for a shy eleven-year-old. When I entered the scene as Bob Cratchit just getting home from his office, and was welcomed by the tall teenager who was Mrs Cratchit, she gave me a loud unrehearsed kiss! I stood there flabbergasted, hearing hoots of laughter from my grandfather and others in the audience.

In preparation for this great evening we had decorated the room and strung a curtain of bedsheets on a wire across the front, with a sheet on either side running back to the blackboard, to form a stage and wings. We had taken all the desks out and stacked them in the woodshed, to make space for the chairs and planks that were brought in as seating for the audience. Light was provided by the kerosene mantel lamp that my father had brought from home and hung from a hook in the middle of the ceiling, as he had done for other community events. And for a time there was some light also from the carefully watched wax candles on the Christmas tree.

It is hard for me to imagine, now, how that room could accommodate such a concert, and all the people who had come from several miles around to see it. But it did, and I don't think anybody had any qualms about it. When all the children and their families and friends arrived in cutters and sleighs, of course the barn was of little use. Sleighs simply stopped in the most convenient place, horses were unhitched and tied to their rigs and covered with their blankets, and usually some hay or green feed was thrown down to keep them happy while they waited. After the last carol had been sung the audience must have been glad to rise from their plank seats to save the King, then to collect their children, find their coats, even to step out into the cold night, retrieve the warmed horse blankets, and head for home. My grandparents had nearly six miles to go but never mentioned the discomfort they had endured in order to see Marian and me perform, and were kind enough never to remind me of my dreadful moment in the Dickens play.

Sometime during every school year, the school inspector would arrive unannounced. He would ask the teacher to carry on with the class for a short time, then he would take charge and ask questions that we always tried to answer as well as we could. Then, unless it was recess time or lunch time anyway, he would send us out to play while he had a session with the teacher. The only inspector whose name I remember was a lively young man named Doucette. He came out to play softball with us, and was surprised to see that our ball was a very hard and lumpy homemade one, strips of inner tube from a car tire wound into a tight ball and covered with leather-sewn out-seam by a local shoemaker. And our bat, a discard picked up after a baseball game in Lavoy, had a slab missing from one side of it. The result of his visit was that we soon had a real softball and a new bat, and inside the school a new water tank with a spigot, replacing the old bucket with a tin dipper hanging on the side. After that we had to bring our own drinking cups; mine was the kind that telescoped into a small leather case, pocket-size.

In December 1928 my three-year-old brother Harold died. He had wakened in the night with a high fever that did not respond to home treatment. At the hospital in Vegreville he grew worse in spite of consultations with a specialist who was brought out from Edmonton, twice. Harold dropped into a coma with encephalitis, brain fever, on Christmas Eve. He lived for nearly two more weeks but never woke to see the new tricycle that was to have been his Christmas present, waiting beside his bed. My father drove to the cemetery at Ryley, where Grandfather Olson had been buried, and hacked a grave in the frozen ground. The funeral service was at home in our front room. Father announced that the men should not remove their hats at graveside. The King had done that recently and had caught pneumonia. When the cars had left for the cemetery I lay on the couch and thought of the good life I would have hoped for Harold to have. I thought about my own sinful nine-year-old life, and resolved to give up swearing and smoking, and not to lie, or repeat dirty jokes, or lock anybody in a dark cellar, or do other bad things, a resolution I have kept tolerably well for more than eighty years.

My father often took me out to the field to be beside him as he worked, quite against the wishes and advice of my grandfather. He let me stand beside him on the long platform at the back of the seed drill, where I was careful to keep out of the way of the lever that whipped back when he pulled the trip rope on the power lift. And he let me stand beside his seat on the tractor, leaning on the fender, looking back over the four-bottom plough followed by the sharp disk and spike harrow. When I was ten he let me drive the Model T the half-mile or so between house and threshing machine, accompanied by sister Marian. When I next write the test for the renewal of my driver's licence and come to the question of how long I have been driving, I will be tempted to write "since 1929." Of course I did not get a licence until I was sixteen; it cost 50 cents and there was no test.

Before I learned how to milk cows, I often stood under the lantern at the back wall of the cow barn while my father did the milking. That was a time for him to drill me in mental arithmetic. "Take 2. Double it. Triple it. Add three. Divide by five. Multiply by 11. What have you got?" He had taught me a neat trick about multiplying 11 by any number up to 100.

When Father replaced the old tractor with a new International 15-30, faster and more powerful than the old one, it was claimed to be so easy to operate that an eleven-year-old boy could do it. I was eleven. After we had gone a few rounds with it in the field, he stopped it, stepped off, and waited for me to do the test. I had no trouble getting it back into gear and keeping the right front wheel against the edge of the furrow. But as I neared the end of the field, I began to panic as to whether I could get turned around at the end without hitting the fence. When I saw that Father was far back in the field, I killed the throttle. When he caught up to me, he just cranked the engine again, and before taking over he rode beside me for a few rounds until I could manage the ends without any trouble.

The autumn I was sixteen I was allowed to drive a team of four horses on the binder, cutting grain. The following year I not only cut grain, but at threshing time had my own team on a bundle-rack, keeping up with the hired men as they loaded their racks in the field and unloaded them into the threshing machine. My grandfather, always present at threshing time, seemed rather pleased with me, and when my left wrist gave out he climbed up to help me unload. But at noon, when he was taking all the men to the house for lunch, leaving our horses in the field, I made a bad mistake. As I saw the truck coming in my direction to pick me up, I unhitched my horses, tied them to the back of my rack, and put down two bundles for them to eat. When the truck came growling over the soft stubble to where I was waiting, and I climbed up into it, Grandfather hopped out of the cab and took the bridles off my team, a thing I had forgotten to do, so that they would be able to eat. That was the day he advised my father to give me all the education I could hold, because I would never make a farmer.

While Father looked after the fields and livestock and machines, Mother ran the household without benefit of running water or plumbing, without electricity or refrigeration.

There was of course the dumb waiter that could be pulled up from the cool earth cellar, and there was the cellar itself at the bottom of steep steps leading down from the trap door in the kitchen floor. The cellar had a few wide boards to walk on, and wooden cribbing around the sides. A potato bin on the bare floor was cool enough to keep all the potatoes we needed for the greater part of the year, when there were none available in the garden. Cabbages and turnips also kept fairly well down there. And shelves along the walls held glass sealers – pints, quarts, and half-gallons – filled with Mother's canning and pickling: wild berries we had picked; vegetables we had grown; peaches and pears and crab apples she had bought in season; and jars of our own chicken, cubed beef, and pork tenderloin, ready to be heated for the table. There were also crocks of butter and lard, crocks of sausages in their own fat, and a crock of eggs preserved in a slimy liquid called "waterglass" that we hated to reach down into.

The cellar also had an oak barrel in which we "cured" hams, sides of bacon, pork shoulders, and beef rounds during the winter. Curing was done by rubbing large pieces of meat with salt, brown sugar, saltpetre, and some smoky flavouring, then packing them into the barrel, which we topped with a wooden lid and a large stone to hold it down. After several such rubbings, and when juices from the meat had risen to the level of the wooden lid, the pieces were taken out and hung from the ceiling beams to dry for two or three months. During that period a person had to pick a way carefully across the dark cellar. When spring came, we buried the meat in oats or wheat in one of the granaries, to keep away flies, and fished for it when it was needed during the year. Our neighbour preferred to hang cured meat high up on his windmill, above the flies, but not above birds and rain.

In winter, when we butchered and had fresh roasts, steaks, and small cuts that were not for curing, cold storage was no problem. About twenty feet from the back porch, and off to the side, Father had built a storehouse, with three rooms. The farthest room was the coal shed; Father would drive about fifteen miles to the nearest mine and bring home loads of lignite, soft coal that split easily and burned well enough. It made large clinkers in the stoves but was much cheaper than anthracite from town. The middle room was for miscellaneous storage, and could be used as a spare bedroom. The third room, nearest to the back porch, was the storeroom, lined with deep shelves on which all our fresh beef and pork would be frozen solid all winter, and brought to the kitchen as needed. In all seasons the storeroom held our supplies of dry foods and other things that did not need cooling.

Storage of milk was not a problem. We had fresh milk from our cows every night and morning, and what was not needed for drinking or cooking was given to the calves, chickens, and pigs. Cream that was not needed for the table was kept in a large can until there was enough to be churned; then it was churned by hand, and the butter taken to the store for credit. At Grandmother Olson's farm, milk and cream were lowered into the well on ropes, and Father worried about the water becoming polluted. The other worry about Grandmother's dug well, with its hinged lid over wooden cribbing, was that some child might fall down it. When we were small our grandmother warned us that a bad troll lived in the well, and we gave it a wide berth. Some other children were less fortunate; one of the boys at Victory School had a big curved indentation and scar across his forehead, made by the edge of a cream can lid that had stopped his fall and held him until his father could be lowered into the well headfirst to rescue him. He had done well to survive, and years later I heard that he was still doing well as owner of a car dealership.

5 The Last Six Grades in Four Schools

My grandfather had given me a Hereford heifer to help me open a bank account. But after having her first calf she died, and I was left with only one steer to sell, not with the steady income that was expected. When my father gave up an experiment with hog raising on a large scale, I was allowed to buy a big red brood-sow, and fed her faithfully. But after having her first litter she became paralyzed and had to be shot, so again my hope of a fortune was lost. At Victory School I had better luck, but on a much smaller scale.

At school it was the custom, on 14 February, for every pupil to exchange valentines. Most of the cards were homemade, but somehow the Gold Seal Company found me and I began selling their cards. The smallest were quite plain and not very wordy, three for five cents. But there were also bigger ones, right up to some swanky ones with real verses, embossing, and fancy paper lace, fifteen cents. After exhausting the school market I walked the district, even the streets of Lavoy, peddling them. Mother was my best customer, and I had very few cards left to send back. The reward was not cash, but a baseball glove. I did the same, for a year or two, with Gold Seal Christmas cards, with different rewards but no cash.

There should have been money in rabbit skins. I bought some copper wire and spent many cold hours one winter setting snares and catching a few rabbits. But when I mailed the dried skins to an Edmonton fur dealer, he sent me a cheque for only 26 cents. There was of course a 1-cent bounty for gopher tails. When the Calgary Power Company reached Lavoy and ran its line two miles south before turning east and missing us, it left a red-topped survey marker at the foot of every pole. I saw those markers as a great improvement over the sticks I had been using to secure and mark the locations of my gopher traps. So I rode my horse halfway into Lavoy, brought home a sackful of markers, and spent all my spare time trapping.

I had received an air rifle when I was nine, and used it for target practice, but it was useless for anything else. I yearned for the .22 calibre advertised in the Eaton's catalogue for five dollars, and at age twelve I was allowed to buy it. It was very accurate and my tally of gopher tails mounted quickly. But cartridges were a cent apiece, and I had to make every shot count in order to break even.

Because of accidents that had occurred nearby, I knew to be very careful with the rifle. One winter a young man who lived only a mile from us had taken a friend with him to get a load of straw, and had taken his .22 along in case they saw a jackrabbit. As they were climbing up onto the load, the trigger caught on something and the young man died. Later, when there was a different family at the same farm, an eight-year-old boy, the nephew of our hired girl, was doing target practice just past the corner of the house and pulled the trigger just as his little brother walked around the corner and got a fatal bullet in the head. The hired girl and I walked over after supper to offer help; only the young shooter was at home, his face purple and swollen; he would not talk. By the time he came back to school the bruises were gone.

The next Christmas evening, as we drove home in our sleigh from dinner at Grandfather's house, a farm woman ran howling out to her gate and begged us to call the police. Her hired man, whose advances to the hired girl had been rejected, had followed the girl out to the barn when she went to do the milking, and shot her and himself. And one midnight my grandfather, hearing a noise from the direction of the chicken house, but not seeing any intruder when he went out in his nightshirt and stood on the front porch, fired his shotgun at random into the air, as a warning. He killed what may have been a romance. A young fellow who had been sitting in his car at the gate, with the hired girl, started the motor immediately and roared away, leaving the poor girl to walk up to the house alone.

One spring I bought fifty baby chicks, Barred Rocks. As they grew and matured, one rooster was larger than all the rest, and had unusually fine colouring. I decided to take him to the Vegreville School Fair. The fair was an annual event, accepting entries from all schools in the Vegreville district, and I got ready to take entries in many categories. I had made a birdhouse patterned after the Pantheon in Athens, painted grey. And there was a map of Europe, watercoloured. I also took many kinds of vegetables, three of each, from my school garden. Mother had let Marian and me have our own gardens almost as soon as we could walk, and we were accustomed to having one or the other of us win first prize for the gardens we grew from the seeds that were given out at Victory School each spring. I took also to the fair a plate of bran muffins and another of macaroons. I took no calf or pig, as some of the boys did. But I did take my rooster, with his nails and legs polished, and his comb and wattles brightened with olive oil. When I went around the fair that afternoon, expecting to see a red tag on his cage, for first prize, there was no prize at all, only a ruffled bird crouched in the corner, his head grimy from his having rubbed it in the dust in an attempt to get rid of the oil.

A few days later we received the names of the girl and boy who had won the most prizes in the whole Vegreville district, and I was the boy! The grand prize was a week at the provincial agricultural school in Vermilion. So at age twelve I went to Vermilion by train, by myself, and among the winners from all the school fair districts in northern Alberta, I was one of the youngest.

All of my fifty chicks survived. I sold them all, killed and dry-plucked as I had learned at Vermilion, dressed as Mother had taught me to do, at 10 cents a pound. Our new teacher bought two six-pounders to send to his mother in Edmonton; in those days the postal service was quick enough that he could do so without worry. I peddled the rest of my chickens from door to door in Lavoy, and earned what I thought was a tidy boost for my bank account. A year or two later I won another prize at the Vegreville fair. There was a yo-yo contest on the grandstand late in the afternoon. There were many contestants but it was a blowy day, and most of them dropped out quickly, until only two of us were left. The other lad was more skilful than I was, but as he was doing a fancy cloverleaf his string broke, leaving me as the only contestant in action. The $1 prize was enough to pay our family's admission to the fair, and ice cream cones all around.

My last teacher at Victory School was Charlie Jenkins, for grades seven to ten. He had a wife and two small children, and a brown-and-yellow roadster. He was a solidly built young man with solid teaching experience behind him, and was new to our district. Apparently he had been told that the previous teacher had been slack on discipline, and he set out to cure that problem on the first day, with a nearly disastrous result.

One of our boys, Stanley, had great difficulty learning to read and write. Nowadays he would likely be seen as dyslexic and given special help, but the word dyslexic was unknown in those days. As well, Stanley wore thick glasses and had to sit in the front row to see the blackboard. He had fallen behind in his grades and was twice the size of other members in his class. But he was a great talker and had a loud, nervous laugh to make up for his misfortunes. On his first day, Mr Jenkins spoke to Stanley twice for turning around and whispering to the classmate behind him. When Stanley did it again, Mr Jenkins, who happened to be at the blackboard drawing lines with the yardstick, spun around and brought the stick down so hard on Stanley's desk that the stick broke. Stanley laughed and laughed, in spite of orders to stop it, until he was ordered to stand beside the teacher's desk and hold out his hand. As the strap came down on his hand several times he continued to laugh, until the teacher dropped the strap, took hold of him and threw him into the corner of the room. Stanley burst into tears, got up slowly, and limped back to his desk sobbing, his glasses broken. My father and other members of the school board had a serious talk with Mr Jenkins that night, and there was never such an outburst again, nor any occasion for one.

There was some grumbling among the farmers in the early 1930s about their taxes that went to pay the teacher $450 a year. Compared to their own labours, his looked very light, only a few hours a day, five days a week, ten months a year. They themselves were working hard, early and late, all year, but having crop failures and hard times. They might have to join the trail of the covered wagons they saw going past on the road, from farther south, headed north toward the Peace River country. They knew that the school had to be kept open, and they acknowledged that Jenkins was a very good teacher with a wife and children to support. But they shook their heads when they saw him whizzing to Lavoy in his roadster.

He did not drive when he came to our house for a quart of milk. There was no artificial refrigeration, of course, and he had to come every night, except in winter. I think Mother charged him 10 cents a quart for milk, 20 for cream. Full bottle in hand, he used to stand in our kitchen with his other hand on the doorknob, and go on talking with Mother on all sorts of topics for what seemed a very long time before finally leaving for home to prepare for the next morning's classes. His other contact with the outside world, at least during the week, was his

Charlie Jenkins with his pupils at Victory School, 1934. Arrows point to Marian and me. Stuart MacFarland is just below the double windows, and George Morris is the tall boy at the corner.

radio. For a time he stayed after school with a few of the older boys to teach us how to make our own radios, but he had to give it up.

Having children of his own, he took an interest in our health. When the smaller children were standing in a row at the front for their lessons, he often had them hold out their hands for inspection, and sometimes sent them out to the pump to wash. Or he would put his hand on a feverish-looking forehead, and sometimes send a child home with a note. One of the youngsters who had a bare circle of ringworm on the side of his head was called up to the teacher's desk every day for a careful painting of iodine. And the teacher made sure that all the older children knew the rudiments of first aid.

When three of us, all boys, reached grade ten, we were supposed to begin learning a language other than English. Mr Jenkins had taken French in his high school days but did not feel able to teach it. He offered us Latin instead. He had never studied Latin himself, but got four textbooks and undertook to go through the course along with us, chapter by chapter. He soon found that he was unable to keep up or to correct the exercises we handed in each week, so he took them in to the principal of the two-room school in Lavoy, who was a Scot and a good Latinist. Thus all three of us were able, the following spring, to pass the provincial examination in first-year Latin. We had acquired also the textbook for first-year agriculture, studied it independently, and passed the examination. I did not see Charlie Jenkins again until eight years later, when he was teaching gunnery.

School in Lavoy

Being ready for grade eleven in the autumn of 1934, we three boys rode horseback to the two-room school in Lavoy. I rode my sister's horse, a fine neck-reined trotter that could trot as fast as my own old plug could gallop. Some of the girls at school called us "the three musketeers," and we did our best to make a good show of trotting along the middle of the street through town, on the way to and from school. The effort was somewhat hindered by impedimenta: I had a large black-leather schoolbag slung over my shoulder and secured by a leather shoelace tied around my waist to keep it from flopping. Of the three musketeers, I had the farthest to ride from home, five miles.

Approaching Lavoy from the south, we crossed a new gravel road that later became part of the Trans-Canada Highway. Then there was a row of five grain elevators on their own siding, south of the railway

With my sister Marian and our horses, Beauty and Daisy.

track. Past the railway station and past the first cross street was the hotel, with a high veranda and balcony wrapped around two sides of it. The veranda opened into the hotel lobby with its leather chairs and brass spittoons, and into three other establishments: the poolroom/barbershop, the beer parlour, and the bank, where we had seen the teller standing behind a metal wicket, a nickel-plated revolver handy to his right hand. Beyond the hotel were the town pump, the lumberyard, a Chinese restaurant, and Bricker's general store, which had a long hitching rail in front and carried everything from safety pins to horse collars and a drum of cheddar sitting on a turntable beneath a hinged blade to cut it with.

At the store we turned our horses westward and passed Dr Arthur's drug store/post office/telephone exchange and his house/office across the road from it. Then beyond the end of the board sidewalk there were two churches and a curve in the dirt road leading to the two-room school. The school had its own barn where we unsaddled. It also had its own pump and privies. Beyond these were the basketball court, baseball diamond, and soccer field with real goalposts.

At school we sat in the principal's room with grades seven to eleven. Among other subjects we took second-year Latin, first-hand now, instead of second-hand as in the previous year. There being no laboratory, we could not take chemistry, to me a serious lack as I was hoping to go on into medicine.

The two other musketeers were Stuart MacFarland and George Morris. We had been in class together all our years at Victory School. Stuart was a bit younger, a quick learner, well informed and thoughtful. As a small child he had a severe case of polio, and the doctor had expected him to die, but his father had given him constant massage and manipulation, and he pulled through. Stuart came to school with a severe limp and could not take part in our running games, but he could take two or three quick steps without falling, and so could serve as goalkeeper or catcher, and could take his turn at bat with somebody to run for him. His father, who farmed only a quarter-section, specialized in growing hogs; Stuart often tired of roast pork sandwiches and would trade for my sandwiches of peanut butter or cheese or dried-beef gravy or raisins or whatever else mine might be. On very stormy days, Stuart and I used to play chess at noon. I did not hear of him finishing high school.

George Morris's father had asthma and could not shovel his own grain. George, too, was asthmatic, and was not good at sports. He was a thorough and methodical student, and when there was a test he usually got full marks for the part he had completed, but seldom did he have time to finish a test. After high school the last I heard of him was that he had moved to England, had married, and was working in a pharmacy. His mother boasted that he had become a "Boots unqualified chemist."

Our principal at Lavoy was an enthusiastic coach and referee at our noontime soccer games. For a few weeks that autumn an Indian band from the Saddle Lake Reserve, about one hundred miles north of Vegreville, camped in the woods beside the schoolyard, and the young men used to come over to play soccer with us, reds against whites, very good fun. I was quite used to seeing Indians, as a matter of course. One summer several families of them had camped in or around a deserted farmhouse where there was a well, about half a mile from Victory School. One or two of their men came to our kitchen door asking for food, and Mother always had something for them, maybe some loaves of bread or a dozen eggs, or a cup of sugar or salt. One time she gave them a whole ham that had been stored under the oats too long and become rancid; she told me they didn't mind, but I wondered about that. Come September, we schoolkids went to look around the vacant campsite, but found nothing interesting except two or three old porcupine skins.

In his memoirs my father wrote about hiring a young Indian, who rode into the yard, to shovel a load of grain from wagon to granary. It was a cold day, but before beginning, the young man stripped to the waist. When asked whether he didn't mind the cold, he brushed a hand from his face down across his chest, and said, "All face." Another time my father hired a proud young chief named Cardinal to cut brush for us on our east half-section. Cardinal, after a long delay, brought his whole band with him after Treaty Day; they all pitched in, women and children and all, to complete the contract. Father took me along to the field sometimes to check on their progress, but all I really remember seeing was a clutch of duck eggs, charred in their nest, where a brush pile had been burned.

I remember seeing another Indian, an old man, sitting on the edge of the board sidewalk in Lavoy, in front of Dr Arthur's house, waiting to be served in his own language. Dr Arthur had come out from the Maritimes as a medical missionary. We did not know the story of his mission work, but apparently it is reflected in one of Ralph Connor's novels, in which one incident is the birth of the doctor's elder daughter as the first white child born in the Northwest Territories, as the Prairie provinces were then known; we knew the daughter only as a farm wife who was active in our church. Dr Arthur knew classical Greek also, and was ready to apply some of it in the pulpit any time our regular minister was not available. On ordinary Sundays he sat in the front pew (for his hearing) beside his prim little Nova Scotian wife; some of us were always on the alert for his stealthy move to ease a cud of chewing tobacco from mouth to handkerchief. He chewed partly for professional reasons. One day our neighbour the carpenter went to the doctor with a splinter that had pinned three of his fingers together. The doctor got out his pocket knife, cut the splinter into three, and began to dig it out with the same knife. When the carpenter asked, "Aren't you going to sterilize the knife?", the doctor just spat on it and replied, "Tobacco juice, the best disinfectant there is!" No doubt he had used it liberally on his Indian patients.

I knew the Indians I saw were from the Saddle Lake Reserve, but I knew nothing about that place. In 2002 I learned that the people there, during my time in Alberta, were parishioners of the Reverend Robert Steinhauer. He was a Cree and a graduate of Victoria College at Toronto. In 1900 he was the only Methodist missionary in western Canada holding a university degree. He served at Saddle Lake from 1919 until his death in 1941. In 1937 he was the first Indian in Canada to receive an honorary Doctor of Divinity degree.

In 1967, when the Order of Canada was being established, my elder son (another Robert) was secretary to the Governor General's committee that was drafting regulations and procedures, seeking and sifting nominations for the first awards of the new honour. My wife Patricia knew the Reverend Ralph Steinhauer, a nephew of Robert, at least by name and reputation, so she and one of her Calgary friends nominated him; he became one of the first recipients of the Order of Canada. Seven years later he was appointed Lieutenant Governor of Alberta, the first Indian to hold such an office in Canada.

It is easy to forget that the modern medicine we take for granted today is very new, and that we who have access to it are a privileged minority. For most of the world's people, modern medicine is too far away and too expensive. We who have access to it forget or distrust the old cures (and admittedly, some of those are best forgotten). Yet medical scientists continue to discover unsuspected virtues in some of the old remedies.

During my childhood on the farm, five miles from the nearest doctor and fourteen from the small hospital where I was born, we depended mainly on remedies that many parents knew and administered, and on our four-inch thick "doctor book" that covered ordinary ailments of domestic animals, poultry, and people. Some of us survived, some did not.

For earache, a frequent childhood malady, there was sweet-oil to be warmed in a spoon and poured into the ear. Then a hot water bottle was applied, or preferably a bag of salt warmed in the oven, as hot as we could stand it. Or sometimes an onion was baked in the oven and the hot core was squeezed into the ear.

For common colds there was a mixture of goose grease and turpentine rubbed into the chest, throat, and forehead. If there was fever, the chest was plied with mustard plasters, one after the other until the fever broke. The best thing about having a fever was the chance to lie on the Winnipeg couch in the kitchen until the day after it went away, and on that last day in bed to taste the first light meal of chicken broth.

For a stomachache or bilious headache, there was castor oil followed by a spoonful of coffee grounds to kill the taste. In fact there was castor oil for nearly every ailment, or at least Epsom salts or cascara, or milk of magnesia, in descending order of potency. For one screaming bellyache of mine, the hired man drove across country to Vegreville in the middle of the night to bring a doctor. By the time he appeared I had confessed to raiding the crate of dried prunes stored under my bed. After checking me over the doctor declared that my only trouble was being full of prunes.

For treatment of any kind to be useful, we thought it had to hurt or sting. For cuts or scratches we used iodine. For chapped skin there was carbolic ointment, which we called "cow salve" because it came in a big tin and its principal use was in the cow barn. For boils there were hot poultices of bread and milk or linseed porridge, or Denver clay, and a breast pump to draw out the core when it was ripe. For the itch I picked up at school there was a homemade mix of sulphur and burnt butter.

For chilblains I found that the maddening itch could be calmed temporarily by pressure, stamping of the toe of one boot with the heel of the other as I sat in school. A somewhat more lasting remedy was to jab the affected toes repeatedly with a clean needle, then squeeze out the blobs of dark stagnant blood. This was almost a nightly ritual for my father and me in winter.

I remember one of the hired men being brought to the house in a wagon at noon, groaning with a dislocated hip. After he was lifted to the ground, other men held him by the shoulders while my father pulled on his foot until the joint snapped back into place. Another day one of the men got something in his eye, and came to the house to bathe it in saltwater. That didn't help. After supper my father, having rolled back the eyelid, could see the end of a barley beard, but he didn't want to touch it himself for fear of cutting the eyeball. The man begged him to do it, without waiting for a doctor, so Father took the tweezers and pulled it out. Mother was ready with a warm solution of boracic acid and a poultice to ease the pain.

In the spring of 1928 my father, after working day and night without rest, up to sixty hours on the tractor to get the spring ploughing done, coughed blood from his lungs. With suspected tuberculosis (of which his mother had died), he had to be nursed through the summer, resting on a cot in a tent in the backyard. Mother took meals out to him, and carefully sterilized his dishes. His doctor in Edmonton told him that unless he gave up farming he would be dead in three years. It took him nearly two years to decide, and by that time my mother, at age forty-two, was having a difficult pregnancy which (she said later) she did not expect to survive. Both problems were resolved happily on 20 April 1930, when my sister Betty was born, and Father received his licence to become an agent for the New York Life Insurance Company.

At school in Lavoy, after the Indians had left, the cold weather set in. One Saturday some other boys and I equipped ourselves with a team of horses, a stoneboat, barrels, and buckets and began to make a skating rink beside the school. All went along merrily until the school's well was pumped dry, and then the town well also, leaving most of the town without a water supply. We were left with a very bumpy rink that we were not allowed to finish.

In December it was decided that our school should have a newspaper, with me as editor. The first issue was three or four sheets of mimeograph, with two staples, and a cover sheet decorated with hand-coloured holly. I don't know whether there was ever a second issue, because I did not return to that school after Christmas.

That autumn my sister Marian, at age thirteen, had been having pains that sometimes kept her out of school. I never heard an explanation but gathered that girls were often delicate at that age. One day, when our parents were away, I got home from Lavoy to find Marian lying in her bed, crying in pain but not wanting me to do anything for her but go away. When the pain continued till next morning, my parents took her to hospital in Vegreville. By the time they got there the pain had eased, but the doctor thought she might be having an attack of appendicitis, and kept her there for observation. As days passed she grew sicker and weaker until they moved her to a larger hospital in Lamont, but by then the infection from the burst appendix was beyond control, and she died on Christmas Day, 1934.

If today's diagnostics and treatments had been available then, Marian and Harold surely would not have died when they did, and the lives of my parents would not have been blighted as they were. Mother would not go back to the farm that winter, with its lonely days when Father was away on business and I was away at school. Instead, our family went to live with her sister Olive in Edmonton until school was out. The next summer our family went to Banff and spent a week there, the only family vacation we ever had.

Edmonton and Vegreville

I approached Eastwood High in Edmonton with some trepidation. I found the principal's office in good time, but the secretary told me I could not see the principal till the bell rang for classes to begin. This gave me a very anxious feeling, because I was accustomed to being among the first to arrive at school, and here I would be late for my first class. The bell rang and still I waited, but presently was ushered into the office. The principal received me kindly, asked a lot of questions, reviewed the list of courses I had been taking, and studied a large timetable. He figured out a list of courses that I would be able to take, with room numbers and times and names of teachers, and finally told me to go upstairs to room 21, to begin in English 3. By then I was feeling very lost and uncertain, and passed many doors, but finally found the right number. I hesitated there, wondering whether to knock or simply go in, or perhaps wait for the next class. But the corridor was along one side of a study hall, with tables full of students watching me, so I simply opened the door and walked into what became the basic pattern of a nightmare that still wakens me from time to time more than seventy-five years later.

As I entered the room, the teacher was standing at a lectern, a smallish man with a grey suit, with flashing black eyes and a plume of white hair. As he swung round to look at me, he cocked his head and shouted, "Was there ever such a man?" There was a roar of laughter from the roomful of students. I stood there dumbfounded, in my best blue sweater, the old school bag over one shoulder and my winter coat draped over one arm. When the noise subsided somewhat the man cocked his head again and shouted, "Where did you come from?" When I answered "Lavoy," there was more laughter until he shouted, "And what do you want here?" I answered, no doubt shakily, that the principal had sent me to join this class. "Join this class! But can't you see the room is full? No room for you here! Desks all full! You people at the back who have only chairs to sit on, stand up and show him how full the room is!" About a dozen boys stood up, and there was more laughter. But when I took hold of the doorknob to leave, he called me back and said he would make room for me somehow, and a chair was found at the back of the room.

When I was finally seated, he addressed me again. He said they were studying Tennyson's poem about King Arthur, and he had asked the class if there was ever such a man. Could I give him the answer? The answer I gave was satisfactory, and then he derided the class for knowing less than this fellow from Lavoy! He treated me well enough for the rest of the year, and gave me good marks. He had forgotten me three or four years later when I heard him speak to the Edmonton Browning Society, of which he was president. But I have not forgotten our first meeting, on my first morning at Eastwood High.

I was gratified that my Latin instruction at Lavoy had been chapters ahead of the class at Eastwood High. My new Latin teacher, Mr Powell, was very good, but he had a large class and some of its members were eager to copy the homework of others who had got it done, instead of trying to do it themselves. Mr Powell was also coach of the Eastwood softball team, on which I became pitcher, but we made a very poor showing against Victoria High, and especially Strathcona High. Years later I attended a chapel service in Wales, where the preacher's name was Powell. The family resemblance was so strong that I asked him whether he had a brother in Canada. He said there was a brother who had gone to Canada many years ago and had not been heard from since. When I told him that his brother had taught me Latin at Eastwood High in Edmonton in 1935, he said only, "Well, he would have been well qualified to do that."

Our teacher in History 3 was a little lady who could rhyme off the names of Ontario counties forward and backward and who seemed to deplore the fact that Alberta had no list of counties for us to learn. One afternoon after the final examination in her subject, she came along as I was waiting in the nearly deserted hallway to go in and write the exam in History 2, a subject I had somehow missed along the way. She asked what I was doing there, and when I told her she was quite angry with me for having dared to enter her class without having completed History 2. But I was saved by the bell summoning me into the examination room.

That winter I had spent many noon hours playing chess with classmate Colin Ross. At year end, while I was waiting in the hallway to write the test in Agriculture 2, which I had studied independently, Colin came along and asked why I was there. He had not even known about that course, but asked what the questions were likely to be, and after we had talked for twenty minutes or so, he went into the examination room fearlessly to write the same test and scored more than 40 percent.

After school was out that spring, my family moved back to the farm. The closest place for me to take grade twelve that autumn was the four-room high school in Vegreville, one room for each grade, with four excellent teachers. There was also a laboratory for the chemistry course I had missed earlier. I was introduced to trigonometry and calculus, my favourite subjects that year. The English teacher encouraged my early efforts at verse writing; she also invited our whole class to a Christmas party at her house, and saw to it that all the girls were properly escorted home afterward. Mr Miller, the principal, agreed that I would need to know German to enter medical studies, so he got me the textbooks and stayed after school twice a week all year to help me through the first two years of German. About twenty years later, when I was president of the Canadian Library Association and our annual meeting was on the University of Alberta campus, we included a special session on school libraries. Mr Miller was there as a delegate of the Alberta Teachers' Association, so I had another chance to thank him for his generous help. The much-worn German grammar he had given me to study had been written by W.H. Van der Smissen, a name that meant nothing to me at Vegreville High. But years later I found that he had been lecturer in German at the University of Toronto while serving also as the librarian for twenty-seven years up to 1891.

At the celebration of high school graduation in 1936 in Vegreville, the Vimy Theatre was full. When the graduates were called up to the stage, one by one, for us to receive our VHS pins, I went down the aisle and up the steps on crutches, having fallen from a horse and sprained an ankle a week or two earlier. The local newspaper editor, who had published my first poem when I was thirteen, was handing out the pins, after giving us all a stirring dose of encouragement and advice. When he saw my crutches he took my hand and resumed his oratorical tone in praise of those who attained their goals in spite of serious handicaps. My parents were greatly amused, and sometimes found occasion later to twit me about my handicap.

    I could never be persuaded that it was any handicap to have taken my first ten grades in a one-room school instead of a large consolidated school. I see those first nine years at Victory School, followed by two years at three other schools, not as a handicap but as a blessing for which I remain grateful.

6 Coming through the Barley to University

When I graduated from high school in the spring of 1936, my parents and I hoped I might be able to go on to university. But in that dry summer, in the middle of the Great Depression, university entrance looked to be far beyond my reach, and the Vegreville Business School loomed as a poor alternative. Our five hundred acres of wheat and oats did poorly that summer, and the hundred acres of barley that my father had planted experimentally looked even worse. Threshed out, it yielded a thousand bushels worth only 24.5 cents a bushel. But then we were told that the dry season had by some miracle raised the barley to malting grade, doubling the price. On hearing that news we began to wonder whether $490 might be enough for me to have a year at university after all.

The next day my father and I drove the seventy miles to Edmonton and found our way to the office of the University Registrar, who was encouraging. He had heard of students who had made it through first year on as little as $500; registration was to begin the following week, and he could reserve a room for me in residence. So the day before registration, my father helped me carry my things up to my second-floor room in the south wing of Athabasca Hall, handed me the $490 grain cheque, my ticket to the university, and kissed me goodbye at age seventeen. As I leaned out of my window to watch him drive away, my view consisted of the roadway, a one-storey green shack that was the Agriculture Lab, and beyond that an open field of wheat stubble that stretched westward almost to the river.

Exploring the campus that afternoon, I found another small building just west of the residences, the caretaker's cottage, but apart from that and the Agriculture Laboratory, the row of three residences defined the western boundary of the campus. In front of the residences was a level lawn, and then a rather springy boardwalk leading down the slope toward the Arts Building. The walk was barely wide enough for two people side by side. The long boards, laid lengthwise, supported at the ends and perhaps in the middle, were pleasantly flexible to walk on. At the foot of the slope the walk widened and was joined by tributaries from Pembina Hall and Assiniboia Hall. Along the north side of the widened walk was the Engineering Lab, and on the south side was the coal-fired powerhouse. Then came the Arts Building, which, with its front lawn and semicircular driveway, defined the east border of the campus. The south border was defined by the Medical Building. Across the street from it was St Joseph's College, and southeast of that was St Stephen's College; they were neighbours separate from the university but provided extra residential space. So in 1936 the university grounds had five large red brick buildings trimmed with white Tyndall stone, and four smaller auxiliary buildings. I saw no other construction during the ensuing five years, but when I visit the campus these days I have a hard time finding my way. On the way back up the boardwalk that afternoon I noticed a high steel tower, rather like our farm windmill, just south of Pembina Hall, and knew it to be the source of the CKUA radio broadcasts we used to listen to at home.

Registration morning was an awe-inspiring experience. From the line-up at the entrance to Convocation Hall I was directed to one of the small tables across the room, at which sat a lean white-haired gentleman behind a label that read "Professor R.K. Gordon." I had in hand the university calendar that the registrar had given me, and from which I had chosen six courses, three sciences and three others. Professor Gordon advised me quite emphatically that the normal number of courses was five, and suggested that I omit either Mathematics (my best subject) or German. I was taken aback and explained, with one or two tears, that I was used to working hard, that I had passed some provincial high school examinations after reading the subject material by myself without instruction, and that I really needed all six subjects. Reluctantly he signed my application for all six, saying that I should come to see him again if I began to have any trouble.

The most impressive part of the Arts Building, for a farm boy who had spent most of his life without indoor plumbing, was the men's lavatory behind the barber shop in the north end of the basement; the line of urinals along one wall seemed to stretch almost as far as the eye could see. Also in the basement, on the west side, was a combination bookstore and post office that served also as a savings bank. Having become a registered student, I deposited the big end of my barley cheque before walking across the bridge to downtown Edmonton to buy a couple of shirts and a new suit. That year I kept track of every penny I spent, every lead pencil or shoelace, bus tickets home for Christmas and Easter, everything; I wish I had saved that record. The total was just below $490. As I recall, tuition and Student Union fees came to just over $100, a three-piece suit made-to-order about $30, and room and board in residence $27.50 a month, rising yearly by $2.50.

Sometime in that first week, the university threw a big party for all the "frosh." The professors were there in tuxedos or tails, and their wives in evening gowns, the first I had ever seen. One gown even had a train that its wearer had to hold up with a little loop around one finger, while dancing. There were other notable people there too, including Florence Dodd, the Dean of Women. I had been warned that she wore heavy make-up and was inclined to rest a cheek on her partner's shoulder. There were many mixer-dances: when the music stopped suddenly we were to turn away from our partners and take the one facing us when the music resumed. At one such moment I turned into the welcoming arms of Miss Dodd. I did not want a smear of her paint on the shoulder of my new suit, so held her at what she may have thought a disrespectful distance while she pointed out various people and asked whether I knew them. I explained that I knew hardly anyone, being new at the university. She replied: "Of course you are new; if you were any younger you'd be in short pants."

The university official I saw most often, day and night, was Reg Lister, the Superintendent of Residences, wearing a white cotton jacket. He opened the doors at mealtimes, and he passed through every corridor at some time every evening, on patrol I suppose for girls, liquor, electric toasters, or anything else that was forbidden. He lost no time in getting to my room when somebody down the hall told him I had Myrtle in my room; he merely nodded when I showed him my souvenir of California, a paperweight of myrtle wood. He was a short, thick man with a narrow rim of grey around his large head, a wide mouth, and a clipped English accent. He had a quick step, and spoke in short bursts. He could be stern, but only when necessary, and his exercise of authority was informed by almost twenty years on the job.

Reg seemed at first to take a special interest in me, but then I saw that he took a personal interest in everybody. He was caretaker of residences and residents. If on his evening patrol he heard too much noise in a room, his knock and a few words were enough to restore quiet. Or he might join the party for a few minutes with some comment on recent happenings, or some news he had received about a student who had been in that corridor years before. From time to time he would stop at any room to ask how things were going, or to give a bit of advice. He often asked about my family, and he remembered details. Once or twice when my father was in Edmonton on business, Reg allowed him to share my room for a night. And six years later, when the residences had been leased to the RCAF and I had a bunk in Assiniboia Hall, Reg would give me a wink as I passed him on my way into the dining room.

In 1936 girls wore dresses, and men wore jackets and ties and shined their shoes. Professors wore black academic gowns. It was customary for the heads of departments to lecture to first-year students. My classes in chemistry, zoology, and English, far too big for the Arts Building, were held in the amphitheatre in the Medical Building. The daily roll call took a sizeable bite out of the allotted fifty minutes, but gave those of us in the upper rows a good chance to learn the names of interesting classmates.

I noticed a beautiful girl in a red dress, down near the front row. She answered to the name of Ruth, the name of the adored heroine in a red dress in one of Jack London's novels. Her last name was McClure, which I found in several spellings in the Edmonton phone book. Having attended one or two of the weekly Athabasca Hall house dances alone, I decided to invite Ruth to the next one. So one evening I spent time on the one telephone in our residence, starting at the top of the Edmonton McClures and asking for Ruth. Part-way down the list my call was answered by a pleasant-sounding Ruth, who thanked me for the invitation, but she and her husband were having guests that evening. Undaunted, I went on down the list to the last number, at which a rough voice said: "Yeah, dis is Rufe, wadaya want?" I never did speak to the right Ruth until I met her at our twenty-fifth class reunion breakfast at the home of President Walter Johns, where I told her the story, and she was amused. I think she was by then the dean of a faculty somewhere.

I had better luck with Peggy Graham. We happened to be the only people waiting for the bus one morning in front of the Arts Building, and we rode downtown together. She was from Regina and had just entered the BSc course in Nursing. Before our streetcar reached the north end of the High Level Bridge, I had invited her to the house dance that evening. She declined politely. But after two or three weekly invitations by phone, she accepted, and that winter we went to several house dances at which I met several of her classmates and their friends. On a fine winter afternoon a few of us hiked along the river up to Whitemud Creek. And on a fine May afternoon, when my barley money was still sufficient, I took her to see *Maytime*, the movie in which Nelson Eddy and Jeanette MacDonald sang at each other in full colour. In the following years Peggy and I continued to attend house dances occasionally, and even one or two formals.

I was the only freshman and the only farm boy in our corridor in Athabasca Hall. Most of the other fellows had lived there at least one year before, and for the first week or so most of the evening "bull sessions" were taken up with the recounting of the summer's events. My neighbours accepted me in a casual and friendly manner. They were all, like me, from outside Edmonton, but unlike me many of them depended on monthly cheques from home. For a few, when their cheques were late or too soon spent, my barley money became a source of short-term loans, always repaid promptly.

In my first year at university I saw a few people I had known as classmates in high school. There were two from Eastwood High. One was Colin Ross, with whom I had played chess, who registered first in Agriculture but switched to Medicine and would later develop a noted surgical operation for pigeon-breastedness, which brought him patients from around the world. The other was Don Stanley, with whom I had shared a desk in Latin III; he later established a very large engineering firm, and made some use of four Latin words – *admitto te ad gradum* – when the time came for him to award degrees in his role as Chancellor of the University of Alberta.

My only former classmate in residence was my friend David Panar, from Vegreville High; he was a very clever Jewish lad known in his hometown for his quick wit and good jokes. He was registered in Engineering and had a room at the north end of Athabasca, on the lower floor where the windows were just above grade level. Of course life in residence encouraged practical jokes, and David quickly became involved in some, as a victim or as a perpetrator. I don't suppose there were many residents who at some time or other did not find their beds wetted or half-sheeted. David kept a fishbowl full of water on his dresser, and when Reg Lister objected, David said it was for his invisible goldfish; for supporting evidence he showed Reg his small box of invisible fish food. Then one night when David went down to his room, he found it filled with about four feet of snow. This was a story that got around quickly. When I went down to see, the snow and the bowl were no longer there. David told me he had been visited by two senior Jewish students, who had instructed him to be quiet from that moment on, and to keep all jokes to himself. Last time I saw him, he was a Professor of Engineering at the university.

I met another student whom I had known at school at Lavoy. She surprised me with an invitation to a dance at the Normal School, just south of the university, where she was studying to become a teacher. She had grown tall and was a very good dancer. She later married Stuart MacFarland, one of the three musketeers, the lame one, who had become a motor mechanic. A few years later I was sorry to hear that he had committed suicide, as his father had done near the end of the Great Depression.

University residence was not the best place for study. Nearly every evening there would be the distraction of a bull session or two in rooms along the corridor, and traffic to and fro until about ten o'clock. I kept track of my time on a sheet of graph paper, twenty-four squares from top to bottom. In one column, every morning, I coloured the squares red from top downward, representing study hours of the previous day, and black from bottom upward, for hours of sleep; the blank space in between was "waste." I found that any really long red line, indicating an unusually long day of study, was usually paid for by short red lines on the following day or two; clearly, long bouts of work did not pay. I had read somewhere that the first three hours of sleep were the most beneficial, so I tried getting that benefit twice each night by sleeping from just after supper till ten o'clock, studying from ten till three, then sleeping again from three till seven. It worked very well for a week or so, until I found that I could hardly get to sleep at all. Then I wasted another week getting back on to a normal schedule.

The rooms in our corridor were cleaned every day, and the beds made, by a brisk middle-aged woman in uniform. I happened to go back to my room one morning while she was there at work, and she gave me a stiff scolding, with dramatic gestures to aid her thick accent. She waved an arm toward my open clothes closet, where rested my old worn suitcase, skis and ski poles, farm boots, gym shoes, skates, cookie box, laundry, wrapping paper, twine, and my grandmother's ancient Whyte typewriter on which she had taken down court proceedings, directly as they happened, in Denver in the 1890s. With trembling voice Mrs Miller said that Canadian students knew nothing, unlike those she had known when she had worked at a school for officers in Germany; there, everything had been tidy and in its place.

For the first year I mailed my laundry home, and Mother sent it back smooth and fresh. Then I heard that one of the boys knew of a laundress in Edmonton who did the work at home, and charged very little, so I began taking my laundry to his room at St Steve's, and picking it up a week later. When he graduated, I took over his agency, and my room became the laundry depot for half a dozen fellows. When I first saw the laundress I was shocked and conscience-stricken to see her so old, with bent back and gnarled arthritic hands, but she insisted that she wanted to continue, with loads as large as she could carry by bus and streetcar to and from somewhere in North Edmonton. So I could not turn her away.

Mealtime in the Athabasca dining room was a dignified ritual. There was white linen, and places were set. At the far end of the room, the Dean of Residence presided at the head table, which seated several members of the teaching staff, mostly young bachelors whose departments I could not name, except for one historian and Walter Johns of Classics. The room was large enough to seat all the residents of Athabasca and Assiniboia halls, plus the head table and two tables of girls, overflow from Pembina Hall. We saw different girls from time to time. We heard that Miss Dodd considered this trek to Athabasca Hall to be some sort of coming-out experience for the girls; she lectured them on dress and deportment, and made up a roster so that every Pembinite, reluctant or eager, had, for at least one fortnight a year, to traipse in line, twice a day, through the south corridor of this den of men, through the wide lounge, and to their special tables under the south window.

Each table seated twelve, and once placed, each man had the same table and chair for the year. Knowing our stalls avoided confusion and delay. Each noon and dinnertime we waited in the lounge until Reg Lister rang the bell and opened the doors. We stood behind our chairs until the Dean of Residence had pronounced the university blessing in Latin. Then all sat down, and streams of uniformed waitresses brought in the food on trays, each to her assigned tables, and serving began. Plates had been stacked at the head of each table, and the head-of-table (who was also responsible for maintaining order) served the meat and potatoes. Water jugs and side dishes were passed along the table. Dessert was served by the chap at the foot of the table. Nobody could leave before the Dean of Residence gave the signal by standing up, and then the occupants of each table had to wait until all twelve at that table were finished and the plates stacked again at the head. I was at a table of town or city boys who had light or picky appetites; I still had my harvester's appetite but tried hard not to keep them waiting. I was glad for the gracious way in which Bob Barron and Eddie Keruluk prolonged the meal at our table by their endless arguments on any topic that offered.

I sometimes wonder how I came to be invited or assigned to a table with at least four medical students, given that I had planned my courses as an entry into medical studies. It made a difference to my life. There were two from Vegreville, Eddie Keruluk and Fred Reid (whose father had brought me into the world there). There was John Elliot (whose father had been principal of the Vermilion Agricultural College when I was there on a one-week scholarship), and there was Bob Kulberg, who sat next to me at table. Bob took an interest in my plans, and one day offered to take me, right after lunch, for a tour of the Anatomy Lab. In half an hour there he killed any ambition I ever had to study medicine.

In the Zoology Lab I was assigned a bench beside a lively Calgary girl named Marian. She said that her father and most of her friends called her Mike, because she had a sister named Pat. Pat-and-Mike was her father's idea of a joke. His first daughter, born in August 1912, had been named after Princess Pat, who had visited Calgary that month to open the very first Calgary Stampede. In the Zoology Lab, Mike was exceedingly squeamish about dissecting things, and managed to get most of her share done by me or the handsome lab assistant. Back in Athabasca Hall, I made conversation by mentioning this amusing girl named Mike. I soon learned that Bill McEwen, who lived just across the corridor from me, had been Mike's boyfriend ever since they were old enough to walk. He always called her Marian, not Mike. Thus began a period of nearly five years during which I knew Pat Gibson's name and heard about her occasionally without ever seeing her. I heard she was working in the public library in Calgary, and living at home; that she was at the library school at the University of Wisconsin; that her family had driven to Madison for her graduation in 1938; that a fellow in Wisconsin had sent her an engagement ring for Christmas; and that after wearing it for some months she had sent it back. I could not have imagined that she would be my wife for forty-seven years. But at that time I was too busy with the present to be giving much thought to the future.

My Student Union card gave me free entry to all university events, and I went to the opening football game. We had played soccer, summer and winter, at Victory School. At school in Lavoy all the boys had played soccer, and one very windy day I actually scored on a corner kick that drifted in over the head of the goalie. But the game I saw at University Stadium was one I had never seen and did not understand, so at half-time I went back to my room to work on an essay. An engineering student, coming back from the game to his room to get something he had forgotten, saw me at my desk and said, "You're crazy!" That taunt hardened my priorities forever in favour of books and study, and I have never bothered to attend another football game. And I have never owned a hockey stick or golf club.

Learning My Way Around

Though study was my top priority, I was eager to take part in other useful experiences offered at the university. I sampled the Film Club and the Philosophical Society, and joined the German Club. At one of the Physical Training sessions, which were held several times a week and were obligatory for freshmen, I was recruited into the Boxing Club. Being the second-tallest recruit, I was paired with a very tall fellow who, after a few demonstrations of his superior reach and speed, was mercifully taken away to spar with the instructor, and soon became our inter-university champion. My second partner was also too quick for me, but I survived with him for a day or two, until he jarred me with a forbidden blow to the jaw that sent me reeling, with him hanging on to me and saying "Don't fall down, don't fall down!" After that I took up weightlifting, not in any club but just by myself, when there was nobody else in the weights room.

For Sunday exercise, two or three of us used to hike along the river path at the north end of the campus. Eastward, near the High Level Bridge, in winter we could see where the ice companies had been busy with long handsaws, cutting thick cubes of ice and hauling them away in horse-drawn sleighs, for storage. Westward, not far from the campus, the path passed the doorways of some caves cut into the bank and occupied by down-and-outers; one had a stained-glass window that consisted of the ends of a few dozen beer bottles set horizontally in clay, one row above another. Farther along we passed below the Colonel Strickland house, a large landmark overlooking the edge of the bank. On a fine afternoon we could watch cars driving up and down the river on the ice, along lanes that had been ploughed out, some cars hauling one or two long ropes for skiers who swooped over the deep drifts along the sides.

My old ash skis, bought at a farm sale, were wide and very flexible; they had been fine for skijoring on a rope behind the family car on country roads, or across fields behind a galloping horse. But they had no harness, only a leather toe-strap. They were not much use for cross-country or downhill skiing, the options now open to me, so I traded them for a pair of racing skis, which were really too narrow and stiff, but had metal clamps that crossed over the toe and clamped onto the soles of my farm boots. At the south end of my corridor was Walt Harris (later to become Dean of Agriculture), who also had skis, and one afternoon we crossed the river to the steep slope below Government House. We had several good runs straight down the packed surface, very fast. But at the bottom of the last run my points drove straight into a frozen snowbank, and I was catapulted headfirst into the hard surface. Luckily nothing was broken, so Walt helped me home to the infirmary at Athabasca Hall for repairs. I wrote nothing about this mishap to my parents until I could say that the bandages had been taken off my head and that all was well.

My first formal dance was sponsored by the Wauneita Society, to which all girl students belonged. Like most other large events, it was to take place in the Athabasca dining room, but unlike most others, the girls did the inviting. A day or two before it was to take place, I lingered innocently at my place in the Chem Lab to give my sink and glassware a good cleaning. There was nobody else left in the room, except a couple of girls near the door, who seemed to be engaged in the same task. As I passed them on my way out, they introduced themselves and struck up a conversation. Ascertaining that I had not been invited to the Wauneita dance, the older one (much older) invited me to be her guest. It would have been uncivil of me to decline. I forget her name, but I think of her now as Wauneita.

My friend Bill McEwen was my size; he lent me his tuxedo for the occasion, and helped me into it. Wauneita's address was some distance south and east of the campus, an area I did not know, but I knew that Edmonton street numbering was easy to follow. Starting out in good time, I found that the south part of the city still had some open fields, and taking a shortcut across one of them in the dark, I found I was walking over ploughed ground. I lost my bearings for a short time, until I got back onto a numbered street. When I rang the bell at last, Wauneita was waiting at the door, in a long yellow gown and short jacket that would not be nearly as warm as my tux in the evening breeze. As we walked toward the campus we kept to the sidewalks, but she was wearing rather flimsy high-heeled slippers open at the toe, which gave her some trouble, especially on the stretches of cinder walkway. A few times we had to stop while she hung on to me and picked cinders out of her shoes.

When we finally got to the party, I noticed that most of the girls, except Wauneita, had got themselves some flowers to wear. I was not a good dancer, but neither was she, and we kicked toes more than once. She told me she had taught school for several years, but otherwise we found little to say except "Excuse me!" and "Sorry." The best part of the evening, for both of us, was during the final waltz, when she said she had met friends who had a car and had offered her a ride, so there was no need for me to see her home.

Other formal dances were advertised on all the bulletin boards but were expensive, beyond my means. A few of us from our corridor sometimes sat part-way down the stairs to the lobby, to hear the music and smell the roses and watch the beautiful people come and go. In following years I did attend some of the big formals, and enjoyed them all, except one of the last, the Senior Prom. My funds were at very low ebb, and it was not until we reached the dance floor that I remembered I had repaired my only shoes with glued-on rubber half-soles that refused to slide on the floor. After some misery, I excused myself, ran upstairs, and with my jackknife removed the rubber soles. Unfortunately, the rubber cement remained, refused to be peeled off, and would stick worse than smooth rubber. However, the operation had exposed a large area of wool sock in the middle of each sole, and I trudged through the evening somehow. After the last dance, ten or twelve of us piled into two cars to go to a party at somebody's house, and stopped for coffee on the way. I was too embarrassed to say that I could not afford two cups of coffee, so I lagged behind as the other fellows paid their shares on the way out, and as they left I paid with my last nickel and last streetcar tickets.

My partner that evening was Peggy Graham, very pretty in a lacy white evening gown. In our party was somebody we had not seen before, a dashing young policeman (RCMP) from Red Deer, more nimble of foot and tongue than I could be. He told me, aside, that he envied me greatly for having such a beautiful partner, and asked me her name. In due course, true to his calling, he got her for his wife. I met her again, twenty-five years later at the Alumni breakfast. She was still living in Red Deer, pretty as ever.

The population of the university in those days was almost entirely British in origin. Those of other origins were mainly Ukrainian or Scandinavian, from settlements in central and northern Alberta. There was a sprinkling of other national backgrounds. Many of the students were first-generation Canadians, as I was, their parents having come from other countries. And many who had Canadian-born parents were first-generation Albertans. The only non-Caucasians I saw or knew about were two Chinese. David Ho Lem (Commerce), who was in his senior year, lived along my corridor, and was about to become Alberta's first Chinese graduate. I was shocked when one of my friends did not wish to be introduced to him, and told me she would never dance with him because of his race. The only other Chinese student I heard about was registered in Engineering. One day a Mathematics professor told his first-year class to be ready for a test in which there were more questions than anybody could be expected to answer correctly within the allotted time. He told them just to work along as far as they could; the paper he received with the most correct answers would be marked as 100 per cent, and the other papers marked in proportion to that. The class got ready by agreeing that nobody would attempt more than half the questions, so that all would end up near the top, with good marks. But they forgot to tell their Chinese classmate, who went right ahead and answered all the questions correctly. As a result, his classmates received no mark higher than 50 per cent.

At the north end of our corridor lived a senior student who could walk the length of the corridor on his hands. He was the well-balanced editor of the student newspaper, *The Gateway*. I told him about the owner-editor of a small-town daily paper who was related to my mother and had visited our family the previous summer; he had invited me to spend a summer working on his paper, filling in for his staff as they went on holiday. With this in mind, the editor of *The Gateway* offered me my first newspaper assignment: to cover a well-advertised public lecture in Convocation Hall by no less a visitor than Stephen Leacock, on his view of the Canadian economy in 1937. I went to the lecture, pad and pencil at the ready, knowing nothing about economics and expecting to hear a *Sunshine Sketches* version. But the lecture turned out to be really dead-earnest economics: production rates, tax rates, employment rates, interest rates, population, and so on, the speaker holding a blue paper in his hand and glancing at it as he reeled off numbers after numbers. After a few minutes I gave up taking notes and tried – not very successfully – to get even the gist of what he was saying. As a last resort I went up to Dr Leacock before he left the platform, and asked to borrow the blue paper. He handed it to me without hesitation and I took it away hopefully, until I looked at it. It was nothing but a railway timetable. So ended my career as a *Gateway* reporter.

But I still looked forward to spending a summer, some year soon, down in Oroville, California, living with my Beebe cousins and working on their newspaper.

Luckily for my friends and me, the hazing of freshmen had been outlawed a few years earlier, but sophomoric energy still sought an outlet. I saw an instance of it in 1937. Engineering students, unlike those of us in Arts, were usually together all day in the same lectures and labs; they even had their own boastful chant: "We are, we are, we are the Engineers." Their profession seemed to encourage them to show a rough-and-tough face to the world, although most of them would end up as managers behind desks. The other large and cohesive group of students, in Medicine, showed a more respectable and dignified face, one that seemed to be a natural target for the Engineers. Antagonism had become traditional, fanned by an annual Med–Engineer "fight." The one I saw was perhaps the last, because of its violence and its shameful ending. I think it began with a noisy Engineering rally, a march to the Medical Building, strong resistance at the doors, and then an invasion of the building. One side or the other turned on the fire hoses, and there was a great struggle for control of them. There was considerable water damage inside the building, paid for eventually by the Engineering Society. Outside the building, waste bins had been dumped, and papers blew about in the wind. The crowd of non-combatants watching from across the street included many Pembinites. When the noise finally died down, we thought the fight was over. People we knew began to come out of the building, in small groups or singly. We saw Sammy Epstein come out. Sammy was Jewish, a large man, a senior in Medicine, a talented debater, well known and respected on campus. As he came down the steps, some Engineers spotted him and mobbed him. A few moments later we saw him bloody, limping barefoot toward St Joseph's College, with nothing but a torn bit of newspaper to cover himself. I cannot write this without strong feelings of shame and pity. He finished his medical studies in the United States, and never returned.

My inability to buy more than a few of the books I needed led me almost immediately to the library, the first library I had ever seen apart from our glass-covered bookcase on the farm and the small box of University Extension books that hung beside the wicket in the Lavoy post office. The University Library, it was said, then had about 50,000 books,

The Beebe visit from California to Alberta, 1936. Front row: Helena Beebe, my grandmother Olson holding my sister Betty, my aunt Olive Watt, my mother Palma Blackburn, my cousin Glenn Olson. Middle row: Dan Beebe Sr, Alice-Mae Beebe, my cousin Gladys Olson, Dan Beebe Jr, my father John Blackburn, my uncle Ralph Olson. Back row: my aunt Nora Olson, my uncle Ingmar Olson, and myself.

more than any person could hope to read in a lifetime, but a mere fraction of today's annual additions. The library visible to junior students at that time was a long, panelled reading room, entered through an imposing doorway on the left as one entered the lobby of the Arts Building. The five long tables on each side of the centre aisle, eight chairs to a table, were usually fully occupied by mid-morning. The west wall, opposite the windows, was filled with sets of big books. At the south end, in a large alcove, were the card catalogue, a big dictionary stand, some journals, and a counter at which one could apply for other books to be brought up from a mysterious region below. The near end of the loan counter was blocked by a dumb waiter with shelves holding a few books waiting to be sent below. And on the near side of the dumb waiter was the entrance to a narrow metal stairway leading downward. The entrance had no sign beside it but was known to be forbidden ground to anybody below fourth year. Opposite the stairway entrance was an office desk from which Dorothy Hamilton directed operations, dispensed information, and kept a sharp eye on the stairs. At the beginning of my fourth year I entered the stairway bravely, but was called back by Miss Hamilton to show my credentials. There were no fines for overdue books, but none were needed: one did not keep anything overdue again after being spoken to by Miss Hamilton on the first offence. Downstairs in the basement, at the south end, was an alcove containing the collection of English literature, in Cutter classification. Under the window was a large table for the use of fourth-year and graduate students, although there were not many graduate students in the university; I think Alberta had yet to grant a PhD in any subject. Those of us who worked sometimes in the English stacks were vaguely aware of other libraries on campus – one in the Law School on the second floor above us, a medical library in the Medical Building, a few books and journals in the Agriculture Laboratory – but we had no occasion to visit them. Several times I made the trek southward to the Normal School to borrow from the Extension Library that was housed there, and once or twice I looked in at the Edmonton Public Library. In principle the topics for MA theses had to be chosen to fit within the limited scope of the collection in the Arts Building. Eventually I discovered that the library had a workroom on the main floor, along the south wall. Also, between that and the mysterious Wauneita room was the office of the University Librarian, named Cameron. I never saw him until I was about to leave the university and called on him for advice.

Another discovery I made during my first year was that there were some Greek-letter fraternities with their own houses near the campus; each autumn they "rushed" selected recruits. I was in the great majority who were never rushed, and was glad of it. But there was a group of fellows, thirty or forty of us, who used to meet for dinner on Sunday nights, when residence suppers were informal and very skimpy. We met in a private room downstairs in the Corona Hotel on Jasper Avenue. A good dinner, from soup to dessert, with white linen and two forks, could be had for 50 cents. After dinner one of the fellows would give a prepared paper on some pet subject. Gradually, to have an identity, the group began to call itself the Parnassus Society, adopted a high-sounding statement of purpose, chose an executive, decided on a way of voting to select new members, and had some talk of designing a lapel pin. As the first secretary, I kept minutes, and walked down to Whyte Avenue to arrange for a hall and music for a Parnassus dance. Eventually some of the fellows got together and rented a house for themselves; it became a sort of headquarters for the society. For some reason or other they held a raffle, in which the prize turned out to be a large bottle of whisky, which I won and promptly gave back. I think the house rental lasted for a year or two, and then I heard no more about the anti-fraternity Parnassus Society.

Near the end of my first year at university, on the Easter weekend, I went home by bus to plant the garden. My parents had rented a house in Lavoy, but I went straight out to the farm to get an early start next morning. Our Danish hired man, Marius, was looking after the farm and had prepared the soil for planting. Next morning we found two inches of snow on the ground, but he made black rows with the hoe. I planted the seeds and covered them, and the garden was very good that year.

At the end of term I went out to the farm again, and worked again with Marius, who had become our renter (on a share basis). I was his hired man. Out across the summer fallow with team and wagon, picking stones, he told me not to bother with the little ones, but "yust leave them for seed!" When the land was dry enough to plough, we took turns on the tractor. I took the day shift, seven to seven, while he took the night shift, also seven to seven; he also ran the seed drill over what we had ploughed, in addition to looking after the cows and chickens. Each of us cooked for himself, and carried a lunch. In slack times, before harvest, I found other jobs. The most unusual was a solitary job in the annex to one of Lavoy's grain elevators, nailing laths over horizontal cracks that had opened up inside the walls. The lower levels went quickly; at higher levels I had to work very slowly and carefully, moving the ladder, moving the work platform of planks along the interior tie-rods, going up and down for more laths. The only light was from the open door at ground level. And then, after harvest, I could afford to go back to university.

Honours English

Professor R.K. Gordon, my adviser on my first registration day, was head of the English Department, and lectured to our large first-year class. He read us a great deal of poetry. He had a neat knack of pausing, just before he came to any erotic or other questionable line or passage, to make some general comment, and then picking up again just below it. He took his work very seriously; I cannot remember seeing him smile.

At the beginning of my second year, having given up the idea of a career in medicine, I went back to him as he had invited me to do. After hearing my story, and scowling at my marks (in which English was lowest in a list that had won me the Governor General's Award of $100 for highest standing in first year), he rather reluctantly admitted me to Honours English. It would require a total of four years, instead of three.

Near the end of that term, Professor Gordon invited all the Honours English students to his home for a party. The food was plentiful and good, but at one point during the evening I was shocked to hear him steering one of the girls away from the chocolates, offering her a cigarette instead because it would be less harmful. A few weeks after that, assigning essay topics in connection with his course on Chaucer, he gave me the topic of medieval cookery. I wondered whether it was because he had noticed the enthusiasm I had shown for the sandwiches and goodies at his party.

Another professor who had a party for us was Dr Owen, who taught German language and literature, as well as several German songs, including drinking songs. On the evening before our final examination he walked the whole class up to Whitemud Park for a wiener roast and a case of ginger ale. He explained that he wanted us to be fresh and relaxed for the test next morning, not tired and tense from a night of eleventh-hour reviewing. Next morning, I found myself in a large crowd of anxious students gathered outside the examination room; among them my classmates were speculating about what questions were likely to be on the examination paper, and wishing they had reviewed some point or other. All feeling of relaxation had been lost, but I thought of a way to avoid that loss on such occasions in the future. I would go to the doors of the examination room twenty minutes before they were due to open, go from there on a ten-minute walk out toward the river, then arrive back just after the doors had opened, in time to enter the room calmly and go to my appointed table. It was a system that worked very well except on one occasion: as I walked through the door I reached up to my shirt pocket for my pen, but it was not there or in any other pocket! I stood in panic for a moment, trying to think what to do, and then found the pen – in my other hand.

Everybody registered in Honours English was obliged to attend one lecture by Professor Clarence Tracy on the subject of Bibliography, a word that was new to me. His lecture began with a lament over our university's poverty in bibliographic tools. Then he went on in praise of the comparative wealth of such tools he had known and enjoyed at Cornell. I had never heard of Cornell University and had no idea where it was, but Tracy's resonant pronunciation of the word "Cornell" stuck it firmly into my brain. Years later, at Toronto, I learned that Toronto and Cornell, back in the 1890s, had shared the talents and benefactions of a wealthy English republican named Goldwin Smith. They had maintained an important exchange of students and other academics, and had eventually used the talents of the same library architect. Cornell would touch my own career in several interesting ways. I had at least two full courses from Tracy, one in modern poetry and one in seventeenth-century authors. The relish with which he read poems about the inconstancy of women led some of us to assume that he was a woman-hater, but he surprised us after one of the holidays by bringing home a bride.

Another English professor was J.T. Jones, with whom I had a wide variety of contacts. He was Dean of Residence and lived in a suite above the front door of Athabasca Hall. The Poetry Club was small enough to meet in his parlour; at each meeting we read aloud from the poems of an author selected beforehand. For the meeting I was to chair, I asked each member to bring a poem of his own; this was to give each one a chance to show his wares, and, incidentally, for us to see what the professors could do. Our host J.T. Jones was not enthusiastic about the idea, but along with the others he met the requirement very well.

Along with three other boys I took J.T.'s course in Anglo-Saxon language and literature: *Beowulf*, King Alfred's Laws, and so on. The following autumn I met J.T. coming down the boardwalk from Athabasca Hall, and gave him the casual greeting "Hi!" that I had learned from my California cousins. He bridled and gave me a look that told me clearly that he would have expected a "Good day, sir" instead. But that year he got me a grant of $100 for marking half of his share of freshman essays, a job that took me a very long day once a month. Before assigning marks I used red ink to mark corrections and what I intended to be constructive comments, though I discovered that they were not always appreciated. On one of my rare visits to the Tuck Shop I sat down at a table with some friends who introduced me to a young woman whose name I recognized as one in my group of essayists; she was complaining about the rude and sarcastic remarks she had found scrawled in red all over her essays when she got them back.

That winter I was elected to the three-man House Committee that met with J.T. Jones from time to time to discuss housekeeping problems or matters of discipline. One of my duties as secretary-treasurer of the committee was to conduct the weekly house dance in the gym under our dining room: to advertise it, sprinkle wax on the floor, collect the 25 cent entrance fee at the door, pay the orchestra, and so on. For one of those events I advertised a "sweater dance" at which the traditional dress code, requiring jacket and tie, would be relaxed. J.T. objected, saying he could not allow that sort of thing in the residences. So I changed the posters, rented the basement in the Tuck Shop, and found a disk jockey with appropriate music. The sweater dance was well attended, a lively and perfectly respectable success. J.T. and I maintained a discreet silence about it. During my fifth year, when I lived off-campus, he served as supervisor of my work on an MA thesis. I was glad to hear, later on, that before he retired he had his turn at being head of the English Department.

My course on Shakespeare was given by a tall young American who played a lot of tennis on the courts behind Assiniboia Hall. It was a fairly large class, and Shakespeare was well served. Toward the end of the year we had an essay assignment in which each of us was to choose a favourite Shakespearean scene, and explain the choice. Instead, I took the liberty of writing a conspiratorial scene between Falstaff and Juliet's nurse, with as much Shakespearean language and style as I could muster. The professor said he did not know how to mark one of the essays he had received, and would let the class be judge. He read the whole thing through, and asked whether he should give it a 90, the highest mark he knew about, or a zero for being off topic. The class voted, and was generous.

There were only half a dozen of us in the Milton course given by Malcolm Ross, a recent MA from Toronto. He made it fascinating, and told me years later that it was his most challenging and stimulating teaching experience. When we heard at the end of the year that his appointment had been cancelled, we reacted as undergraduates often do, without ascertaining the facts. We suspected that he was the victim of a political conspiracy, based on a report that he had been at the railway station to meet Canadian volunteers just returning from the Spanish Civil War, where they had fought alongside Communist forces.

Our private indignation against the university administration rose to the point where I wrote a satirical poem, consisting of a patchwork of parodies of well-known sources, and handed it around to classmates. The only lines I recall were:

On such a foul sea are we now afloat
and we must take the current as it swerves or lose our vestures!

In later years Malcolm told me that his appointment had been for one year only. He had hoped for renewal, but its lapse persuaded him to go on for a doctorate that would become the foundation of his career, in which he became a prominent promoter and mentor of Canadian writers. As editor of *Queen's Quarterly* he published one of my stories and a poem. As head of the English Department at Queen's University, he invited me to his first conference of Canadian authors and publishers (at which the youngest author was Leonard Cohen, who sang to his small guitar). Malcolm eventually moved to Halifax to be head of the English Department at Dalhousie; I visited him there more than once. When he retired, the University of Toronto Library bought his correspondence and other papers. In July 2002, two months before he died, he wrote: "I have been house-bound for the last couple of months. Various ailments that attend the 'golden years.' I am getting close to 92 and am *beginning* to realize that I am an old guy."

7 California, Here I Thumb

At the end of my second year at university, I went to California for the summer. The first thousand miles or so of my journey could hardly be classed as hitchhiking. It had been arranged that I would ride that far with Jerry Ambler, and help pay for the gas. Jerry, a young farmer from down the line, had bought life insurance from my father, although I wondered later whether the company understood the risk it was taking. Jerry at that time held the bronco-riding championship of Canada, and he was soon to become champion of the world; he carried some scars of his trade, including a long, bony welt from knee to ankle where a horse had fallen on him and split the bone.

In the spring of 1938 Jerry was on his way to Redding, California, to begin another season of rodeos. I was going another hundred miles south, to Oroville. On the day of departure Jerry had lunch with us at the Shasta Cafe, on Jasper Avenue in Edmonton. Mother and I had not met him before, and she asked him questions about his wife and children and how they would fare on the farm all summer. When lunch was over, Jerry led us to his car that was parked nearby and chucked my suitcase into the trunk. Then, as my parents stood on the sidewalk waving goodbye, we roared off on our three-day journey, making very quick time in those days of gravel highways in Alberta.

Jerry handled his Ford V8 as if it were a spirited cow pony. He balanced forward in his seat, shoulders hunched over the wheel, his bridle hand fidgeting, his eyes shifting back and forth as if scanning the horizon for strays while he made his mount "git along" at seventy or eighty miles an hour. In cities he was careful to watch all the traffic lights, but when it came time to move, he would dig in the spurs and dart forward as though he were cutting out mavericks in a corral, and would slip in and out through traffic with a suddenness and precision that must have left other drivers as limp as it did me at first.

That first day we came to mountains and passed them. Some time after midnight, and somewhere beyond Spokane, Washington, we stopped in a small town. The hotel was a faded frame building beside the railway tracks, not at all a fancy place. When the bell had been answered and we had paid $1.50 each, we were directed upstairs to our room by the proprietress, a ponderous old hulk in a flannel nightgown. Before we put our shoes beside the bed, Jerry gave me a short lesson in hotelmanship. Close the transom, lock the window and door, wedge the chair back under the door knob, fold your trousers and put them under your pillow, with your wallet and keys still in the pocket. Then we slept soundly and safely, until wakened in the morning by the whistle and rumble of a freight train just below our window.

On the second day we drove through rolling country where the spring wheat was just beginning to shade the ground, and we saw lilacs in bloom although it was only April. In Oregon we stopped to take a picture in a forest where the snow was eight feet deep along the edge of the road. We saw the splashes of feeding fish, and the floating picture of the sunset for twenty miles along the narrow mirror of Klamath Lake. And we passed miles and miles of stacked green lumber.

In Klamath Falls we found a gas station attendant who happened to know the rodeo rancher for whom Jerry was going to work; that night we slept in the bunkhouse with three of his ranch hands, all professional bronc riders; that is, I slept after being lulled to sleep by cowboy gossip.

"Say," Jerry would ask, "where's Coot's wife?" And a voice out of the dark would answer, "Oh, she's travelling with Ole Nelson now. They say Coot's carrying a gun for her. And Nelson he's riding awful bad these days. You just can't mix women and bucking horses."

"And say, what's happened to Speers, that scar on his neck?" In the house at supper I had noticed the scar, a withered brown patch down his cheek and the side of his neck.

"Oh," the voice was saying, "that breed wife of his took to shooting. Thought he was running with some other woman a little too much to suit her. One night when he got home late she met him on the stairs with a sawed-off and blazed away. Lucky for him she was drunk!" Then another voice chimed in, "First time I saw him I thought Blue-Girl must have piled him and then jumped on him." And then they were away again, riding Blue-Girl and Red-Gold and Shot-out-of-Hell and Phantom and Rocking-Chair and others, until it was too late to listen.

The third day, we started out with two new passengers, hefty cowboys who were going down to Redding with Jerry to look after sixty head of bucking horses. They were still talking about their trade, and how they always hoped to draw a real hard bucker and get into the prize money, and how they couldn't help feeling relieved when they drew a softer ride, and how hard it was to hold your leg grip for the regulation time. When Jerry was out filling the gas tank they quizzed me about his riding technique, because he was such a slim fellow and still a champion. Jerry had told me it had nothing to do with grip, only with balance and keeping one guess ahead of the horse, but all I could tell them was that I had never seen him ride.

About mid-afternoon Jerry dropped me at a gas station, and I started my first honest-to-goodness hitchhiking. Being a novice, I hung around the filling station and asked for rides until the attendant saw me and told me to move on. So I lugged my suitcase down the highway for half a mile or so and stood at the edge of the pavement with my thumb out for quite a long time. Finally an old coupé sputtered to a stop and a well-dressed young man invited me to hop in. He apologized for the state of his old jalopy, and the racket it made at its top speed of about twenty miles an hour, but he had bought it for $12 just to get him the four miles to and from work. He told me he had been across the continent and back by thumb, and dropped me at a spot he said would be better for my purpose, a deserted stretch of road farther from town.

I waited again, a longer time than before. There were fewer cars passing by now, and all in a hurry. There were black clouds overhead, beginning to spit rain, and I was starting to look around for a tree to shelter under. But then an old sedan pulled up, the door swung open, and the driver called "How far you goin', Bud?"

He was the meanest looking codger I had ever seen. I could not make out whether his dark complexion was due to some racial mix, or just ornery-white with a bad sunburn. He was clad in old overalls, and the peak of a dirty cloth cap hung low over his forehead. There was a long scar across his dark three-day beard. And the hand on the passenger seat, as he leaned toward me, was far from clean.

As I hesitated, there was a clap of thunder, so I told him I was on my way to Oroville and wondered whether he was going that far. He said he might, if he had enough gas. That seemed an unusual and rather mysterious answer, but I offered to buy him some gas. Then I tossed my suitcase into the back seat and climbed quickly into the front before my new driver could have a chance to start away without me.

"The name's Jake Taylor," he volunteered. "I can prove it. Them's my papers in the door pocket. Read 'em so you won't be scared. Go ahead, there in the pocket. Read 'em all."

I got the small pack of miscellaneous papers and glanced through them, but my attention was focused, out of the corner of my eye, on his dirty hands and the point of his bearded jaw.

He said, "Them's the papers I got from my boss in Redding. I drive truck for him, an' he's very perticular. Now I need your name and address, right there on the back o' that. You gotta be perticular, these days. Not get in bad company." I could not think of any particular reason for not obliging, so I wrote my name and address and put his papers away.

"Canada, eh? I thought you must be Canadian when I seen you standing there. You got something honest looking. I swore I wasn't ever going to pick up nobody again, but I could see you was right. Us Canadians gotta stick together. I'm Canadian myself, y'know. My mother, she was born there. You might not believe that but I can prove it. Yah, we gotta stick together. But you're all right if ya just keep outa bad company."

It was raining hard now, and I was nervous about the speed Jake was driving as he divided his attention between me and the slippery pavement. But he kept up his side of the dialogue, or rather the monologue, as I kept wondering about his motives and did not have much to say.

"Say, lucky for you old Jake came along, eh? What would you ha' done, with only enough money for bus fare for this last hunert miles, and no bus till tomorra morning?" (I had not really lied when I told him I had enough to take me as far as Oroville; actually I was carrying nine $10 bills.) "Yes, pretty lucky. You know, I was driving home from work and thinking of going the other way, but something kept saying 'Jake, go by the highway.' Lucky for you. Life is pretty tough here for somebody ain't got any friends ... You see that farm over there? House with the new roof? Well, that's my farm. Twelve miles out. Just bought it today. Took every cent, but that's life. Millionaire today an' broke tomorra. Here I am without money for gas. Lucky for you I came along ... I guess you're about nineteen, eh? I have a nephew that age, an' I know how tough it is for him. I have kids of my own, too. Three ... I got the farm for them, that's what I got it for. Keep 'em out of bad company ... My wife died six years ago ... I ain't never been the same since. But I look after the kids ... See those guys on the boxcar? Hi boys! ... Poor suckers, out there in the rain. They all know me, I been all over the country on the rods myself ... Working for the police in Sacramento. I wouldn't say this to anybody but you, but you're Canadian and I can trust you: I'm expecting my reward money any day now. No chicken feed. Ten thousand bucks. I cleaned up a gang for 'em down there. Should have been in the mail today, but wasn't. Be there tomorra, though. Ten thousand. But keep it under your hat, I wouldn't tell anybody but you."

There was a pause while he relished the idea of that much money, then began again. "So you came down to Redding with a bronc rider, eh? ... Say, you better give me his address. My brother has a good bucker he might sell. A real bargain. And if they close a deal you'll get a cut. Sure you will, trust old Jake! ... Remember when I rode broncs myself. Jolts the liver right out of a guy. You wouldn't believe it to look at me now, but I was a pretty salty cowboy. My mother's cousin, too, he used to ride with Buffalo Bill. All over the world. An' my great-grandfather was Zachary Taylor. You know, President Zachary Taylor. You may not believe that, but I can prove it."

I bought him some gas at Red Bluff, and he said to the garage man, "I see you took my picture down since I was here last time. Don't you remember? On that post, good picture too."

That really made me wonder, but there was more. He had me go with him into a newspaper office where he inquired about a paper that his brother had ordered and not received. And he asked the girl whether they had any hot news about the case, "You know, the murder case!"

Then he insisted, in spite of my protest, on driving down a narrow side street and stopping at a cheap-looking café for lunch. There was only one other customer, a young chap with very blond hair. While Jake went into the kitchen to wash, I sized up the young man and the sloppy little waitress, who both seemed to know Jake, and I recalled some of the dime mysteries in which I had read of situations rather like the one I was in.

Jake came back and ordered a full dinner, which he ate lustily while I sipped a Coke that I ordered for myself. I hadn't eaten since breakfast at the ranch house at six that morning, but had too much imagination to want a meal in that place. When Jake had finished he went over to whisper something to the waitress, and while she fumbled in a drawer he called me over to the counter and said he had something to show me. The girl handed him a worn roll of paper, and something hard and flat in an envelope. Jake unrolled the paper on the counter, for me to see a picture of a cowboy on a horse, and the hand-printed inscription "Jake Taylor on Fire-Eater at Denver Rodeo." Then Jake untied the envelope, showed me a framed photo of a tigerish girl reclining in a silk robe, and retied the envelope while I paid for the lunch.

I was greatly relieved to get out into the street again, and as Jake lit a cigarette I slipped my camera out of my pocket. Just as he was about to step into the car I said, "Oh, Jake!" and snapped his picture as he turned my way. He did not seem to realize what I had done, and asked whether the waitress had called after him; he seemed disappointed that she had not.

The fair-haired customer then appeared and asked whether he could ride to the next town with us. It did not quiet my nerves to have him sitting silent in the back seat while Jake glued his eyes to the road and was also silent for a change. I turned half around to watch both of them, and tried to make conversation. But my anxiety turned out to be baseless, for the young fellow got out at the next town, and Jake opened up again.

"You know," he said, "last time I was in that town they had my picture up all over. Sheriff was after me. They had a rodeo there last month, and I was on a spree. Old rider, you know, and you gotta have some fun, long as you keep outa bad company. They had some Indian riders too. Those guys hate me like poison. They had this girl doing some stunt riding. They called her the Indian Princess, but I just laughed and said who she really was. Against the law to give them liquor too, but I did it just to get even with them, eh? They had their knives out when I left. They sure hate me! ... The sheriff kept me in the jug all through the trial. They sure do!" As he relished that thought, I spent a few minutes trying to put his story together and fill in the blanks, before he spoke again. "Say, you know that Filipino girl in the picture? To look at me you might not think I had a girl like that. Down in Sacramento. And all mine. Carries a knife for anybody else. You might not believe it, but I can prove it!"

I was still trying to figure him out. Was he some kind of crook? Or some kind of loony? Or maybe only an old, lonesome, broken-down type of Jerry Ambler, an old bronc rider, going far out of his way to do me a good turn? I began to repent of my unkind suspicions. But when we reached Oroville, and he offered to drive me to wherever it was I was planning to stay, I declined with thanks. I preferred to find my way on foot. I didn't want to risk getting my cousins, the Beebes, into bad company.

Helena Beebe was my mother's cousin, who had been taken into mother's family at age two, in South Dakota, and had finished high school in Tofield, Alberta, before moving away to Seattle to become a nurse. Her husband Dan Beebe was owner of the *Oroville Mercury*. When I reached their house they greeted me warmly and called the movie theatre to have their two children sent home; Dan Jr was about my age, and Alice-Mae a sixteen-year-old beauty. The children got home just in time to say hello before I was shown upstairs to bed. When I woke the next morning I saw yellow roses against a yellow stucco wall, and took a few moments to think where I could be.

The *Oroville Mercury* occupied a former Safeway store across the street from the courthouse on a street lined with crepe myrtle trees, the leaves barely visible among the masses of pink bloom. Oroville had a population of about five thousand, and its newspaper was unique. Most small-town papers in those days got all their pictures as boilerplate from large news agencies, but Dan Sr carried his camera wherever he went, and Dan Jr ran a one-man photoengraving plant. Any local news photo taken before two o'clock in the afternoon could be in print by the time the press rolled at four. The *Mercury* was published daily, Monday to Friday. On Fridays, Dan Jr and I did a two-hour circuit by car for regional delivery of the *Butte County News,* a mostly advertising rag that we tossed into every driveway as we sped along.

My job was to replace some of the staff as they went on vacation. I learned how to run the switchboard, take classified ads, read proof, and do the photoengraving as well as stereotyping (which involved pouring hot lead against the news agency mats of advertisements and pictures from out of town) and sawing them to size, ready for the press. Boilerplate advertisements for San Francisco hotels were paid for in credits. Using some of those credits, Dan Sr and Helena took me to stay in two or three of those hotels while seeing the sights of the city. In the lobby of one of the hotels, the Drake, was a replica of the inscribed metal plate that Sir Francis Drake is reputed to have left when he careened his ship in the bay about four hundred years earlier.

My beat as a reporter was the daily coverage of births, deaths, and marriages as registered at city hall, and police reports. At Oroville the Feather River flows out of the Sierras, and there were many reminders of the great Gold Rush days. Not far above the town bridge was the stone Chinese Wall, which ran for some distance up the centre of the river and was said to have been built by Chinese miners so that they could divert one side of the stream, then the other, as they took gold out of the dry bed. The table mountain just north of town had been cut into on one side by hydraulic miners with powerful hoses, to wash down the muck into their sluice boxes. South of town there was a very large mining barge floating in the centre of a big pond. It had an endless revolving belt of large buckets slanting downward and undercutting the terrain, scooping up earth and rocks to be washed for gold. As it ate its way slowly through the orange and olive groves it took its own pond along with it, with another endless belt at the back hoisting the cleaned rocks into barren heaps behind it. I was assigned one day to go and interview the barge man, but when he heard I was from the newspaper he simply hauled up his gangplank and turned away.

One Sunday, Dan Jr and I drove around to the other side of the mountain, looking for the village of Paradise. We stopped where there was a narrow rope bridge across a deep ravine, and thought to explore it, but an old man appeared and waved us away with his shotgun. As a reporter, I attended a court case in which one school trustee from Paradise was charging another trustee with attempted murder. Evidence given by the witnesses revealed that the issue was really a family feud; the name calling and shouting from both sides drowned out any testimony that might have been given, until the judge dismissed them all for contempt of court.

Gold panning up the river was still good enough to support a colony of winos. They lived in packing boxes and other makeshift shelters, straight out of Steinbeck's *Cannery Row*. When they had panned enough to buy jugs of wine, there were often a dozen or more men sleeping it off peacefully the next morning on the courthouse lawn. If any of them caused trouble, I would find them in the police record in the morning. I remember one entry in which the note under "property" was "one shoe and pair of pants." The typical charge was "disturbing the peace," and the penalty "one hour to get out of town."

One police story told of a gathering of winos drowsing in the afternoon in front of one of the brothels down by the river. One fellow, asked by another to share his jug, refused and went back to sleep, whereupon the other fellow began bashing his head with a large stone. One was taken to hospital, the other to jail. A week or two later, as I sat at the front desk reading proof, a young man with bandaged head came in asking for the paper of a certain date, the date of that incident. He was just out of hospital, had heard that his name was in the paper, and wanted a copy to send home to his mother. I was reminded of a similar instance in one of Chekhov's stories.

Oroville had no rain that summer, and the hot days were seldom without the smell of grass fires. It was before the days of air conditioning, and we spent most evenings, after supper, in the basement taking turns at the billiard table. Carom billiards is a game for two players, on a large table with no pockets, and three balls on the table, one red and two white cue balls. A point is scored when a player strikes his cue ball (maybe the one with the black dot) so that it hits the other two, perhaps after hitting a specified number of cushions. The Dans, Sr and Jr, were old hands at the game, and taught me so well that now and then I could make a successful three-cushion shot, and occasionally win a game.

One evening a farmer came to the door with a gold nugget the size of his fist, embedded in some quartz, that he had found in his orchard that day. He asked Dan Sr to keep it in his safe overnight, as a precaution. Another evening my cousins were hosts at a community picnic at Bidwell Bar, a wide stretch of gravel in a clearing beside the river, reputed to have been an important location during the Gold Rush. Cousin Helena had prepared a very large kettle of lamb stew with noodles and black olives. When supper was over we had a big bonfire on the beach, and Dan Sr told stories. As the moon came up over the forest across the river, the setting was such a good fit for the words that I could not resist reciting a poem we had learned at Victory School, "Dickens in Camp" by Bret Harte:

Above the pines the moon was slowly drifting.
The river sang below;
The dim Sierras far beyond uplifting
Their minarets of snow.
The roaring camp-fire with rude humour painted
The ruddy tints of health
On haggard face and form that drooped and fainted
In the fierce race for wealth;
Till one arose, and from his pack's scant treasure
A hoarded volume drew, And cards were dropped from hands of listless leisure
To hear the tale anew;
Then while around them shadows gathered faster,
And as the firelight fell,
He read aloud the book wherein the Master
Had writ of Little Nell.

To my surprise, it seemed that nobody else there had known of it.

I had begun to think I would like to be a journalist, until the city editor strode out of his office one afternoon and threw down on my desk a list of marriages that I had given him. He pointed to an item that consisted of the names, address, and ages of two octogenarian newlyweds and asked loudly, "Where's the story?" I had not written one. I had found the couple in rocking chairs on the front porch of an old folks' home nearby. They had been childhood friends, and happened to meet again in that home in Oroville, but did not want any news coverage because it could embarrass their families. When I told this to the city editor he grabbed his camera and told me to lead him to them. He badgered and bullied those dear old people until he had a full column of their life stories, to print beside their picture. It was then I realized I would never make a journalist.

8 The English Department

When I returned to the campus in the fall of 1938, I found Malcolm Ross's former office occupied by a Professor F.M. Salter, who was full of surprises. He was offering, among other things, the University's first course in Creative Writing. I applied for it.

He was a man of medium build, with a round face, round eyes, small moustache, and ready smile. On the first morning, after introducing himself, he began by announcing that there was only one good textbook on the subject into which we were about to launch. He paused for a moment, as we sat with pens poised, and then told us he was referring to the book he had begun writing the previous evening. Later on he did suggest another book for us to read, Sir Arthur Quiller-Couch's *On Jargon*. Years later I discovered that Sir Arthur had been a close friend of Kenneth Grahame at Fowey, in Cornwall. On long walks across the harbour from Fowey, I have stopped several times at the Q monument that marks his favourite spot from which to view the village.

Salter told us there were to be no assignments during the year, except that each of us was to write something every week and drop it into the box beside his office door. Our grades would depend on quantity and quality. Then he counted us, found there were thirty, and jolted us by saying that number was twice too large a class for him to handle properly. It would have to be reduced. He invited each of us to drop a page of new writing into his box by next morning, and he would conduct interviews during the week. I gave him a poem, making sure that it scanned perfectly. When I kept my appointment, he looked me up and down and asked whether I knew that I was deaf. Dumbfounded, I begged his pardon, and he repeated the question in a louder voice. When I said that I didn't think so, he explained that poetry was meant to be heard, not read. Then he read through my poem aloud, pointing out the awkward sounds and misplaced emphases that I should listen for.

The fifteen of us who met with him the following week were a mixed lot in age and experience, but all were excited to be there. Salter said that he himself was excited to be back in Alberta, one of the few places left where he might expect to have some students who were seeing streetcars and indoor plumbing for the first time, and for whom the Maple Leaf, our national emblem, was as mythical as skylarks and cherry blossoms. He spoke about writing what we knew, or what we could imagine on the basis of what we knew, in plain words.

He did not give formal lectures, only stories and general advice. Mostly, he would read to us some piece that a member of the class (unnamed) had dropped into his box, and would lead a discussion of its merits and faults. At the end of each session he gave us back our writing of the previous week, marked with fine red handwritten corrections, and suggestions that might run to half a page or more. Each of us had personal attention, as well as personal interviews from time to time.

Salter was the same age as my father, born in 1895. While a student at Dalhousie University he had worked, summers, underground in a coal mine. On warm dark nights he was still sometimes wakened by mining nightmares. He had taken his Master's degree under Professor Archibald MacMechan, whom he recalled as "the love of God that will not let you go." After graduation he found a job in the Marmon (auto) factory somewhere in the American Midwest. There he received a note from MacMechan, saying that he had been recommended to a lectureship in English at the University of Alberta.

After a year in Edmonton, Salter went on to the University of Chicago to earn a doctorate while serving as one of the two assistants to Professor J.M. Manly on his great eight-volume edition of *The Canterbury Tales*. Just as that work was going to press, Salter received a note from R.K. Gordon, asking whether he might be available for an opening that would soon be available at Alberta. Salter answered, "Whistle and I'll come to you, my lad." Gordon whistled "rather feebly," but Salter, having a wife, a small daughter, and a Chicago job that was drawing to a close, returned to Edmonton.

He and his wife Ben (family Benbow) occasionally invited a few of us to tea at their home, a short distance east of the Arts Building. One spring day at class he told us that their five-year-old, Elizabeth, had announced at breakfast that she had decided to run away. Her parents

My mentor Professor F.M. Salter, Professor of English, University of Alberta. Courtesy of the University of Alberta Archives. Accession# 79-52-1883.

had helped her gather a bundle of things she might want to take with her and kissed her goodbye. She had walked halfway to the corner, sat down to rest on a strange doorstep, and was home again before an hour had passed. He turned the story into a homily for writers, in praise of having an adventurous spirit but respecting practical limitations.

Another day he warned us, as writers, to persevere in spite of the many bitter disappointments we were likely to face. For an example, he held up a thick book in lavender binding, the first volume of Manly's *Canterbury Tales*. Manly's other assistant in the work for that grand edition had been E. Rickert. On publication of the work she had received a doctoral degree; Salter had not. Her name, and Manley's acknowledgment of her work, were prominent in the preliminary pages; Salter's name did not appear. And the book's cover was exactly the colour of her eyes!

Our marks were handed out to us as we left the last class. Mine was at the end of a fatherly letter, handwritten in red. Near the middle of the first page, it read: "I need not say that I shall be glad to read more of your work, and I hope you will soon pass beyond the need of such help as I can offer." I did continue to hand him some of my work from time to time. At the end of my final year, he asked me what I was planning to do. I told him that I had decided to enlist in the RCAF. On hearing that a few of my friends had already been killed in action, I had given up my conscientious objection to voluntary enlistment. But I had no plans for what I might do if I should happen to survive. He said that nobody in Canada could make a living as a writer, and therefore I should plan for a career that would leave me plenty of free time for writing. His only suggestions offhand were the full-time army, or else library work, for which he thought there was a short preparatory course somewhere in eastern Canada; Mr Cameron the librarian would know. So it was that before enlisting, I spent a year at the Library School at the University of Toronto, as preparation for a possible future.

I will have much to say about the war years, but will continue this present thread for now. After the war I sent Salter a story I was pleased with, called "Recipe for Pork". He sent it (without telling me) to the prestigious *Atlantic Monthly*. I was astonished to receive an acceptance and a cheque for $250 for my "Atlantic First"; the *Atlantic* had earned a reputation for publishing the first work of unknown writers; they had published Mark Twain's first. Mine was published that spring in time to amaze my classmates in the MS course at the Columbia University School of Library Science in New York. For a month or so I received letters from a few publishers and literary agents, wanting me to call them and show them some of my other writings, but I had to tell them that all such things were in storage at the bottom of a barrel in Calgary. Salter was excited when I told him that Dudley Cloud, editor of the distinguished Beacon Press in Boston, had taken me to breakfast in Toronto and wanted to talk about a novel, but nothing came of it because I was already fully committed to other tasks.

After settling down in 1947 as Assistant Librarian at the University of Toronto, I wrote a verse drama on the last voyage of Francis Drake. It was produced on radio on *CBC Wednesday Night*, a great institution in those days. Salter, after hearing it, advised me to rewrite it with a different narrator (I still have not found time or energy to do it). About that time he referred one of his recent graduates to me, Doris McCubbin, who was in Toronto writing copy for the *Eaton's Catalogue* and who was living in a boarding house where the bathroom tap, having no handle, had to be turned with pliers. We had her to Sunday dinner but never heard of her again until she became a prominent feminist and editor of *Chatelaine Magazine*.

Salter spent one summer in Toronto, seeing his book *Mediaeval Drama at Chester* through the University of Toronto Press. He invited me to his room at Victoria College to see a set of woodworking tools he had just bought to provide him, he said, with a quiet alternative frustration to the daily frustration of academic work. We took him on a family picnic beside Lake Ontario, with our children. We took him to a play at the Stratford Festival, where he was especially interested in a novel portrayal of Shylock as a madman.

One day the president of the University of Toronto, Claude Bissell, remarked to me that he was tired of handing out honorary doctorates to tycoons, celebrities, university presidents, and other politicians; why couldn't there be one for somebody who was simply a good scholar and teacher? Of course I mentioned F.M. Salter, whose seminar at Toronto, on the miracle plays at Chester, had been attended by students and English professors, including Bissell. And so it was that Salter received a doctorate after all. He reminded me that it was an "unearned degree, only the kind a person works for all his life."

On one of my later visits to Edmonton I found the Salters very worried about Florence Dodd, who was sick and long retired from her deanship at Pembina Hall, and whom they had befriended. They themselves were feeling very insecure because the university, having sold its large block of farmland west of the campus, was planning to expand eastward and had expropriated their whole street. He was carving a small wooden screen with an intricate pierced pattern. After his death in 1963 his wife allowed me to have his woodworking tools; I still use them occasionally.

When I was president of the Canadian Library Association, in 1959, we had the annual conference on the Alberta campus, and Salter agreed to be speaker at our banquet. By that time his fingers had become so arthritic that he could hardly hold a pen. In introducing him, I spoke about the textbook he had recommended at our first class, which he was still trying to perfect, and which I thought might never be published because he kept so busy following former students through their lives. And so it turned out. The manuscript he left behind was nearly complete, and I took some part in getting it to press with the title he had given it, *The Way of the Makers*. It is a great text, but a shoestring production that is not a great example of the book-making art.

I thought there should be a Salter Memorial Bursary, and one afternoon in Edmonton I dropped in on President Walter Johns at the university. His secretary said he had another visitor in his office, and he had to go immediately after that to a five o'clock appointment at the legislature. I said I did not need more than a very brief time with him, and could have it while walking downstairs with him on the way out. When he opened his door just after five o'clock to let his other visitor out, he spotted me, hailed me by name, and invited me in. I objected because of the appointment for which he was already late, but he waved me to a chair. He said he was reminded of a story that would explain his situation. The story was about a man from the city who visited his cousin in the country. The cousin showed him all around the farm and insisted that he stay for supper. After supper, before leaving to drive home in the dark, he said he really needed to use the toilet before starting out. He was told that the privy was just around the woodpile and to the right. Waiting on the porch, the cousin heard a loud twang and a groan. He called out "Sorry, I forgot to warn you about the clothesline!" The gloomy reply was, "It's all right. I probably wouldn't have made it anyway." Walter Johns was pleased with the idea of a Salter Memorial Bursary, but I could not find the addresses of very many of Salter's other former students. The fund was small and must have been exhausted long ago.

Last Two Years at the University of Alberta

At the end of my third year of university I had gone to Banff with Doug McKecknie, a Dentistry student who lived in my corridor. We camped on Tunnel Mountain. As he had planned, he got a licence to use his father's car at the public taxi stand on Banff Avenue, next door to the police station and across the street from the Veterans' taxi stand. I applied for work at the Banff Springs Hotel, but there was no place for me. Canadian Pacific Railway, which owned the hotel, had hired all the students it needed in Toronto and Montreal before the season opened. I happened to be nearby, however, when one of their elevator boys got tired and decided to go home to Montreal. He had not bothered to tell the hotel manager, but I did and got the job. The pay was $35 a month, the first $5 going to the head bellman. There were, of course, other benefits: a shared room in the staff quarters and meals in the staff cafeteria.

I began work on one of the staff elevators that carried room service up to the guests. One of the upper floors was occupied by King Farouk of Egypt and his retinue; we saw wagonloads of delicacies on the way up to them. When the wagons came down again, many of the trays were untouched; we had a place to park them on their way back to the kitchen, and enjoyed them with due care. I was soon promoted to the front elevators, where we wore the liver-coloured CPR livery. The head bellman inspected us daily, and for a while gave us each two pairs of white gloves a day, in expectation of a surprise visit by the president of the CPR, Sir Edward Beatty. The surprise was that we never saw him. But there were other notables. Sonja Henie, the world champion figure skater, was there in her white Cadillac. And the comedian Jack Benny was there briefly, strangely silent. The Governor of New York came and went in his private railway car. There was rumoured to be another private car at the station, and one evening a pudgy middle-aged fellow, rather unsteady, told me two or three times on the way up to his floor that he was the Duke of York. He may have been a Duke from the Carolinas.

That was in the days before self-operated passenger elevators. We stood in or beside our cars during shifts of six, nine, and fourteen hours, twice a week. We were just outside the main lounge, and every evening heard the Murray Adaskin quartet there. After the concert, there was the dance music of Mart Kenney and His Western Gentlemen at the far end of the hall.

The big event of the summer was Canada's declaration of war against Germany. There were mixed reactions. A sweet old German guest went up to her room in tears. A fearful young couple, chambermaid and busboy, jumped into a taxi to rush downtown and be married, hoping to avoid the draft.

The bellhops apparently prospered on tips, but there were few tips for elevator boys. My total for the summer was about $2, most of it from my share of what was left by the Duke of Sutherland to be divided among the whole staff of the hotel.

At the end of August, when the great hotel closed for the winter as usual, I stayed on for two days to help put it to sleep. We rolled up all the carpets and rugs, then covered them with sheets. We also covered good furniture and pictures on the walls, and stripped the beds. It was a dismal sight, and I was glad to get home in time for threshing.

My friend Bill McEwen had finished his Engineering course in the spring of 1939 and took a job at the copper mine on Britannia Beach on the west coast. His girlfriend Marian Gibson (the girl I had met in Zoology Lab) graduated in Household Economics at the same time, and entered the University Hospital in Edmonton for a year's internship in dietetics. I was entering my fourth year in Honours English, and Bill asked me to take good care of Marian for him in his absence that year. That task was complicated by a senior medical student who had his eye on Marian and was in pursuit. Marian, always resourceful, devised a neat compromise by introducing me to one of her apartment-mates, a charming Maritimer who had come west to intern as a dietitian. The four of us began going out on double dates.

Because this Maritimer had never seen real mountains, I thought she should do so before she left for a job at Gravenhurst in Ontario the following spring. When I took our family Ford to Banff in June 1940 to drive it on the public taxi stand, I had company.

Mother and my sister Betty went along to keep house for me, and my Maritime friend went along for the ride. She stayed with us for a few days, and I showed her Banff as I had got to know it the previous summer. The night before she left we danced at the hotel to Mart Kenney's band, right up to the closing waltz. Next day she went on to Calgary for a visit at Marian Gibson's home.

My friend Doug McKecknie was back in Banff again with his father's car, and lived with us, paying his share of the rent. Except when we had taxi fares, we stayed by our cars from morning till night watching the passersby, offering them private tours at bus rates. While sitting near the back of the taxi line I had time to work on a few poems; these were slipped into the glove compartment whenever I got close to the head of the line. I did get a few trips to Lake Louise and one to Jasper, but most of our trips were up to the big hotel or other local spots. My net income for the summer was $200.

When Mother, Betty, and I were on the way home we found that Marius Christensen, who had been renting our farm, had moved to Vancouver to a job in the shipyards. Father had found other renters who were occupying our house. He had also decided to pursue his insurance work more aggressively by moving to Vancouver, where his firm had its western Canadian office. He had put our furniture into storage. He had also arranged for Mother and Betty to live temporarily with Grandfather Blackburn and Aunt Lila on their farm near Vegreville, Mother to keep house and Betty to take her grade six at Imperial School three miles away. He had taken a room at a boarding house in Vancouver. This sudden and unexpected turn of events was a shock to all of us. It left Mother feeling abandoned by her husband and bereft of her belongings. It was a most unhappy prospect for her. I was due back at the university. For 1940–41, my fifth year in university, my MA year, I lived in an upstairs room at a home just east of the campus. I took my meals at the Stacey house, four or five blocks south. I paid $12 a month for the room, $14 for meals.

The Stacey house was a remarkable institution. Mr and Mrs Stacey looked as though, twenty years younger, they might have stepped directly out of Grant Wood's painting *American Gothic*. They had moved to Edmonton so that their children, a large family, could get to high school and to university. Mr Stacey had built the house, providing a room for each child. And next door to it he had built another house, identical in size and outward appearance but filled with bedrooms for other students. As the Stacey children graduated and moved away into their careers, both houses had become filled with students, who were still treated as sons of the family.

The first house had, on the main floor, a large parlour, a bathroom, two bedrooms, and a very large dining room. The boys waited quietly in the parlour until the door opened, and then went in to their appointed chairs. I think the table seated fourteen or fifteen, with Mr Stacey at the head. When all were seated, he asked a blessing and served the plates. Mrs Stacey carried the food up from the kitchen; it was nourishing and plentiful. We were a mixed lot and had good conversation at table, but nothing rude or loud or prolonged, or else Mr Stacey would rap on the table; he was waiting for everybody to finish and leave, so that the table could be cleared and reset for the second sitting, the fellows waiting in the parlour. At the second sitting, an extra chair had been set at the foot of the table for me. I was the only non-resident, but Mrs Stacey took me aside and invited me to bring my laundry in to be done with that of the other boys, at no charge. I was glad to do so, but sometimes thought my shirts had a faint aroma of soup. We knew that the basement was one large room for kitchen and laundry, a fact that for some time had posed a mystery. Mrs Stacey used one of the bedrooms on the main floor, and the two boys who occupied the other room there would hear Mr Stacey say good night to her and go downstairs. Eventually it was discovered that the kitchen table, large and sturdy, had a hinged top that, when raised, disclosed his bed.

A couple of weeks after graduation, I was passing through Edmonton and called Mrs Stacey to ask whether I might have a room for the night. She welcomed me, would take no money, and kept apologizing for not having made me a white shirt for graduation. She had always made white shirts for her graduates, but had been just too busy that year.

My room that year was a good place to study, except when the son of the house, another student, thumped out current dance tunes on the piano downstairs, to accompany his own falsetto voice. Next to my room upstairs there was a Ukrainian Household Economics student, and at the end of the hall a secretary who also danced in the Edmonton Ballet. I shared the bathroom with them but seldom saw them, except occasionally to share some cake from the Household Economics laboratory.

When the Second World War began, all able-bodied male students, except those who had a medical exemption, were obliged to join the Canadian Officers Training Corps (COTC). Twice a week we had lectures, parades, inspections, and basic military training. I was surprised to see Professor Tracy turn up as captain of our company, very dapper in uniform complete with flat hat and baton. He had the voice for it, but on parade he was not always well coordinated. When he gave the order to march, he sometimes caused muffled merriment in the ranks by starting off with left arm as well as left foot.

Another surprise was to see Professor J.T. Jones, still Dean of Residence, as leader of our platoon. Our platoon consisted of graduate students and members of the teaching staff. Our natural stride was a bit longer than J.T.'s and on the march he had to skip ahead now and then to avoid being trampled. On one route march he suggested that we strike up a song to march by, and started it off with "Tipperary." Soon, however, he was hearing improper versions of that and other soldierly songs, so he called a halt and ordered a silent march.

The two-week COTC camp, at the end of term in 1941, was at Sarcee Camp on the southern edge of Calgary. We arrived on a blistering hot afternoon. After finding our bell tents, stuffing our mattresses with straw, and drawing blankets and rifles, we had a route march and rifle drill. Before supper we were drawn up in companies for inspection by a cocky young regular army drill sergeant who was out to show us schoolboys what army life was all about. Peering at us belligerently as he paced along the ranks, he pointed and shouted in front of Professor Elliot, and ordered him to step forward. Elliot, the oldest among us, was already a distinguished economist, and already sagging a bit in his woollen battledress. The sergeant shouted orders at him, insulted him, cursed him in vile language; Elliot stood silent, obviously unable to suck in his gut to a satisfactory degree. The rest of us were too cowed, or too wise, to do anything about it, but the thought of it still burns me.

My tent mates were Ted Miller, my former lab technician soon to become head of Zoology; Ottomar Cyprus, a German immigrant just graduated in Theology; and Fred McKinnon, a prominent leader in student affairs. We woke next morning to four inches of snow and the prospect of open latrines and of shaving at cold taps out in the breeze. It was a gentle reminder of the horrors of trench warfare in the First World War, as they were portrayed in a book of cartoons in our bookcase on the farm, Bruce Bairnsfather's *Fragments from France*.

The other candidates for Master's degrees in English that year were Chet Lambertson, Alice Frick, and Edith Fleming. Alice had taught school for several years. Edith was a pleasant girl who knew much but said little. Chet was a gifted fellow who had got his BA before I entered university; the University Cheer Song was his composition. He had then taught school for several years, and in summers had toured Alberta in an old Ford, with three of his friends, making music for country dances. During his MA year he found time to compose and perform on the piano for two productions by the Edmonton Belasco Players: *Alladin, or The Genie with the Light Brown Hair,* and *Cinderella, or Godmother What Have I Done!*

The four of us were working at our theses but continuing to take various English courses as well. On days when we had lectures, we often studied together at the large table in the stacks, and sometimes went across to St Joseph's College for coffee. Marion Conroy, an Honours English student who had a part-time job shelving books in the library, would sometimes join us. I knew her years later as a senior officer in the National Library of Canada.

In one of Professor Tracy's courses I sat at the back between Chet Lambertson and Bill (W.O.) Mitchell. Bill was taking a characteristically casual route toward a BA. He had not taken Salter's course, but was writing stories that eventually attracted Salter's attention and advice. Bill was courting Myrna Hirtle, beside whom he had played a leading role in a Drama Club production in Convocation Hall. One evening several of us were invited to the Hirtle home for a critical reading of some of Bill's stories. Myrna was his sharpest critic and would interrupt his reading with: "Bill, you can't say it that way!" Some of the things he read that night turned up later as chapters in his novel *Who Has Seen the Wind*.

Late one morning Bill arrived at my room with an urgent need to borrow my razor and use it on the spot. The examination for his History course was slated for that afternoon, but his history professor was also the Commanding Officer of COTC and had taken Bill's name off the examination list because he had failed to take any part in COTC. Apparently Bill had been exempted earlier from physical training and thought the exemption would apply also to military training. He was now on his way in a hurry to his professor's office to make an appeal, and could not appear with a week's growth of beard!

A few years later, starting out on the way from Calgary toward New York and Columbia University, with my wife and two-year-old son, we parked our house trailer beside the Mitchell house in High River and had supper with Bill and his family. The house was pink all over. Bill had rented a paint sprayer, and to be sure of finishing the job in one day, he had painted everything, windows and all. He had not yet got around to scraping the glass, and Myrna was not amused.

I met Bill again when he was fiction editor of *Maclean's* and was living on Toronto Island. He borrowed my old bike but lost it one day by parking it unchained beside the ferry. I recovered it later from the police department. Another day he drove our family to see the house that Pierre Berton was building in the hills north of Toronto; the journey was enlivened by an excited exchange between our six-year-old sons, concerning their favourite characters in *Winnie The Pooh*. Years later, Bill was invited to be the after-lunch speaker at the annual conference of the Canadian Library Association in Ottawa, and I sat beside him at the head table at lunch. As we were finishing dessert, he turned to me and asked, quite seriously, what I thought he should speak about!

During my final year, when Chet Lambertson and I got to the stage of writing our theses and could not leave our books and notes over-

My MA graduation photo, spring 1941.

Myself (front row left) with other muckers and miners in front of our bunkhouse at the copper mine at Britannia Beach, summer 1941.

night in the library, he brought a card table and folding chair to my room, and we worked there side by side. It was a good arrangement. After working for a couple of hours we would stop for him to have a cigarette, and for us to try out our ideas and problems on each other. He sometimes told me about the young woman to whom he was engaged, who was continuing to act as principal of an Edmonton girls' school that could no longer afford to pay its staff. He was eager for me to meet her, and it was agreed that I would do so at the Graduation Ball. We did meet at the very beginning of the evening, but Chet had momentarily forgotten her name, and had to ask her before he could complete the introduction.

When we four MA candidates had our theses completed and accepted, we sat together at McDougall Church in downtown Edmonton, Convocation Hall being too small for the ceremony. That evening we spent a relaxed time at the house of a friend who had a fine collection of classical records. When the hour became very late, the four of us walked to my street and I collected my thesis notes, two shoeboxes full of white slips neatly tagged in categories. We carried them to the middle of the High Level Bridge, and dumped both boxes over the rail at the same moment. The slips scattered and fluttered down to the water, in the rosy light of dawn. And we turned away toward our new lives.

Edith Fleming, the brightest in our class, turned down a chance to study for a doctorate in Toronto. When I last saw her, she was professing English at Mount Royal College in Calgary. Alice Frick I saw again in Toronto, when she was assistant to Andrew Allen, director of drama at the CBC. From there she moved to England and the BBC. Chet Lambertson decided to go on for a doctorate, and after being turned down by Toronto, earned a PhD at Harvard. He and his wife, on their way home, stopped overnight to see me in Portage la Prairie, where I was an RCAF instructor in the Commonwealth Air Training Scheme. I visited them later at their home in Victoria when he was teaching at the university there. My last visit was to their acreage near Butchart Gardens, where she was raising Irish setters while Chet and their Japanese son-in-law raised fruit and vegetables for market. Chet remarked that his family was accustomed to mixed marriages; he himself, an Edmontonian, had married a girl from Calgary.

And I, having taken up F.M. Salter's suggestion, had a long and interesting career in library work. But there were some things to do before that could begin.

9 Preparation for a Career

When I went to the COTC camp Sarcee near Calgary that spring, I knew that Marian (Mike) Gibson had finished her internship at University Hospital in Edmonton and was home in Calgary. When I phoned her from the camp she invited me over one evening to discuss her wedding plans. Bill McEwen would be coming from his job at Britannia Beach and had asked me to be his groomsman. As Marian fed me cookies and cocoa before sending me on my way, her sister Patricia came in. She was just back from a hike with some other public library staff, including the librarian, Alexander Calhoun, who was an alpinist and had carried the ladies piggyback across a stream. That is all I remember about my first sight of Patricia, but at least we had met.

Later that week I received two telephone messages at the camp at Sarcee. The first was from a classmate with whom I had walked home from the graduation party; she had now arrived unexpectedly from Edmonton, was staying with friends, and wanted to see me. The second was from Marian Gibson, inviting me to Sunday dinner. I said I had just promised to spend that Sunday with a friend, but she said to bring my friend along, and I did. Marian had assumed that my friend was another chap and was rather surprised when I arrived with a girl who worked part-time in the university library.

The dinner had its unusual moments. Part-way through, Mrs Gibson suddenly lowered her head, covered her face, and retreated to the kitchen. The two Gibson daughters followed quickly, and all three were gone for some minutes. They came back to the table smiling bravely but looking rather red-eyed, as though they might break down again at any moment. It was a strange incident, and the Edmontonian asked me about it as we wandered around Calgary that afternoon. I could only say that Mrs Gibson was very worried about her son, who was a doctor in wartime London, and perhaps she had received bad news. Years later, Patricia gave me the real explanation. The Gibson ladies had been highly amused by my seeming unawareness of the tender looks the Edmontonian kept sending across the table in my direction, and they fled to the kitchen when they could no longer contain their laughter. Thus at our second meeting I had at least provided Patricia with a good laugh!

Our third meeting was a month later, at Marian's wedding. From Sarcee army camp I had gone back to my grandfather's farm south of Vegreville. It was seeding time and I had given up the idea of going back to Calgary, but Granddad said I would not be needed on the farm that summer, because his land was rented. He did not want me to lose touch with my university friends, and he urged me to go to the wedding. When I said I had no money or opportunity to buy a present for the bride, he went to his china cabinet and brought out a cut glass bowl that had been one of his own wedding presents. Then Mother suggested that I go on from Calgary to Vancouver to find work and keep my father company for the summer. So, carrying Granddad's old portmanteau, I hitchhiked to Calgary the day before the wedding.

Some friends were giving a party for the bride that evening, but when Bill McEwen and I walked around the corner to the Gibson house after supper, Marian came to the door with her face so swollen with allergies that we hardly recognized her. Patricia, however, was ready for the party, so she and I walked down to the friend's house. Bill and Marian arrived later, and the evening was spent in charades and chatter. By the time I walked Patricia home again, we had begun talking about books we liked.

The wedding was at the Gibson house the next afternoon. The June weather was perfect, and Marian's face had returned to normal. Patricia was bridesmaid, and after the ceremony we stood beside the happy couple for a picture. Social kissing was not in vogue then, at least not where I came from, but when people lined up to kiss the bride I saw that Patricia was in tears, and I kissed the beautiful bridesmaid instead. A bit later my attentiveness led me to get her a cup of tea, and when I somehow managed to spill some of it on her pink gown she assured me that no permanent damage had been done. Later she and I drove the newlyweds to their car, which Bill and I had hidden that morning, but which now, as a result of my own perfidy, had its luggage stuffed with confetti and windows scribbled with soap. There we waved them away toward their honeymoon at the Banff Springs Hotel.

When we got back to the house the lingering guests were supping on leftover refreshments, and some of the younger couples were deciding it would be fun to give Marian and Bill a surprise party at Banff and to dance at their wedding, so to speak. That idea fitted my plans perfectly, and suited even better when the car in which Patricia and I rode was so full that we had to sit close together for the whole eighty-five miles. Marian and Bill received us politely, if not joyfully, when we all trooped up to their room to renew congratulations and use their bathroom. Being a shy country boy, I hung back until I could slip into the bathroom unnoticed as everybody else started to go downstairs, and presently I found myself alone in the bridal chamber with the door locked from the outside. Luckily, an urgent phone call brought a bellhop to the rescue in time for me to catch up to the wedding party before I was missed. For the rest of the evening Patricia and I danced happily to Mart Kenney. Then we went up to the top floor of the hotel to look down on the Bow Valley by moonlight.

When the Calgary folks left for home after the final waltz, I borrowed Bill's keys and drove down to Bow Falls to clean out his car and wash it, and dozed in it till sunrise. Then I turned the keys in at the desk and set out for Vancouver on foot.

From Vancouver I wrote Patricia about a bear that had followed me parallel to the road for some distance, mostly out of sight in the bush, west of Lake Louise. And about being overtaken by nightfall near Abbotsford, finding my way into a hayloft when the ditch turned out to be too chilly for sleep, and having to charm my way out of a tight spot when the farmer came up the ladder in the morning. And about not finding any work in Vancouver, except peddling cheap magazine subscriptions door-to-door, a job that I quit after one day. And about an interview I was to have next day with the hiring man from the copper mine at Britannia Beach, where the company was advertising for muckers. Next morning I stood in a hotel corridor on East Hastings Street, with about twenty other men looking for work at the mine. After brief interviews, two of us were chosen – the youngest, I think – and were sent up along the coast by boat to Britannia. The other chap had some mining experience. At Britannia we were given brief medical examinations, and he was turned away on account of silicosis.

At Britannia, the townsite and mine entrance were halfway up the mountain, reached by a "skip," which was a flatcar on rails, hauled up the slope by cable. To ride up or down, passengers held on to a railing or sat on crates that were roped down. The townsite had a company store, bunkhouses for the miners, a row of apartments for the upper staff, and beside the mine entrance a cafeteria and the "dry." The dry was a large room with a row of showers down the middle, with hangers for mining clothes on one side and for dry street clothes on the other.

The miners worked in pairs, in three eight-hour shifts, ten days on and then two days off. I had several partners during the summer, the last one being the Big Finn. He was a powerful man, rambunctious, short-tempered, and with little respect for the safety rules. He would stride along the drift carrying a hank of fuses around his neck, the metal detonator ends clacking together as he walked. He would tip a fifty-pound box of dynamite off his shoulder to the floor and bash it open with his shovel, instead of using the regulation copper wedge. When we were blasting, he would cut the fuses short. When I set a new steel in the chuck of the drill, he would switch on the air and water before I had a chance to get out of the way.

As his nipper and mucker, my first job every shift was to take a set of dull drill steel, on a tram and tugger, back down to the main level. There I had to pick up a sharp set of steel and take it back up to the work face. A set consisted of six rods of different lengths, from two to twelve feet, the diameter of the drill-head diminishing in that order, to allow for wear. The trick was to get the sharp steel up the fifty-foot raise on the pneumatic tugger without the rods catching on some obstruction or other and come spearing down. Once it was up safely, I would climb the fifty-foot ladder beside the tugger track, up to our work level. Back at the workplace, my jobs included mucking out the broken rock, or turning the crank of the liner that forced the drill forward, or slitting sticks of dynamite and tamping them firmly, one after the other, into a hole that was ready.

Now and then I saw my friend Bill McEwen at work as mine surveyor, checking the direction and level of our work. Our shift boss, another young engineer, was catcher to my pitches in a pickup softball game one evening. A year or so later I heard that he had missed his footing at the top of a fifty-foot ladder, and fallen to his death.

On arriving at the mine I had written Patricia to give her my new address. It was a pleasant surprise when she arrived at Britannia for a week's visit with the McEwens. I happened to be on graveyard shift that week and so had mornings and afternoons free. We swam in the company pool and hiked up a mountain trail that overlooked Howe Sound.

One afternoon I was having tea with Patricia and Marian in the McEwen apartment when we saw two women coming up the boardwalk, the mine manager's wife and the mine superintendent's wife, self-appointed social arbiters in that company town. A visit by these ladies counted as a sort of Royal inspection, and it was against their rules for engineering staff like the McEwens to fraternize with riff-raff from any bunkhouse. Before the visitors passed the front window, I ducked into the kitchen, and found that the only way I could keep out of sight was to lie down under the stove. Patricia managed not to laugh when she came out to replenish the teapot, and I managed to stay awake throughout the visit in spite of being on my back. Thus we continued to build up a fund of shared experiences to remember and laugh about.

The summer's shortage of employment in Vancouver had turned out to be a blessing for me. On her way home to Calgary, Patricia stopped in Vancouver for a few days with her cousins there. At the end of my ten-day stint I ran down the hill beside the skip track to be sure of catching the boat. Bill and Marian McEwen were weekending in Vancouver, too, and their uncle took us all to dinner at the Hotel Vancouver. The next day Patricia invited the whole company, including my father, to lunch at the White Spot. My father was still in his Vancouver office, but he had enlisted in the RCAF and was to report for duty that week.

In the early years of the war I had thought of myself as an objector. I was patriotic enough, but thought that in fairness there should be systematic conscription of industry and wealth, as well as manpower, and I did not intend to volunteer until that came about. By the spring of 1941, however, with my father enlisted in the RCAF and some of my friends already reported as missing in action, I felt obliged to join up. I decided to join the Air Force but to take a year of library school first, so as to have some kind of professional qualification in case I survived the war. My application to the Library School at the University of Toronto, accompanied by a character reference signed by Marian McEwen, had been accepted, but it called for two weeks of practice work as a prerequisite. The public library in Edmonton had agreed to take me, so I left the mine early in August to hitchhike to Edmonton, making an overnight stop with the Gibsons in Calgary.

While I was in Edmonton, Patricia turned up at the library one day. She had been recommended for a job in the children's department and had come to discuss it with the librarian. She was staying with an old friend, but was to have dinner at the librarian's house that evening, and by some miracle I was invited, too. Because the contents of Granddad's old portmanteau offered limited choice, I went to dinner in my wedding outfit, including Bill McEwen's old white trousers that he had given me for his wedding, and the white buck shoes left over from my summer in California.

That day must have been Patricia's birthday; at least I turned up with a corsage of roses for her. There seemed to be an assumption around the table that we were an engaged couple, an assumption neither of us did anything to dispel. I was seriously in love and would have proposed marriage that very evening if Patricia had not been so painfully aware of the six-and-a-half-year difference in our ages, and if there had been any way for me to offer her any prospect of comfort and security. Maybe after the war, I thought. I knew she shared the feeling and that she understood my reasons for not speaking out.

Next afternoon she came into the library again to see the librarian and decline his offer of a job. I did not see her until she came up to me as I was tidying the magazine rack in the reading room. She said she had had a long talk at breakfast with her friend's mother, who had told her in tearful earnestness, and from her own experience, that a woman's being several years older than her husband was no bar to a happy marriage. Without other preliminaries she said she would wait for me until I got back from Toronto and that we could see how things were by then. I can't remember what I said, if anything, before she left me standing on the library steps and went home to Calgary.

After a two-week stint at that library, I spent a few days on the farm at Vegreville. Mother and Betty were about to look for a house in Edmonton, and Granddad was to live with them there. I shipped the old portmanteau to Toronto and set out afoot, carrying my typewriter and raincoat and no map.

Hitchhiking was easy in those days, and I spent the first night with my father at the RCAF station at Saskatoon, where he had become the Aerodrome Control Officer. Two days later in Port Arthur I discovered that the Trans-Canada Highway, about which there had been so much publicity, was not yet open north of Lake Superior; some other route had to be found. Train fare and boat fare were beyond my budget, but I learned that the *Hamonic* would be docking at noon to pick up passengers for its end-of-season sailing to Sarnia. When its gangplank came down I stepped up with an empty but official-looking envelope in my hand and asked to see the captain, who kindly hired me to clean the empty cabins as we crossed the lakes.

The winter of 1941–42 was a busy one for me. Besides the course at the Library School there were two afternoons a week of Officers' Training in khaki battledress; the midweek sessions were in the armouries on University Avenue, the Saturday parades were on the front campus. I was a private in C Company, which was commanded by the University Registrar, Joe Evans; B Company was commanded by the Librarian, Stewart Wallace. Wallace had kindly given me a job, ten hours a week of cleaning books at the University Library for 50 cents an hour. Today that seems like rather a skimpy rate of pay, but really it was quite generous; as an hourly rate it was very close to what I had been paid for working underground at the copper mine, and more than twice as much as I had received as a regular worker from sunrise to sunset on the threshing crew. I think it was better than what I was paid during that Christmas week for twelve hours a day as clerk at a haberdashery.

Wallace was also a lecturer at the Library School, in Canadian Literature. It was there that I realized he was the W.S. Wallace who had written *By Star and Compass,* a book about early explorers in Canada, the first history book we had read at Victory School. I was surprised to have the same author as my teacher and employer and could not have imagined that within a few years I would occupy his chair.

Our class at the Library School consisted of thirty girls seated alphabetically and a secondary alphabet of two Toronto boys and me at the back of the room. A few of the girls used to ask me in for tea, but I had little time or money for social life. I did hitchhike up to Gravenhurst one day in the autumn to visit my Maritime friend, who was dietitian at the sanitarium. She later moved to the diet kitchen at Toronto Western Hospital. She came to Sunday dinner at my boarding house once or twice, and I invited her to a waltz night at the Royal York Hotel, providing she would buy the tickets and let me pay her back when I got my next fortnightly pay of $10 from the library. We went with one of my classmates who had a car. When the other couple decided to go down to the coffee shop for a snack, I tried to persuade her it would be more fun just to keep on dancing, but she was thirsty. Although I told her, as we went down the stairs, that she could order anything she wanted as long as it didn't cost more than 25 cents (coffee was a dime in those days, most places) she unfortunately thought I was joking and had to dig into her mad money to help pay the bill.

The one thing I did make time for that winter was to send Patricia a letter at least once a week, and a poem now and then. She wrote, too, and knit me a pair of spiral no-heel socks, one size fits all. At Christmas I ordered her a dozen short-stemmed roses from a Calgary florist, to learn later that one of her Calgary admirers had taken her a dozen long-stems. For her part she, having heard about the temperature in my third-floor room on Brunswick Avenue, knitted me a sleeveless sweater, so wide in the shoulders that it would barely fit inside my jacket, so wide that it made me realize how far I fell short of her estimation. In fact I lost about twenty pounds on that winter's boardinghouse fare, down to 140. My aged landlady that winter was a retired nurse and church organist, a kindly spinster but not a great cook.

At the end of term I took the streetcar out to its western loop on a Monday morning and set out for Calgary. The *Huronic* was sailing from Sarnia the next day, and after sitting on the dock all afternoon, I got a job waiting tables across the lakes. From Port Arthur I travelled by foot, cattle truck, railway boxcar, and auto. Saturday evening I reached Calgary. I called Patricia's house immediately, only to hear that she was out dancing at the YMCA.

I rented a room for the week, hoping to spend a lot of time with her. But she was very busy. By now Dad was in charge of the control tower at the Service Flying School near Currie Barracks, and I spent many hours in the tower with him. Mrs Gibson invited us to dinner, but the chicken had to be sent back for more roasting and the evening was not a great success. After dinner Mrs Gibson suggested that the weather was so fine that the young people might like to go and sit out in the garden. My father (always young at heart) irked and embarrassed me by deserting her and Dr Gibson and following Patricia and me.

My Library School graduation day was that week, and I wanted to celebrate by taking Patricia dancing, but she had promised to visit friends that evening and I was allowed only to walk with her as far as their driveway. Trudging homeward I stopped on a bridge until dark, feeling sorry for myself and watching a dance of swallows over the river. Another evening she had to attend a staff farewell party (for her!) as she had accepted a library job in Wisconsin, where one of her former classmates had hired her as head of his children's department. In fact she was leaving at the end of that week, and when I wanted to see her off at the station she refused. She was, she told me, being seen off by an old friend, a medical officer in naval uniform! She had promised to see how things were when I got back from Toronto; now I had to interpret her actions as unstated but deliberate discouragement.

Next morning my father got me onto a duty flight to Edmonton (the final lap of my trip homeward), and after spending one day with Mother, Betty, and Granddad, I went downtown to enlist in the RCAF. It was 2 June 1942. I didn't want to waste any time, partly because the

Officer Training Corps adjutant in Toronto had been very angry when I declined to go to his spring camp at Niagara and had threatened to have me called up for the army as soon as he could. (He later spent some post-alcoholic years lettering book labels as a clerk on my staff.)

10 Enlistment, Military and Marital

One of the conditions of enlistment in the RCAF was an undertaking not to marry within six months, and there was no reason for me to hesitate in signing. Most of those who took the oath with me that day were shipped straight off to distant parts, but half a dozen of us were loaded into a panel truck and hauled to the manning depot in Edmonton's old fairground, where we were assigned bunks in one of the old sheep barns.

Patricia wrote again, from Calgary. She had not reached Wisconsin, having been turned back at the border by Canadian officials intent on keeping able-bodied young Canadians in Canada. So she was home again, and had written to me. Maybe there was hope for me yet, if I could just get to see her before being shipped away myself.

Canada, as the centre of the Commonwealth Air Training Scheme, had to keep a pool of potential air crews on hand for posting into the training schools. After a few weeks of boot training at the manning pools, groups of new recruits were being sent to do various routine chores at RCAF stations all across the country, to wait for their serious training to begin. And there were several stations in or near Calgary, if only they could be reached! This is where my wisdom teeth came into play.

Part of the initial screening at the manning pool was a dental inspection in one of the old hog barns, which had been upgraded to a clinic with a long row of chairs. At the first chair an inspecting dentist called out his discoveries to an orderly who marked the bad news down on a chart. I had been letting my teeth go for some time, but in my Toronto boarding house I had shared the third floor with a dentistry student who had made me acutely aware of my teeth and their shortcomings.

The dental inspector in the hog barn clinic took about a minute per customer. He stuck his mirror into my mouth and called out several findings, but when he stood back to call for "next" I startled him by saying I thought he had missed something on the left side – caries on the distal surface of the lingual-distal cusp of the second molar mandibular. He growled a bit but looked in and had the orderly write it down. When I said also that there had been periodic eruption of my third molars, he glanced in again and called out "Extraction! That means we'll dig all four of them out!"

Dad had told me the name of one of his policyholders who was a dental officer at the manning pool, and I was able to make appointments with him. After doing all the other things that were called for, he offered to take out the wisdom teeth one at a time and give me two days of "light duty" after each one. This meant that after picking up paper around the grounds for an hour each morning I could spend most of the day around the small arena called the "bullpen," where groups were assembled to be posted away for guard duty.

One day, as I sat at the edge of the bullpen, with one wisdom tooth still to go, the sergeant was calling for volunteers to make up a "flight" for posting. There were always rumours about groups being sent to desolate stations on the prairies, so it was taken as an ominous sign when the sergeant failed to name the destinations, and volunteers were reluctant. Finally, when the three ranks were nearly complete, he shouted that he needed one more man "for Number 2 Wireless". Half a dozen of us leapt over the board wall and ran for the spot, but I was first one there.

Number 2 Wireless was an RCAF school for radio operators in the old Technical School on the north hill in Calgary, only a half-hour walk from the Gibson home. I was one of those assigned to guard the front gate. The duties were to stop and query all incoming traffic, to patrol twenty paces of high wire fence on either side of the gate, to report any suspicious circumstances, and otherwise to stand in the sentry box beside the gate. Equipment consisted of white spats and a white belt and holster with revolver (but no ammunition), a close haircut, and highly polished buttons and boots. We worked shifts, two hours on and four off, night and day, with a day off every week or so. Both the location and the timetable were perfect for me, as I could usually trade shifts so as to get an afternoon or evening off when I wanted, say, by working two or three unpopular shifts in a row between midnight and six in the morning.

And so at the price of three teeth I had won seven wonderful weeks in Calgary. Patricia said she had finally made up her mind not to go on worrying, as her father and my mother did, about the difference in our ages, and would not try to run away from it again as she had been doing. And she agreed to marry me after the war was over.

As an AC2 (Aircraftman 2nd Class) with $39 a month and no fixed expenses or incentive to save for the future, I felt richer than I had ever been before; I could afford to take Patricia dining and dancing sometimes, and to buy a small gold wishbone pin that she was willing to wear. She had me up to the house for lunch now and then, with her Aunt Jennie as chaperone. She had a little black Austin to drive, and sometimes called for me at the gate. On those occasions I gave her a corsage of sweet peas, the sweet-smelling annual kind that climbed the fence behind the sentry box.

One afternoon she invited me to go on a picnic with her father and her friend Georgina Thomson from the library. We drove out to Dogpound Creek, where Dr Gibson angled up and down the stream, planning to catch fish for supper. While the ladies gathered sticks for a fire beside a large pond, I followed the doctor from one pool to another. He was not a patient man and never stopped to dangle his bait in one place for more than a minute or so. Finally he retorted, "Oh shoot, the fish are all gone!", and we trudged back to join the ladies.

Not being a fisherman but being curious, I picked up the rod he had laid down to light the fire, and swung the hook over into the pond. Almost immediately there was a nibble, and when I jerked the rod, a trout came shining through the air and landed on the grass at my feet. Unfortunately it was no longer on the hook, and in its struggles it was sliding down the slope toward the pond. I pounced and grabbed, but it squirted out of my hands and slithered halfway down the bank. I went after it again and got it, but the bank was slippery and I ended standing up to my knees in the pond in my best summer uniform.

I had caught a fish, my first and only trout, but shouts of laughter from the bank did not help me feel like the hero of the moment, and there was to be yet more merriment at my expense.

Mrs Gibson, well acquainted with the doctor's prowess as a fisherman, had put a good supply of bacon into the picnic basket. After bacon and other food, and one small fish, had been divided four ways, tea was poured into an assortment of cups. The cup I got was tin, very hot on the lips, and when I could finally take a sip from it the liquid congealed immediately on teeth and tongue. I was too startled to hide my distress, and when I was done spitting and spluttering it was found that my cup was the one in which wax had been melted at canning time, and the dregs melted again by the tea!

From Calgary I was posted to an initial training school in Edmonton. The transfer was made late at night by train, in an old coach in which the wicker seats had heavy brass edges. It was almost impossible to find a comfortable place or position for sleep, especially after one of the seat backs came crashing down and whacked my left kneecap hard enough to give me a classic case of housemaid's knee. For some weeks I had a painful limp and had to be driven to class every morning, to the evident chagrin of our sergeant, who had to arrange transport.

Number 4 ITS (Initial Training School) occupied parts of the University of Alberta campus. Parades for roll call and inspection were held in the gym or on the playing field beside it, and from there we were marched down to the old Normal School twice a day for classes. We were quartered in the three original residences, surrounded by a high security fence. I had an upper bunk in Athabasca Hall, just down the corridor from the corner room I had once occupied as secretary-treasurer of the house committee. Reg Lister, who never forgot a student, was still in charge of the buildings and used to give me a wink as I passed him at the entrance to the dining room.

Posting to ITS as potential air crew did not carry with it any promotion from the lowest RCAF rank of Aircraftman 2nd Class (AC2), but it did bestow the right to wear a white flash tucked into the front of the uniform wedge cap. Every new white-flasher wanted to become a pilot, but along with most others who carried the handicap of a university degree, I was soon declared unfit for that trade, and was steered toward navigation instead. After wearing reading glasses for twelve years I had discarded them before enlisting, so perhaps did not really have pilot's eyes despite a rating of 20-15, 20-15.

Medical inspection at ITS included electrocardiograms. After the war was over, a doctor at the University of Manitoba gathered these cardiograms and other medical records of about four thousand young airmen, all of us in perfect health, to begin what has become known as the Manitoba Heart Study, the longest-running such study in the world. It still monitors our health records, and there are still about six hundred of us answering annual questionnaires about our physical activities, social activities, diet, smoking and drinking habits, and so on. Many important articles have been published on the basis of that study, and as government support of it waned and finally stopped, we guinea pigs pitched in to help support it. Our average age is just above 91.

During those first weeks of ITS I looked forward eagerly to Thanksgiving weekend, when Patricia was to come to Edmonton to meet my family. By now she had agreed to marry me in April, during my embarkation leave. For this weekend she was to stay at the home of her old friend Pudge Williams again, and I was to pick her up in time for supper at Mother's. But difficulties arose.

The sergeant in charge of our platoon had been having trouble with two or three of the lads, and was fed up. On the morning just before Thanksgiving weekend he found three beds improperly made, so he confined our whole platoon to barracks for a week, saying he would not issue any new pass for any reason. This meant that the only way I could keep my date that evening with Pat was to go out through the hole in the back fence, as many of the boys had been doing. Before going out, I took the traditional precaution of arranging my greatcoat and a few other things in my bunk to look as much as possible like a sleeping airman.

When I got in again, after a nice evening with Mother, Betty, Granddad, and Patricia, my roommate woke up and told me I was in trouble. One of the young lads in our corridor (Eddie Broadbent) had been greatly amused to see an aged twenty-three-year-old like me sneaking out through the fence, and when he heard the orderly officer coming down the hall after lights out, he humped up in his bed to look as much as possible like a rolled greatcoat. The orderly officer, seeing the hump, pulled back the blanket and was annoyed when his flashlight was reflected in smiling eyes instead of the expected brass buttons. Thereupon he opened every bed along the corridor and found one greatcoat, mine. Next morning I was paraded before the Commanding Officer, who sentenced me to two half-hours of pack-drill, that is, drill in full equipment plus a backpack filled with sand.

That evening it was rather late before I could go out, because my pack-drill was after dark and I needed to shower and dress after. This time my bed was to be occupied by one of our lads who was married and had a living-out pass but whose wife happened to be away. That evening Pat and I had a long visit in the Williams parlour, with tea and cookies brought in by her friend Pudge and Pudge's mother.

That night, not daring to return through the fence and risk a meeting with the orderly officer, I bunked in with an old friend at St Stephen's College. In the morning I woke late, just in time to run down the street and mingle with our lads on the way to morning parade. Because there had been no time for me to borrow a razor, I did not pass inspection and was up before the CO for the second time in two days, for a stiff reprimand. But Patricia had met my family, and there had been time to do what planning we could for a very uncertain future. We had decided to marry before my April graduation and expected overseas posting, and to do it as soon as I could get a few days leave and we could save enough money, between us, to set up housekeeping. From then on, all my spare moments were used in studying food prices, adding them up against my $39 per month, and scanning the housing ads in vain for a place we could afford, or any place at all. My last wisdom tooth, no longer needed, was surrendered to the station dentist.

When our course at ITS was finished in early December, our class was split up and posted away in all directions, but by chance I was one of the four sent to Number 2 AOS (Air Observer School), just across Edmonton at what is now the municipal airport, within walking distance of Mother's house.

Our classroom work alternated with navigation exercises in Mark I Ansons, the kind that had been bombers at the beginning of the war. Some had patches over what we thought were bullet holes. They were two-motored, propeller-driven (jets had not yet come into use), and designed without any provision against Edmonton winters. There was no heating system. To measure wind drift, the navigator had to crawl past the pilot and up into the nose, slide open a tin panel, and lie facing into the wind as he twiddled the bombsight to take his reading. To take a bearing on the sun or moon or a geographic feature, he opened a side window, mounted an astro-compass on the sill or farther out, and took a reading with the wind whistling around his ears. To take a sextant reading on a star (this was before the days of radar), he opened a trap door in the roof. It was cold work with bare hands, and the three layers of issue gloves (silk, kid, and leather gauntlets) were not very useful for accurate work with dials, dividers, straightedge, protractor, and pencil.

Trainees flew in pairs. My partner was Doug Barr, another farm boy, from Saskatchewan. On our first training flight, Doug and I were in the first aircraft in line. After a cold three-hour flight we got home to find that nobody else had taken off; the throttle had frozen open on the third plane as it taxied into line, so that it crashed into the rear of plane number two and blocked the runway. The whole exercise had to be rescheduled, but not for three weeks, as the temperature during that time never rose above −30 Fahrenheit. Although American military planes of all kinds kept streaming in on their way to Alaska (and many crashed on takeoff because of the cold), all our training flights were cancelled and our class got seriously behind in flying time.

Near the beginning of the long cold spell, Patricia's mother wrote me a very warm letter, urging me not to worry about money. But I had other problems besides lack of money.

Having picked up athlete's foot, I was reminded that my father, at about my age, while hauling feed to his cattle shortly before he was to be married, had frozen his toes in such weather and was married in shoe-packs. I was still searching the housing ads and had been to the housing services at the YMCA and YWCA, but without any success. Since our class was to have a four-day leave beginning after work on 30 December, our wedding date was set for New Year's Eve, and my senior instructor had got me special permission to marry two days before expiry of the six-month ban. Our class was put on duty watch, which meant that I was confined to barracks for a week. And I had not yet found us a place to live!

At the end of our week of duty watch, with Christmas looming, the situation was desperate. I got an evening's pass and left camp on the dot of five o'clock. Beginning west of the airport, I went knocking at every house that looked big enough to have a room or two to rent. I worked southward toward the river, then eastward toward the centre of the city, but Edmonton was full of service wives and "northwest staging route" Americans. Finally, around nine o'clock or maybe ten, I found a room in a large old house on 107th Street about a block south of Jasper Avenue. The landlady had a houseful of roomers from cellar to attic, but one vacancy was coming up. She showed me the former living room, pointing out that the present occupant, standing beside her, was due to go into hospital the next week to deliver a baby and then with the baby would be going home to her mother. So I paid the first month's rent of $15 and went around the corner to the Corona Hotel to phone the good news to Pat.

On December 30 the evening bus was so crowded I had to stand just inside on the step for the first hour or so. In Calgary, Patricia in her Austin met me at the depot, and I slept that night at a neighbour's house, a few doors down the hill from the Gibsons.

Next morning we had a number of chores to do. We went to the jewellery shop to pick up the wedding ring that Pat had ordered because I was not there and could not afford it anyway; it was the wrong size but would be ready later in the day. (She never did have an engagement ring, unless we count the ruby I got her for our twenty-fifth anniversary.) We went to the marriage licence bureau, where the man behind the wicket, noting our ages, advised us to reconsider. Luckily it was early in the day or we might have. At a millinery shop we picked out two long feathers, red and blue, for her going-away hat, and proceeded to the bakery to pick up cakes. At the florist's we picked up corsages and other flowers to take home and decorate the house. At the airport late in the afternoon we picked up her Aunt Amy from Vancouver, who just looked at Pat and said, "My dear, you shouldn't be here. You should be home resting!"

At that stage I think we were both feeling bewilderment and rising panic, wondering how we had ever got ourselves into this and how to get out! But there were all those presents at the house, and ninety guests due at seven o'clock! One good thing to be said about weddings is that both parties get locked into the arrangements and cannot bolt when they start wanting to at the last moment.

After supper I gave my buttons and boots a final polish, put on the new pearl-grey shirt and black tie Mother had got to go with my blue serge uniform, and marched up the hill to the Gibson house, where Bill McEwen in his army officer's uniform was waiting to take charge of me. A head-cold I had been nursing for two weeks turned suddenly into a severe nosebleed. The two doctors who followed me upstairs to the bathroom got it stopped by plugging my nostrils and packing my upper lip. I remember the Reverend Andrew Lawson coming upstairs to brief me on my part in the proceedings, and presently Patricia and I stood facing him in the living room where we had first met nineteen months earlier.

Bill and Marian McEwen were beside us. Breathing through my mouth, I found myself in a very ungainly posture with feet apart (at ease) and hands at my sides (at attention) but was too paralysed to shift either pair. My parents, sister, and grandfather were there, and a whole houseful of Gibson family and friends. It was a fateful moment and we were both scared stiff. And the words were said.

First Home, RCAF Style, Edmonton

We had planned to spend a couple of days in Banff after our wedding. The Banff Springs Hotel was of course closed for the winter, and the other good hotel was fully booked, but a tour operator had reserved a comfortable suite in his house for us, and promised to meet us at the train.

After Dr Gibson had dropped us at the Calgary station we found that the train was two hours late, and the waiting room was so full there was no place for us to sit, except back-to-back on Patricia's suitcase in the middle of the room. So we sat for at least three hours, with gusts of –30 blowing on us every time one of the outside doors was opened. Eventually the train arrived, and set us down in Banff long after midnight. There was nobody to meet us. The driver of the last taxi had never heard of our tour operator, but he drove us to the hotel, where we would at least be warm. There was one vacant room there, but it was reserved for people who had not yet arrived. So we dozed in the hotel lounge for an hour or two, and were wakened when the desk clerk decided that the other people were not coming, and let us have the room.

After breakfast next forenoon we went for a walk, but the temperature had dropped to –40. We decided to return to the hotel and catch the afternoon train back to Calgary, where Patricia's parents were glad to see us. The next day was spent packing. I had nothing to pack except my shoulder bag, and most of the wedding presents had to be put into a big barrel in the basement for indefinite storage. There were suitcases of Patricia's clothing and other necessities, a supply of sheets, blankets, and towels, and finally a large carton of essential utensils and basic groceries that we would need in Edmonton.

On the fourth and last day of my leave we took the CPR to Edmonton, and it landed us at the old station on 109th Street, on the north side of Jasper Avenue. This was only about three blocks from where we were to live, so I carried the first load of baggage and left Patricia to guard the rest till I got back. When I reached our place I found my father there waiting for us. Apparently his holiday leave was a day longer than mine. He was shocked to see me alone, and to hear that I had left my bride sitting on luggage at the station, but we had little money and needed to save when we could. Of course he returned to the station with me, so Patricia had little to carry on the second trip. Dad had some soup ready for us on the hotplate, and Mother had sent with him a hamper of other food to see us through the first day or two.

Our landlady Mrs Carey lived in a room just inside the front door, and our room was next to hers. The bathroom was across the hall, just beyond the stairs, and there were other doors beyond it. The door at the end of the hall was that of our station Medical Officer and his wife; he was brother to the woman who had been my chemistry teacher in Vegreville. Our room had been the original living room, and there was an unused stone fireplace. A partial partition had been built to close off that corner as a kitchen, with a small sink and some shelves beside the fireplace. Facing the sink was a small cupboard with a two-burner hotplate on it. Beside our entrance, on the left, was a "Toronto couch" that served as a sofa and could be widened to form a bed. The opposite wall had a double window, with Venetian blinds that raised to provide a close view of the brick wall of the house next door. Beside the window was a cardboard clothes closet. To complete the furnishings there were two or three kitchen chairs, a padded armchair, and folding card table. The light was an old chandelier in the middle of the ceiling, with a frayed silk shade and hanging fringes. My first act was to remove the shade and set it on the top of the clothes closet.

Patricia, having heard how difficult it had been for me to find any place at all, surveyed her new home briefly and sat down cheerfully to her bowl of soup. Dad lingered for a chat, being careful not to say what he was thinking. Mrs Carey broke the tension by coming in with a welcoming tray of cookies, a pot of tea, and three cups, and left after assuring Dad that she would take good care of us.

The RCAF navigation school was in a row of low buildings beside a hangar on the south border of what is now the municipal airport, on what was then called Portage Avenue. I had to be there by seven the next morning for roll call, breakfast, and a mid-term examination. There was no flying from our station that week, only classroom work, because of the persistent low temperature. When I got home in the early evening, Patricia had done some shopping and had supper nearly ready. Her mother had warned me that Patricia knew very little about cooking, and for the first weeks she found that it took her nearly half the day to make supper. Meal planning was complicated by the fact that such things as meat, butter, and sugar were limited to her own ration tickets, which had to provide for both of us. When she had gained a bit of experience, she invited some people in for an evening tea party: Mother, Betty, my cousin Doris Watt, Patricia's dear friend Pudge Williams, and my flying partner, Doug Barr. Meanwhile she had found a part-time job, mornings in the public library.

Before our night flying began, I had to bring my sextant home at night for practice. That meant standing out in the back alley with sextant, pencil, paper, and flashlight to record the instant at which my reading of the height of a particular star was to begin. Having taken two or three readings on two or three stars, I would go back to our room to warm up before getting busy with the star almanac and a palm-sized mechanical "computer" to plot the resulting lines on a chart to see how close they came to our actual location on earth.

Doug Barr spent several evenings at our place helping me make a new kind of "computer" that would be a short cut in plotting our sextant readings, bypassing the star almanac and the hand computer. My version consisted of two twenty-inch squares of beaverboard, glued together. The top piece had an eighteen-inch disk cut out of it, cut and buffed so carefully that it could rotate easily inside the hole it came from. With a fine mapping pen and India ink, the edges of the disk and of the hole were marked and numbered in degrees and minutes, and the values of certain useful stars were marked on the disk. There was a second disk, smaller and thinner, graduated in minutes and seconds all along its edge and around the base on which it rotated. The whole thing was held together by a small short bolt in the centre, and each disk had, glued to it, a neat cardboard thumb tab with which to rotate the disks. When we demonstrated our creation to our two navigation instructors they were amazed, and when we took it to the next briefing, where our pilots and classmates were getting instructions for the next flight, it was the centre of much curiosity. We used it on two or three flights and it worked well. But it was too big to fit into our flight bags, unhandy to carry, and rather unwieldy to use on the small table under the small light provided for the navigator on our Anson Mark 1, so we left it behind and forgot about it. But it may have helped improve our final grades.

Besides the two officers who taught us navigation, there were other instructors, mostly sergeants, in other subjects. One was Sgt Charles Jenkins, who taught us about machine guns, including how to take them apart, clear stoppages, and reassemble them again within seconds. Jenkins had been my teacher in grades seven to ten at Victory School, but in gunnery class we never gave any hint of our previous acquaintance.

When our flights were at night, I did not get home until nearly midnight.

On one such night I found that Patricia had jammed the door shut with a chair under the knob and was very frightened. She told me there had been shouts and sounds of fighting in the basement below us, and there was still an occasional shout or moan. Mrs Carey, having heard me arrive, knocked at the door and asked me to go with her to the basement, where she had rented the space to two men who had been passed on to her by the YMCA. We found one of them snoring loudly on a cot near the furnace. The other was lying face down in the coal bin, mumbling and groaning. When we turned him over, his face and one hand were covered with coal dust and blood. Mrs Carey hurried upstairs for towels and a bucket of water. When the man sat up to have his face washed, we saw no damage there, but the hand was cut and bleeding slowly. It looked as though he had cut it on a broken bottle that lay on the pile of coal beside him. While I washed the hand, Mrs Carey got some clean water, disinfectant, and bandages. When we had washed him again and bandaged the hand as well as we could, Mrs Carey pointed him to the other cot and told him he would be all right until morning. He still seemed to be in a daze, but said, "Thank you doctor, thank you very much," and with his good hand pulled a $5 bill out of his pocket. When I refused it, saying I was not a doctor, he insisted, and Mrs Carey snapped it out of his hand, saying, "Take it! Take it!" So I did. Next morning, when Patricia told her how frightened she had been, Mrs Carey said, "Lord, woman, it's not the drunk ones you need to be afraid of, it's the sober!" And I think she was glad for me to have the five dollars. She had been passing her daily newspaper along to us when she was done with it, having said she knew we could not afford one. She probably knew also that Patricia had been obliged to leave her part-time job at the library because of morning sickness.

Our class or "flight" had begun with the standard thirty-two trainees, mostly Canadians and New Zealanders, but a few dropped out along the way, for various reasons. A few were married men, but only three of us had our wives in Edmonton. When the end of our course drew near, we had a big flight party at the Masonic Temple. After a very good dinner, Patricia gave a short but touching valedictory address, and we went home before the dancing began. No doubt the New Zealanders performed their Maori war dance before it was over.

The day before our class was to graduate, we were still two night flights short of the required number. A standard training flight took three hours, so it was planned that we should have two flights that night, the first outward to the navigation school at Pierce, in southern Alberta, then refuel and return. As it turned out, we took off in a snowstorm in the dark, passed through a weather front along the way, and landed at Pierce during a chinook. One of our planes, wandering off the runway, was stuck in the mud and had to be pulled out by tractors. We all gathered in the airmen's mess, waiting to be briefed for the return flight, when word came through that Edmonton airport was closed, completely fogged in, and might or might not be clear the next day, graduation day, April Fool's Day.

Our two instructors were with us that night, sitting at a table by themselves, looking very worried and helpless, so I joined them with an idea. There was no train or bus service from Pierce to Edmonton, but my father was traffic controller at No. 2 Service Flying School in Calgary; if we could get clearance to land there and stay overnight, we could fly to Edmonton in the morning. But in case Edmonton was still shut down, we should have reservations by train. So it worked out. Dad was waiting for us when we landed in Calgary, and gave me his bed in the officers' quarters while he made other arrangements.

In the morning I was woken up by an urgent message that our whole gang was waiting for me outside, in the back of a cattle truck, and a train was being held! It was the "fish train," with one old passenger coach and no services, so we reached the CPR station in Edmonton in the late afternoon, very hungry. There were three wives on the platform to meet us, all in tears; until an hour before train time they had not been able to get any word of us since the previous morning.

Rushed back to the airport, we hardly had time to do what was required: locate our planes (which had flown in earlier) and retrieve our things; turn in all our navigation equipment; shave–shower–shoeshine and polish buttons on our dress uniforms; receive sergeant's stripes and sew or pin them to the proper sleeve; have supper; fall in for a rehearsal parade and final instructions in the hangar; be wafted off to the old Edmonton arena; march in smartly; halt in front of the official party, left turn, right dress! One of our lads fainted and fell flat on his face.

Of the thirty-two beginners in our class, only nineteen graduated; seventeen were posted overseas in time for the concentrated night raids over the Ruhr. I know of only three, including Doug Barr, who got back safely to Canada; I hope there were more, but I heard of only three.

The seats in the arena seemed to be packed with spectators, but each of us had been given two tickets for reserve seats, so I knew that Patricia and Professor Salter were there to watch. To our surprise, a large "honour guard" in American uniforms marched in and formed lines off to our left. The official party consisted of Wop May, the famous Canadian bush pilot whose company was then providing planes and pilots to the RCAF navigation schools, as well as a US Air Force general who for some reason had been given the honour of presenting us with our navigation wings. I was called forward in my turn to have him pin the N-wing to my jacket, and marched back to my place in line. When all had been awarded, to my surprise I was called forward again to receive a gold wrist chain with my name and number on it, as leader of the

Our graduating class at navigator school in Edmonton, April 1943. I am pictured in the back row, fifth from the left. My flying partner, Doug Barr, is seated fourth from the right.

Patricia Gibson Blackburn with her new navigator, April 1943.

class. It was a thrill to know that Patricia and Salter were there to see it; Salter claimed later to have told his English class that morning that it would be so. He himself was studying the RCAF navigation syllabus, besides teaching it to cadets at the university's COTC.

Next morning the lead headline in the *Edmonton Journal* was ROMMEL ESCAPES DESERT TRAP! Rommel was the German general facing our allies in North Africa, but our class that morning had other things to think about. It was announced that two of our lads would continue as sergeants; all others would be promoted to "pilot officer" rank. After two weeks of leave, all but two would report to the RCAF embarkation depot in Moncton, New Brunswick, for overseas posting. Two were to be held back as instructors, and one of them was me: I was to report to the Navigation Instructors' School at Rivers, Manitoba. Mrs Carey was one of the many who were glad to hear that I would be in Canada for at least a while longer.

During my month at Rivers, Patricia stayed in Calgary with her parents. On the last day of my course, we received our list of postings to navigation schools across the country. I had been listed for Winnipeg, but one of my classmates, listed for Portage la Prairie, was eager to trade with me because his wife's home was in Winnipeg. After being assured by our Medical Officer that Portage had a good hospital for Patricia, I agreed to the trade, and had a few days of leave before going to my new posting.

11 Navigation Instructor, Portage la Prairie

The day before my leave ended I arrived at Portage la Prairie to find us a place to live. When it was found, Patricia would follow from Calgary.

The girl at the Accommodation Centre in Portage had only two places to offer, one at Mrs Pigg's house and the other at Mrs Buggie's. And she could not recommend one listing above another. There were two chaps waiting behind me, so there was no time to hesitate or consult. Thinking that dirt was easier to cope with than bugs, I chose Pigg. It was the wrong choice; I learned later that Mrs Buggie had a fine home, and a daughter Ruth whom I met later when she was Acting Librarian at the University of Manitoba.

The upstairs room at Mrs Pigg's house was fairly clean but quite bare except for the bed, a couple of kitchen chairs, two orange crates and a hot plate. It had a window facing the street and a side door that opened into space – a potential death trap for a sleepwalker or a stranger looking at night for the hall door and the shared bathroom. Since I knew of no other place, I paid one week's rent and hoped for an early move.

Next day I began my career as an instructor. The airport was a fifteen-minute bus ride south of town. About mid-morning on the appointed day, I reported there for duty. The adjutant assigned me a shared room in barracks and asked me to wait for a few minutes while he called the Chief Instructor's office. After a short time, a young instructor came in to say that he had just been called away and had been told that I would be taking his class for the next hour, a class on the geography of the Pacific. This was a nightmare! I knew very little about the Pacific except what I could remember of the wall map that hung on the wall at Victory School, and I now had only a few minutes to find the right classroom! Worse yet, when I opened the door and saw the class, I knew from their uniforms that they were Australians!

My introduction to Australian airmen had been at the manning depot in Edmonton, the day about 150 of them arrived from Down Under across the Pacific by ship and then by train, without any stop along the way. At their arrival parade and roll call they had been told they were confined to barracks for the first week, for documentation and so on. There were shouts of protest from the ranks. After supper they got hold of a saw, cut down the high flagpole at the head of our parade ground, and used it as a battering ram to knock down a section of the board fence; they were not seen again for several hours or several days. As I walked into a roomful of thirty-two Aussies to teach them about the Pacific, I had visions of them uprooting a gatepost and carrying it around the station with me astride it. How on earth could I begin the lesson? I do not remember much about that hour, but after introducing myself and naming the assignment, I must have asked each of the men to say where he was from, and what he had done there. The one thing I do recall is one of them explaining how he and his cobber had tracked their secret route across the Pacific. They had used a small square of plywood with a nail stuck upright in the centre; by marking the height and direction of the nail's shadow exactly at noon each day, they knew how long they had sailed eastward before turning north toward the equator, and how far south or north they were from the equator.

When the hour was over I had time to wonder whether my assignment had been legitimate, whether it was just a spontaneous practical joke or a deliberate rite of introduction to deflate a green instructor. After that, I was given a regular full-time assignment and gained confidence as a teacher.

Midway through the first week, at the end of a very hot day, I met Patricia at the railway station. Our room at Mrs Pigg's had been closed since I had first been there, and there was no ventilation except by the window and the side door. We decided to leave the door shut, with suitcases in front of it as a barrier. During the rest of the week Patricia spent time exploring the "city," looking for shady places to rest, and making useless visits to the Accommodation Centre. She did, however, find that there was to be a vacancy at the end of the week at a hotel on the main street. It was not a big hotel, but a low building that had a coffee shop, bar, a few hotel rooms down the corridor, and a large basement room used for dances, flight parties, and other noisy events. She had booked the room, and when I was about to go downstairs to tell Mrs Pigg we were leaving, she came up to evict us because I had not paid in advance for a second week, and she had another party ready to move in. Besides, Mr Pigg had mumps and she did not want Patricia, in her condition, to be exposed. We were glad to decamp without delay, and in leaving we saw Mr Pigg in a rocking chair on the porch looking miserable, his extended jowls glistening with a coat of black bristles.

After we had been at the hotel for a few days, Patricia located a better place at Mrs Tom's. It consisted of the upstairs of a small house. We had two small rooms, kitchen and bedroom, and at the end of the hall a bathroom in which the basin served also as our washtub and bathtub. The bathroom was shared with Mrs Tom, who trod the stairway and hall so quietly in her bare feet that she often startled us as she passed our doorway or met us in the dark hallway. We saw nothing of Mr Tom except as a corpulent old man in a rocking chair on the front porch, with a wreath of white hair around a pink and smiling face. When his wife happened to be nearby she would nod in his direction and declare, "He's no good, dear, he's too old," but he continued to smile; maybe he was deaf. His wife, when she received mail, was unable to read the addresses, and brought it to Patricia to pick out whatever was for us. So we gathered that her husband was useful at least as a reader of their mail.

Mrs Tom was already using produce from her garden at the side of her house. When I commented on her success, she advised me to go to the town hall to apply for an allotment of garden space. They gave me a good plot in a vacant lot several blocks away, and I bought a spade to turn the sod that weekend. With hoe and rake lent by our landlady, I planted the usual variety of seeds. As the weeks went by, I found time to do the necessary cultivating, weeding, and hilling of potatoes, while Patricia sat on a camp chair and read to me from our current book. Some neighbour across the street found our activities amusing enough to describe in a paragraph for the "I Saw This Week" column of the *Winnipeg Free Press*, where we found ourselves in print.

Meanwhile, after my first hour of nightmare as an instructor, I had been assigned as full-time assistant to an experienced instructor, with whom I shared an office and the lecturing as prescribed in the syllabus. One of us would take part in all briefings of our students, before and after their flights, and from time to time we flew with each of them to see them in action. We marked, very promptly, all their written tests, and the charts and logs of every flight. Our class of thirty-two trainees was the usual mix of airmen from three countries, and the course ran for three months.

Every two weeks there was a new intake with two sections, A and B, so our full complement consisted of 384 trainees and 24 instructors. During the time I was an assistant in an A section, the assistant in B section across the hall was Frank Rooke. Frank and his wife Lib were expecting their first child a month after ours, and we became lifelong friends. (In July 2009 my wife and I attended Lib's 90th birthday party in Toronto.)

After that first class graduated I was given an office and assistant of my own. The first of my assistants was an Englishman who had already done a tour of duty over Germany and was very worried about his wife in London, where bombs were falling. The second was Jack Sword, unmarried, a Manitoba schoolteacher who had enlisted after working in the Wartime Information Board in Ottawa.

I had permission to live away from the RCAF station. I had a room in barracks where I kept my flying suit, but I never slept there except when I was Duty Officer or after a night flight. My roommate, by the name of Hamilton, was from Saskatchewan; I hardly ever saw him and did not really get to know him. He later served as federal Minister of Agriculture. I later chanced to meet his brother (because we were both in RCAF raincoats) while we were both waiting for a train at Orangeburg, New York, and our families became good friends.

Most of the young instructors had brought their wives to Portage, and most of the wives were pregnant or had small children. Patricia was expecting in early October and was suffering from the heat. In the evenings we often crossed the bridge over the oxbow lake to enjoy a cool walk in the park. Our two rooms under the Tom roof were never cool, and Mrs Tom was not a great comforter. On a morning visit to our kitchen she had pointed to the house across the street to where a woman had been brought home after a miscarriage. There followed a series of daily reports: "She has a fever now, dear," then "She is worse today, dear," then "The doctor came early today, dear," then "They took her back to the hospital today, dear," then "She died today, dear" and "The funeral will be tomorrow, dear." And after seeing Patricia waddle carefully down the stairs, she said, "I hope it lives, dear."

In late September, Dr Gibson, Patricia's father, an obstetrician and gynaecologist, came from Calgary for a day's visit and told us that no grandchild of his would come home to two hot rooms in an attic! He said that Patricia would simply have to go home. Next morning I happened to sit beside Art Buller, our Chief Instructor, on the bus; he asked how my wife was surviving the hot weather. I told him I had left her in tears, having decided she would have to go home to Calgary next day.

Midway through that morning, the intercom box on the wall of my classroom, the intercom that connected every classroom with the office of the Chief Instructor, came alive with a message for me to report immediately to the Chief Instructor. I did, and he told me he had just received word that he had been posted to another station. He told me to leave my class to him before anybody else could hear the news, and to run to the gate where the next bus was about to leave for town. In Portage I was to go directly to Sam Marmel's general store on the main street, to tell Mr Marmel quietly that his renters would be moving out of their apartment in his house two days later and that my wife and I would like to move in. Mr Marmel agreed. I gave him the first month's rent and ran to tell Patricia before going back to the station.

The rent was $45 a month, more than twice what we had been paying, but was worth the difference. It was upstairs, but there was a banister. There were two bedrooms at the front, a three-piece bathroom at the middle, and at the back a large living room and kitchenette with an icebox. Four windows gave through-ventilation, west to east. As we were moving in, Mr Marmel told me he would not have accepted us if I had told him my wife was pregnant, because they liked a quiet house. I replied that he had not asked, that his former renters, whom we were succeeding, were expecting only about a month later, and that we would be as quiet as possible. So we were allowed to stay.

On 18 October we left the supper table in a hurry, by taxi, and at the Portage hospital I had only about an hour to wait before the nurse came and offered to show me my son. She took me to a window in the corridor, through which I saw a row of cribs and two or three babies. She went through a side door and lifted the baby with the blackest hair and reddest face for me to see. I knew the hospital was near the Indian School and reserve and assumed she was showing me an Indian child by mistake, but she was not. When I went down the hall to see Patricia, she said dreamily, "Isn't he beautiful!" Of course I had to agree without mentioning my reservations. When I saw the doctor, I asked him whether the child was normal, because his head looked three-cornered, like a buckwheat, but he merely smiled and said it would soon take a normal shape, and it did so. When it was time for me to take the family home, I carried the baby upstairs, laid him on the bed, and asked, "What do we do next?" I felt rather lost, with a new sense of responsibility. Patricia insisted that the boy be named Robert, to be sure that she would always have a Robert in the family. He gave promise of being a sturdy one, having weighed in at nine pounds twelve ounces. My class of nascent navigators marked the occasion by presentation of a birth spoon, engraved with name, date, and weight.

It was not long before Mr and Mrs Marmel and their small daughter Linda came upstairs to see the baby. After a month or so, when they had visitors downstairs, Mr Marmel would knock and ask to borrow the baby for a little while. When we bought a regular baby carriage (perhaps at Marmel's general store), it was too awkward to be taken up and down the stairs, but we were allowed to park it on the glassed-in front porch. Our landlord also gave me permission to build a crib in the basement. It was patterned after the one my father had made for me, but was a rougher version, as my tools were limited to hacksaw, hammer, screwdriver, kitchen knife, and sandpaper. The knife was for carving teething knobs at the top of the corner posts. The crib was demountable with twelve screws and was to follow us wherever we went. About forty years later I gave it to a family of Vietnamese refugees, and it may still be in use. Sam Marmel used to bring visitors upstairs to see it.

One morning, when Patricia got home with some groceries and was about to haul the carriage up the front steps, she found a package in butcher paper on the top step. Knowing that the Marmels would both be at the store until noon, she took it up to keep cool in our icebox. When she heard Mr Marmel come home at noon, she presented it to him with an explanation, but in handing it to him she chanced to turn it over and see a large hand-printed message saying "Mr Marmel yur meet it steenks."

Portage was a watering depot for both the CNR and the CPR, and all trains stopped there for fifteen or twenty minutes to take on water for their boilers. The tracks ran on either side of the water tower, the stations faced each other across the tracks, and we lived only about four blocks away. Friends travelling east or west would often let us know in advance, and we would meet them on the platform for a short visit. Once or twice, after meeting one group, we walked across the tracks to the other platform to meet somebody else coming in on the other line. Once, as we stood waiting, a trainload of war prisoners stopped, with armed guards stepping down to the platform while men at the windows flashed swastikas and Iron Crosses for me to see.

We had met a reliable teenager at church, and she sat with Robbie while we celebrated our first anniversary by attending the New Year's

Eve dance at the Officers' Mess. Next morning we were wakened by a phone call. Sam Marmel was on the line to wish us a happy new year, and then to add, "I think your ice box is leaking." It was, and had leaked through the newly painted ceiling of their bedroom. After that, we were careful to empty the drip pan every morning and night.

One morning the new Chief Instructor, Whit Shannon, an ex-banker, must have been on the alert at his end of the intercom, and tuned in to my classroom. He slipped through the side door, sat at the back of my class for a few minutes, then asked what topic I was teaching. When I named it, he said it was not even on the syllabus. I replied that I had begun by telling the class so, but that it was an extra bit that might save their lives some day. He listened until I had finished the lesson. When one of the lads asked me to go over some point that he had not understood, Whit strode forward to the blackboard, presented the point in a slightly different way, and asked, "There now, is that better?" The lad replied, "No, that's worse!" Whit put down his chalk and left the room. Poor Whit, his alertness failed him one day as a civilian soon after the war. He looked the wrong way before stepping off a curb in London and was killed by an omnibus.

Another morning, just as I finished writing some problems on the blackboard, I was doubled up by a sharp pain in my middle. After telling my assistant, next door, to look after the class, I went to the station infirmary. Before I even spoke to the doctor there, he made a diagnosis on the basis of my posture and colour, then lifted his phone to call for an emergency aircraft and the ambulance to take me to it. The pilot said he could not take me without my flying suit and parachute harness, but when I groaned that I would be quite unable to put them on even if they were at hand, I was lifted on board and placed on the floor. In Winnipeg, on the way to the military hospital, the siren on the ambulance was music to my ears. As the surgeon came into the operating room, he asked, "Which one is this?", and the nurse answered, "Blackburn from Portage la Prairie." The doctor retorted, "I just finished with him, take him away!" The nurse said, "No, that was John, from Portage la Prairie; this one is Robert, acute appendix!"

I was well acquainted with instructor John H. Blackburn (my father's name) at Portage, whose face was badly scarred from a flaming crash in Egypt. He had shown me his logbook signed in Egypt by his Commanding Officer John H. Blackburn (another man with the same name). The Adjutant's Office at Portage had misdirected the child allowance to John H. instead of Robert H. when our Robbie was born.

A day or two after the operation, I had a surprise visitor, my Grandfather Blackburn (another Robert!), who had got off the train at Portage to see us (including his only great-grandchild) on his way homeward to Edmonton from a last visit to his birthplace, cousins, and old friends at Union, Pennsylvania. After spending a night in our spare bedroom (and nursery), he had doubled back to Winnipeg to spend an hour with me in the hospital before resuming his homeward journey. Then Patricia and Robbie came to Winnipeg and stayed with some old family friends until we could all three go back to Portage together.

The weakest student in any of my classes had a Master's degree but too little aptitude for figures or orderly procedures, and he dropped out tearfully. My best student was a Manitoba farm boy with a grade ten education. Another Manitoba farm boy was lacking in confidence and came to me wanting to drop out. I encouraged him to wait at least until I had flown with him on his next flight. Until then his flights had been based mostly on map reading and bearings on visible landmarks, plus wireless bearings on a few radio stations. The next flight was to use only radio bearings, and the day happened to be clouded. After taking off we climbed through a tight layer of cloud, and there was nothing to see below us but sunshine on a white blanket. The student became quite rattled, and shouted to ask what he should do. I simply told him to follow his flight plan. He did so, and at the end of the flight was delighted to see it work out very well; as we descended through cloud three hours later, our base at Portage was a mile or two straight ahead. After that he stayed on and graduated, although with a rather low standing in class, and went overseas with the rest. Two or three months later, when he would have been in operational training in England, I saw his name on one of the yellow sheets, the weekly listing of RCAF casualties. I could not help thinking that he may have become rattled there, made some fatal mistake, and gone down with all his crew, on account of my pushing him through when he wanted to drop out. After that, when a trainee lost confidence or showed signs of incompetence, I would call him to the office and say, "Today I am going to save your life by dropping you from the course."

In the summer of 1944, Frank Rooke and I were posted to Rivers, Manitoba, for the Staff Navigation course. It was three months of advanced training in climates, tides, the insides of navigation instruments, and the latest developments in tactics. With Sam Marmel's permission we sublet the apartment to a new arrival at Portage, so that Robbie and

Patricia could spend the time in Calgary. After some weeks, however, Mr Marmel phoned her to say that our renter's wife was an alcoholic, that he could no longer stand the shouting and banging upstairs, and that unless we put those people out he would have to call the police and we would lose our place. The only way for us to put them out was for Patricia to return to Portage, which she did.

While Frank and I were at Rivers, the war in Europe ended, and we were volunteered for the war in Asia. At the end of the course the other members of our class, from navigation schools across the country, were to have seven days of leave before reporting back to their stations. Frank and I assumed that we would be getting the same, but when we phoned our Chief Instructor to confirm it, he said for us to get straight back to Portage, as a new double intake of trainees would be arriving. For me this was very awkward news, because Mother had already come to Portage to look after Robbie while Patricia and I had a little holiday in Kenora.

The day before our course was to end, I spotted the Medical Officer on his way to lunch. I told him my tonsils had been removed when I was only eighteen months old and had partly grown back in, and that since then I had been subject to recurrent sore throat and tonsillitis. And I should not be sent for duty in Asia with a bad throat. He said for me to meet him at his office after lunch. In his office he sat me in a chair under a strong lamp, and did see tags of tonsil in my throat. His nurse rummaged through the cupboards to find the proper tools, and got them sterilized. As the doctor administered some freezing, the station's Security Officer dropped in for a chat and asked what was going on. So he was given a peek into my throat and became a close observer of the whole procedure until I was tucked into bed. When the freezing wore off I had a very sore throat indeed, and it was some time before the orderly brought me ginger ale and a straw. The orderly I recognized as a neighbour lad who had been a few grades behind me in school at Lavoy, a grandson of Dr Arthur. He was very attentive and helped me dress next morning in time to totter to the classroom just as marks and passes were being given out.

The doctor had given me four days' leave, and Frank Rooke helped me get onto the early afternoon train with him to Portage. Getting home, I found that Mother had baked a batch of my favourite bran muffins and had one buttered for me. The bran felt like gravel in my throat, but I had to make a show of enjoying at least a part of it before secretly flushing the rest; any mention of the operation would have sent me straight to bed. I did mention it to Patricia when we got off the train at Kenora, and that night at the hotel I supped on spaghetti and ginger ale. Next day we walked in the park and took a scenic boat ride, and by the end of four days I was fit to report back to work, with my final class.

The main sidewalk of Portage la Prairie in those days saw a morning parade of baby carriages, mostly in pairs, most of them carrying Air Force babies. They could cause traffic problems in front of the tea room, which served good chicken sandwiches. Sometimes the fathers joined the parade in the evening, although officers were not supposed to be seen pushing prams. Linda Marmel, about seven years old, was determined that Robbie should walk before another Air Force baby, about the same age, who lived next door. She played with him daily, set him up on his feet, coaxed him, and finally he met her deadline about the time of his first birthday. Jack Sword, who after finishing a term as my assistant had become the station Education Officer, was the only guest at the birthday party and gave Robbie his first bib overalls, in red corduroy.

About that time, Sam Marmel received a very severe shock; he got word that his brother had died in a Nazi extermination camp. He went into deep depression and was sent to Winnipeg for treatment, leaving his wife and daughter to tend the store.

The Commonwealth Air Training Scheme was winding down, and it was announced that all navigators then in training would, on graduation, be sent home on indefinite leave. Classroom morale was not high, and it received a severe blow when some Canadian journalist referred to the unused navigators as "zombies." This caused real bitterness in my class. Next morning I tried to alter their perspective by saying that William Shakespeare had a word for them, and read them his sonnet that begins "When in disgrace with fortune and men's eyes." They asked for more. After they graduated and went home, Frank Rooke and I were posted to three months of Operational Training at Comox, British Columbia.

Operational Training at Comox

My father was then in charge of Air–Sea Rescue at Pat Bay, north of Vancouver. He wired me not to take my family to Comox; he had heard that housing was so scarce there that the Commanding Officer was living in a chicken coop. Patricia, however, would not be deterred. And our new Commanding Officer at Portage, just arrived from Comox, had already arranged for the Rookes to stay at the place he had vacated—the main floor of an old house perched high above the beach about two miles east of the RCAF station.

After shipping the crib and selling our other bits of furniture to the incoming tenant, we piled my kit bag and Patricia's suitcases onto the carriage and wheeled it to the railway station at Portage, with the baby safely stowed in the bottom of the carriage. In our tiny bedroom on the train that night, we put the baby to sleep in the upper bunk, with the webbing barrier carefully in place. In the middle of the night, however, we were wakened by a loud thump, and found the baby on the floor with his head wedged between two suitcases. He gave us a fright by seeming to be still asleep, but soon wakened and was apparently unharmed.

After a few days in Calgary, where we left the carriage and got a small wicker go-cart, we went on to Vancouver and had dinner with my father, before boarding one of the Princess boats that carried passengers, mail, and groceries to settlements along the coast. We had reserved a room in Comox at the Elk Hotel, which turned out to be a sprawling half-timbered structure beside the dock. After we got into our room there in mid-afternoon, my first errand was to find the kitchen and warm the milk bottle. In the corridor I met Frank Rooke on the same errand, as they had just arrived by train.

The desk clerk assured us that there were no vacancies in the village. Using the tactic I had found successful in Edmonton—just knocking on the door of every house that looked big enough to have space to spare—within half an hour, we had located two empty rooms. Because of size or location, neither was suitable for us, but within two days both had been taken by some of my classmates. Having found nothing for ourselves in the village, we set out, with go-cart, eastward along the coast road. There were few houses there, and after a couple of miles we began to lag. Then a car came along and the driver stopped to ask whether we were lost. When he heard that we were newly arrived and homeless, he told us that he had just built a new house and was on his last trip to lock up his old cottage. He took us onward for about a mile to see the cottage, and rented it to us at a very low price.

Our landlord was a young man who said he was on extended leave from the University of Manitoba. When we told him we were Albertans, he said, "I know Albertans; they are an aggressive lot." He drove us back to the Elk Hotel for our things, then to a grocery store to stock up, and back to the cottage again in time for supper. When we thanked him for all his help he said, "But that's what people are for, to help each other!"

Our cottage was white clapboard, set well back from the road, with the forest at its back. There were several windows facing the road, and one at each end. The rooms were three in a row, one step above grade. The front lawn was obviously grazed by local cows, and the privy was off to the west, closer to the road. Fifty yards to the east was a dug well, with pump. Fifty yards east of that was a small square plywood cottage, newly built, the only other building in sight. Our only visible problem was the woodpile outside our kitchen door; it had no proper cover and the wood was wet. There was a can of coal oil to help start fires in the stove, and as long as the fire would burn we had to keep wood in the oven to dry. There was a fireplace in the middle room, but never enough dry wood to keep a fire going there, and the bedroom beyond was always cold during the spring weather.

The morning after our arrival I walked to Comox in time to catch an early bus to the RCAF station. At breakfast I met an old friend from Vegreville, at whose home I had boarded when I was in grade twelve and he was away in Edmonton for his first year at university. He had just arrived from the RCAF Service Flying School in Calgary and was looking for a navigator for his crew. Together we found a co-pilot who had been an instructor at a school for flying instructors. Our WAG (wireless operator/air-gunner) was a sergeant newly graduated from the Bombing and Gunnery School at Macdonald, just north of Portage.

The Commonwealth Air Training Scheme was closing down its stations and sending its instructors into operational training for transport work. Our class of navigators included several officers more senior than I was, and even one wing commander. We expected to fly the supply route from Dum Dum airport in Bengal and "over the hump" (the Himalayas) to Chungking in China. Our course was to take three months; we were given "jungle shots" and some lectures on survival in the jungle.

On our first day in the cottage, Patricia found a retired English couple half a mile down the road who had a telephone. She had called our families and left the neighbours' number, in case anybody needed to send us a message. The first message was from Dr Gibson, saying that he was sending a bicycle (by express) to save me the three-mile walk to and from the bus. The second message was on Easter Day, for Patricia to call home. Her parents had gone to Banff for the weekend. Easter morning, Patricia's mother had been sitting up in bed reading her Bible when her father went downstairs to get a newspaper; when he returned she was slumped forward over her book, dead. Patricia flew home for the funeral, and of course took Robbie with her.

By the time they got back from Calgary, my bicycle had arrived and I had found a shortcut between our cottage and the station: a rough path through the forest and then over a wire fence, followed by half a mile on the gravel highway. Frank Rooke also had a bike, and we usually rode home together as far as my short cut. One day the grocery store just outside the station gate had hams for sale, and we had one cut in half to share it. Our wives were dismayed to have so much ham on hand without refrigeration. We were invited to a ham supper at the Rooke house, a two-mile walk along the shore road. After supper the ladies thought it would be fun to bathe the two small boys together in the round washtub, but the boys would have none of it. When the Rookes came to us for supper (ham again!) Robbie took Howie around the cottage and wagged his finger at each electrical outlet, saying "No! No!" He had experimented on one of them with a hairpin, getting a shock and a burnt palm.

In operational training at Comox, the standard exercise was a flight that went three hours out to an imaginary landfall at sea, then back to Estevan Point on the west coast of Vancouver Island. We flew Dakotas (DC3s), in which the gas tanks did not carry enough fuel for six hours; there was a large auxiliary tank (the size we had later for our furnace) bolted to the floor in the middle of the aircraft, with a valve to open it when needed. Navigation at sea was by sextant shots on the sun or moon and stars, when they were visible, and by bearings on a number of radio stations—bearings that were very unreliable because of coastal refraction and therefore had to be used with care. A navigator in those days had no time to rest. For the pilots, on the other hand, these flights were dull work. Our co-pilot, whose main duty was to sit and wait in case he was needed, developed a rash on his arms, so severe that he had to be hospitalized and sent to Vancouver. I took over the mechanical part of his work, which was simply to crank the wheels and flaps up and down for takeoff and landing. My pilot, alone at the front with nobody to talk to, began to suffer from nervous exhaustion and found it increasingly hard to stay awake and hold a steady course. When I felt him wavering I would shout forward to wake him up, but he refused to see the doctor about his sleepy condition. One afternoon, about three hours out over the Pacific, with bright sky reflected in the water and no visible horizon because of haze on the water, there was a sudden hush as both our motors stopped. I happened to be in the privy at the back of the plane but ran forward and found the pilot sound asleep at the controls. He had switched to automatic pilot and forgotten to switch the fuel tanks. When I opened the valve to the spare tank, my pilot got the motors going again and climbed back to the required height. When we got home I told him I would report him to the doctor next morning unless he did so himself. After a few days of sleep in the infirmary, he was sent to hospital in Vancouver, where he was invalided out of the RCAF. (After a complete recovery he served for several years as Deputy Minister of Tourism in Ontario and then in Manitoba.)

Having lost both pilots from my crew, I was assigned to a different crew that had lost its navigator, in the course behind ours, so my time at Comox was changed from three months to four. My new captain, another former flying instructor, had been a hardrock miner in British Columbia and was rather rough-handed as a pilot. Our only smooth landing was on our very last flight, and I congratulated him on it, knowing full well that it was the only landing for which he had allowed our co-pilot to take the controls.

About the time of my change of crews, Patricia broke a filling in a tooth. The station dentist, with whom I had shared the third floor of an old house in Toronto when we were students there, could not invite her to his office at the station. But he drove over in the evening to take us to his own cottage and give her a new filling, working with an emergency drill that was driven by treadle. Not long after that, Patricia had a miscarriage and spent some time in the Courtenay hospital. I was given one day of leave, and that afternoon Robbie and I went to see her. Robbie was in his go-cart, with the handle lashed to a strong, crooked stick, the other end of which was attached to the saddle of my bike. On the same trip I arranged for Marnie Clay to drive over every day from the Elk Hotel to look after Robbie while Patricia was away; Marnie's husband Don was an old family friend from Calgary. At the end of Marnie's first day, Robbie had a fever, which the doctor diagnosed as measles, from which he recovered in a few days.

Patricia's stay in hospital was longer than expected. While she was there, there was a knock at our door one night. I opened it to a young man I had never seen before. He was from the new plywood cottage next door and had just had word that the Canadian Navy was posting him to Halifax. He and his wife had to leave early next morning. He handed me the key to his cottage, saying he had paid the rent for the next two weeks. Would I please try to find another renter, if possible in time to recover part or all of his prepayment, and then send him the money? When he mentioned that his cottage had hot and cold water and a bathroom, I refunded his prepayment immediately and became the new renter myself. On my next free afternoon, Robbie and I carried our belongings to our new home. And by the time Patricia was able to come home to it, our friend the dentist and his wife had been glad to move into the one we had vacated.

For one of our morning flights we were to turn over Sitka, Alaska, and come back over the Queen Charlotte Islands. We were in cloud most of the way, officially at 11,000 feet, but our pilot could not coax the engines to take us above 9,000. By the time we turned back, in cloud, over what I had calculated to be Sitka, ice off our propellers was clattering against the fuselage. We had no idea what load of ice there might be on the wings. We had no de-icers, so I decided not to return over the mountainous Queen Charlotte Islands. We knew from observation that mountain heights as shown on maps did not always correspond to the heights indicated on our altimeters; we knew also that we would be in cloud the whole way and that some clouds had hard rock centres. We descended into warmer air and made a long dog-leg out to sea, well clear of the Queen Charlottes, before heading home. By the time we landed, our pilot had noted several other deficiencies in our plane, in the instruments and controls, in addition to the lack of engine power; after landing he turned in a detailed report that he reckoned would put the plane out of service for a week or so for repairs to be made. Next morning the young Commanding Officer called me in and delivered a severe reprimand for disregarding the official flight plan, and did not seem greatly impressed by my account of the circumstances.

That same afternoon one of our planes, with an English crew in the class ahead of ours, failed to return and could not be reached by radio. Our class was to fly that night, and I had got permission to take my dentist friend along for the ride, as he had been hoping for. When we got to the briefing we were told that the exercise was to be a parallel search for the missing plane. Our tracks were laid out five miles apart, from the north end of Vancouver Island to the boundary of Washington State. Each crew was assigned to patrol one of those tracks for six hours, back and forth, on the watch for an emergency flare or a weak SOS on radio. We were to fly at 11,000 feet. Our crew was to carry a "screen" pilot and "screen" wireless operator; the word "screen" was used for an officer who was to inspect performance in the air. When we reached height and turned on to our track we were above a thick layer of cloud that lay white in bright moonlight. There was little or no chance of seeing any flare, but our dentist watched for me as I kept busy trying to maintain our track above the mountainous coastal area. We were above the altitude at which oxygen begins to be needed, and with seven men aboard, instead of the usual four, we had to share the four available masks. I shared mine with the dentist as much as I dared, and he, not having any place to sit except the floor, had a miserable time of it. The only complaint he made was that I had not told him we would be flying above the moon; in a tight 180-degree turn at one end of our track, he had braced himself beside a window and seen the moon far below the wing. He must have been glad to get back to the comfort of his dental office next day.

My father had official as well as personal worries when he got word that a plane was missing from my station, he being in charge of Air–Sea Rescue on that coast. When nothing was found that night, he had daylight searches continued for about a week. During that time, fourteen other wrecks were found, but not that of our English crew. The saddest part, for me, was discovering later that the English boys had been in the same deficient machine that we had taken to Sitka the day before.

At the end of training at Comox our class was given two weeks' leave and a posting to the RCAF Embarkation Depot at Moncton, New Brunswick. I spent the time in Edmonton and Calgary, where I left Robbie and Patricia with her father, sister Marian, and Marian's baby. About two hours before I was due to take the Calgary train to Moncton, we heard on the radio that an atom bomb had been dropped on Hiroshima, and the Japanese war was over.

At the Moncton Embarkation Depot I found that Frank Rooke had already been there for about a month, and I took the upper bunk above his bed. The barracks were full of waiting crews. The only duties were to attend the morning parade and roll call and to wait for further instructions. Frank and I made several excursions by bus to the beach near Shediac, and spent a rainy weekend seeing the sights of Charlottetown.

Then at one morning parade a list of selected crews was read out, including mine, with an announcement that they would all be leaving next day for Halifax to take ship for England for transport duty in Europe. Around noon I received a second message, from Patricia's father, saying that Patricia was in hospital with another miscarriage, and that I

Four generations of Blackburns: my grandfather Robert P., my son Robert G., Flight Lieutenant Robert H., and my father Flight Lieutenant John H.

should come as soon as possible. I tried to see the Commanding Officer but was told he had left for the day. As I stewed about what to do, Frank Rooke, whose crew was not being posted overseas, offered to take my place, but I could not accept his offer.

Early next morning I waited beside the parade ground until I saw the Commanding Officer coming across on his way to breakfast. I went out to him and made my request for leave, but he brushed me off with a remark that miscarriages were very common; his own wife had had some, and I should not be worried.

An hour later the crews being posted overseas were formed up in a special parade, given detailed instructions and documentation for the coming journey, and called to attention for inspection. The CO himself led the inspecting party at a very slow pace along each line. After some parley at the front, the inspecting party did something we had never seen before; they came around again, peering carefully at each of us. After another parley at the front, the Warrant Officer marched back along the line to where I stood and asked whether I was the officer who had spoken to the CO on the parade ground early that morning. Hearing that I was, he marched me back to the CO, who told me he was cancelling my posting and giving me indefinite leave to begin as soon as I could be cleared from his station.

Getting clearance from the station was not a simple matter, but by taking an unemployed bicycle to get from one office to another I got it done by mid-afternoon. Frank Rooke went with me in a taxi to Greenwood, the nearest RCAF flying station, to see whether there might be a westward-bound duty flight that night. There was not, but we got back to Moncton in time for me to catch the evening train to Montreal. The train was so full that it was standing room only for the first couple of hours. But by dint of a touch of provincial aggressiveness, I was on my way home to Calgary and an honourable discharge from the RCAF.

So ended three years of military life.

12 Calgary Public Library, and Hail Columbia

By the time Patricia was safely out of hospital in Calgary I had applied for discharge from the RCAF. We had decided to live with Patricia's father for a year to be company for him. His daughter Marian would soon be leaving him when her husband Bill McEwen returned from his posting in charge of a Canadian base in Holland.

I applied to Alexander Calhoun for work at the Calgary Public Library. I was surprised to see that he was a very slim old man who looked rather too frail to be the man who had carried Patricia and other ladies of the library staff across a stream only four years earlier. He invited me to join him for lunch at the Round Table, a group of worthy citizens who met at a café once every month to settle the affairs of the world. On the day I was to meet him there I could not remember whether he had said Beaver Café or Buffalo Café, so I went rather early to one of them and asked whether I had come to the right place for the Round Table meeting. The girl at the desk looked me up and down as if considering what to say. For the sake of economy I was wearing my officer's uniform, but without navigator wing or brass buttons or sleeve stripes. After a few moments she leaned forward and said in a low voice, "Yes, are you the exterminator?" However, I passed muster at the luncheon, and Mr Calhoun launched me on my library career, to begin on 1 September at $96 a month. He himself retired at the end of August, and was replaced by William Castell, who thus inherited my services for a year.

My plan was to spend one year at the library in Calgary and then, using my veteran's credit, go for a year of advanced study at the Library School at Columbia University. Then I would return to Canada to some good public library with a strong program of adult education through which I could help change the world.

After learning the ropes in the main library, in the old stone Carnegie building in Calgary's central park, I was put in charge of opening a new branch library in what had been a shoe store in the east end of Calgary, near the railway roundhouse; I learned some things in the process. In looking through the books that had been assembled for it, I rejected the one by Zane Grey, but Mr Castell told me to put it back—I would need it. During the first week in the new place, a stout middle-aged man in overalls came in to register, looked around, and seeing the cowboy picture on the cover, borrowed the Zane Grey book. A few days later he brought it back and asked for any other book I had by Zane Grey. He said he was night watchman at the roundhouse and needed something good to read at night. Having no more Zane Grey, I offered him a new biography of Billy the Kid, and he took it. Two days later he was waiting for me when I arrived to open the shop. Handing the book to me, he exclaimed, "This is real! It really happened!" He asked if there were any other real books, and I gave him *Nanook of the North*. After that he read *Maneaters of Kumaon*, and then anything else I would give him. It was exciting to think that I had really enlarged his outlook on the world.

I was allowed to hire two teenagers to help me shelve the books and keep the room clean. They had some time on their hands, and I had the idea of sending them out to deliver books without charge, in response to phone calls from members of the library. The service was advertised and began, but then I bragged to Mr Castell about it. He reminded me that we were responsible for the safety of these youngsters and should not be sending them out into strange buildings. So that was the end of my bright idea for free delivery service, until I applied a version of it as a delivery service to professors at the University of Toronto; in due course it spread far beyond Toronto.

One morning, as I was hurrying across Calgary to work, on my bicycle, a taxi came cruising through an intersection and hit me broadside. In the Colonel Belcher military hospital nearby, I woke up with a blinding headache and a certainty that both legs had been broken above the knee, where they had hit the handlebars. I thought my plans for Columbia were at an end. But next morning a nurse, who must have had training as a sergeant major, ordered me to roll over and I found I could move my legs. A thorough examination showed that I had no injuries except bruises and abrasions, which would keep me in hospital for a few days only.

I recall only three incidents that occurred during those days. The doctor decided to strip the varicose veins in my legs, and did so. I had a game of chess with my neighbour, who was a brother of the future prime minister, John Diefenbaker. And one afternoon a dear old lady volunteer, wheeling a cart of books and magazines through the ward, stopped at the bed of a young fellow who was well bandaged and had one leg suspended in traction. She said, "Poor boy, what service were you in?" He replied wanly, "The British Thermal Unit, bringing coffee up for the troops." She said, "Oh you poor boy!" and pushed on, shaking her head.

The next spring, Patricia's father married again, moved to an apartment, and arranged for some old friends to rent the house when we moved out at the end of August. He assigned most of the contents of his house to his two daughters, so Marian came on a visit from Toronto, where Bill MacEwen had found a job after returning from military duties in Holland. After the sisters had agreed on a division of the furniture, piece by piece, Marian shipped the McEwen share to Toronto, and we put our share into storage pending our return from New York the following year.

The move from Calgary to New York was a nightmare wished on us by two American agencies: the American consul in Calgary, and the housing office at Columbia University. I had been accepted by the Library School at Columbia to enter the old Master of Science course in September 1946. The Department of Veterans Affairs had agreed to pay my fees plus a living allowance of $90 Canadian a month, and I had given notice that I would be leaving my job at the Calgary Public Library. But there was a snag.

When I applied at the American consulate for a visa for myself and family, I was told that a student visa (the only kind available to me for the purpose) would not cover wife and two-year-old son. They would have to stay in Canada. When I suggested that my wife could take a course, too, and apply for her own visa, the man said that would be allowed, but of course that would not cover the child. When I said he could go to kindergarten and so qualify for another student visa, the consul said that might be permitted if we could show him we had arranged in advance for a place to live (living accommodation was very tight in New York City just then). My father took our case to the consulate in Vancouver and sent me a copy of the existing regulations, which, when I read them to the American consul in Calgary, solved the visa problem.

We had, in fact, applied to the housing bureau at Columbia University, which was in charge of housing for families of students who were war veterans. Their only response was that I should come to their office upon arrival as they could make no assignments or promises in advance. So it seemed that we were stuck, unless we could find a way to take housing with us.

Although we had little money and no car of our own, we went hunting for a house trailer, and ended up one evening being offered one out on a campground south of the city. The people who were living in it wanted $1,800, about half of our savings. We knew nothing about trailers and it was the only one we had ever seen inside, but it looked cosy enough and was perhaps our best chance, so we bought it.

Patricia's family home was on a corner lot; the trailer was parked behind the hedge, at the curb at the side of the house. There we became better acquainted with it and prepared it for life in New York. Inside the door there was a small metal plate bearing the name Elkhart Trailers Ltd., although we could find no trace of a trailer company in Elkhart, Indiana. In fact it began to look rather homemade and became more so as we worked on it. Six months later we would translate Elkhart as Hellkart! At the front end of it was a closed cupboard that we changed easily into a private bed for Rob. A lidded storage box just inside the door became a chemical toilet, with a ventilator pipe up through the roof. Near that we invented a shower-bath that consisted of a galvanized bucket hung above the kerosene heater, with a spigot and rubber hose that drained into a tub that was only a rubber sheet in a folding frame. Gradually we made the thing ready for the great excursion, except of course that we had no way of moving it, except by hope.

In 1946 new cars were scarce, and were rationed. Nobody could get one without having an old one to trade in, or without being a veteran who needed a car in order to carry on a business. Going to Columbia did not qualify as a business. Pat's father owned a tiny, worn-out Morris Minor that we had been using in Calgary, but it would never pull the trailer, and its market value was so small that we could not afford to trade it for a new auto. Finally, about a week before our deadline for departure, Patricia's father happened to hear that one of his friends was planning to trade his 86,000-mile Oldsmobile for a new one, and our plans were rescued by trading the Morris plus $800 for the Oldsmobile. Dr Gibson had the motor and brakes checked, the tires retreaded, and a trailer hitch bolted on. So we were away to the races, almost!

Before taking on cargo I decided to take the ship for a trial spin, alone. Around the corner and down the long 11th Street hill it went very well. The electric brakes also worked very well, except that when

I applied them the front end of the trailer bowed low, and the hood of the Oldsmobile responded by rising in graceful salute. Around the corner and homeward up the 10th Street hill was quite another matter; the motor laboured in low gear and finally conked out. After failing several times to get the parade started uphill again, I tried to turn around in the rather narrow street, and the whole thing jack-knifed on me. Backing up with an eighteen-foot trailer was a trick I had not until then even thought about, let alone learned. There I was halfway up a long hill with car and trailer locked in a tight V, in danger of breaking the hitch and seeing the whole shebang go looping and galumphing down the street to the utter destruction of itself and anything or anybody in its path. Memory has drawn a curtain around what happened next, but somehow the trailer resumed its accustomed place beside our house, and stood ready for loading.

Loading was something of a community effort. Meat and sugar were said to be unavailable in New York City, so kind friends had been dropping by with offerings of canned meat and shares of their own precious sugar rations. These gifts, plus our own additions, filled our cupboards, shelves, and bins with more than 180 cans of food, besides canisters of sugar and flour and boxes of such things as Red River cereal. Then there was our clothing for the year on hangers in the closet, and bedding, plus toys and a few necessary books and medical supplies, dishes and kitchen utensils, plus anything else that at the last minute looked useful, including a large electric fan that turned out to be our salvation during the following winter. It was not a light load. So it was with mixed feelings of relief, expectation, and trepidation that we waved goodbye to our well-wishers in Calgary and in late August set off down the hill toward the future.

In Madison, Wisconsin, we stopped for an hour for Pat to walk us around the State House and point out the library school from which she had graduated. Nearing Chicago, one of the two tires on the trailer exploded, and we parked it at roadside while we waited all night in line behind a factory in Chicago to buy two new tires. Near the Canadian border the other old tire on the trailer blew out, and again there was the job of mounting and pumping up a new one. We stopped in London and Toronto to call on the directors of those public libraries, and to visit Pat's sister and her family, the McEwens.

Patricia had written ahead to an elderly cousin on her mother's side who was a judge and lived in a place called White Plains, a suburb of New York City. She had asked for advice about trailer parks in or near

New York, and was told that he knew of none. He advised strongly against bringing a trailer; trailers were what some people had in Florida, but of course they were not allowed to enter White Plains. He had suggested that we stay at his house for a few days instead, until we could get a place of our own.

As we neared New York, Pat phoned her cousin the judge to get directions to White Plains, and was told that the easiest route was straight down Highway 9W and across the Alpine Ferry to Yonkers. The word alpine should have warned us, but we were tired and did not realize the full significance of it until we turned off at the ferry sign. After one or two curves in the rather narrow road, we found ourselves descending the steep switchbacks of the Hudson Palisades, to the river. There was no hope of us ever climbing back up that road. The ferryman, understandably, had never seen a house trailer before, and was reluctant to take us, but when faced with the possibility of having us in his parking lot all winter, he relented and accepted double fare.

The Yonkers side presented its own problem: a street ran straight uphill from the ferry to a stoplight at the top. We decided to make a run for it, and when the light turned red, I carried on regardless, but with one hand on the brake lever in case an emergency stop was needed. And that is how we were able to get to the top, make a right turn through the light, and proceed down Broadway. Broadway? The signs said Broadway! A million lights they flicker there, and the first one was red.

Just past the Yonkers Public Library there was a commercial parking lot filling up quickly in the early darkness of Saturday night. The attendant was reluctant to accept our strange conveyance but agreed to do so if we would unhitch and get the car out of the way quickly.

The trailer door had a cheap lock, and we did not dare leave our year's supply of clothing there, so we piled as much as we could into the car, as quickly as we could, some things just loose and smaller things stuffed into pillowcases. An hour later, at the stone mansion of the cousins in White Plains where the east wing was being opened for us, we unloaded in some disarray, feeling like very small and hungry country mice.

Two days later, when I gave my name at the Columbia University housing bureau, they simply pulled out the file, took my deposit and handed me the key to an apartment at Camp Shanks. I told the girl at the counter that one brief letter of assurance two months earlier could have spared me my life's savings and a nightmare of travel across the continent, but she was already busy with the next arrival.

Next day I went back to Columbia to register, a process that provided some anxious moments. I went first to the School of Library Science and lost little time in signing up for three courses there. The school was willing to let me take two courses in other parts of the university provided I could obtain the signatures of the relevant professors. It took me most of the afternoon to find the right offices and wait for the professors to be in. Then with all applications finally signed, I handed them in at the Graduate Studies office, where there were several clerks behind a long counter. Joining the cluster of applicants near the clerk who was handling the top part of the alphabet, I waited a long time for my name to be called. At the call for Blackburn I stepped forward quickly, as did an attractive young woman; apparently there were two Blackburns! The clerk repeated "Blackburn?" and I replied "Yes, R.H. for Robert Harold." The young woman beside me said "R.H. for Ruth Helen" and received the necessary certificate. When the clerk looked in her in-box and found no other Blackburn, I turned away with the lost feeling Rip Van Winkle must have felt when he woke up and found that nobody knew his name. But mine was called again shortly before closing time.

Camp Shanks, our new address, was on the west side of the Hudson River, twenty-five miles north of Columbia University. It had been the principal US Army embarkation and debarkation centre, and most recently had also been a POW camp, from which the last prisoners had been removed only two months before we arrived. The long, one-storey barracks were set on concrete blocks, roughly built, covered with asbestos siding, and lined with sheets of "ten-test" (pressed wood pulp) about half an inch thick. They had been divided into small apartments for married students who had at least one child. Our unit happened to be across the street from the old parade ground, a perfect place to park the trailer without charge after towing it across the bridge (no ferry!) from Yonkers.

The trailer still presented a problem, however. It had crossed the border on a six-month permit, and had to be taken back within that time, or else be sold. It could not be sold legally without an import permit, even though I pointed out its American origin as attested by the Elkhart label. After lying awake most of one night fighting the temptation to set a match to the plagued thing and collect the insurance, I spent $25 and many hours getting an import license. About that time we discovered that somebody had broken into the thing and camped there, leaving it a somewhat less valuable commodity. We did get one offer for it, of

$1,000 American, but that was only about half what we had paid, and it could not be considered.

So we hauled the thing back to Toronto one weekend in March. I invited one of my Texan classmates to go along for the ride, and he did. His clothing was mostly of Texan weight, so he was glad to hold Rob on his lap the whole way to help keep him warm, there being no heater in the car. We were delayed along the way by an ice storm and had to stop for the night beside a filling station. Pat and I were warm enough with Rob between us, but the Texan was left to his own devices and said next morning that he had spent most of the night standing sheltered in a doorway with his two blankets wrapped around him to survive.

On Monday morning in Toronto we left Pat and Rob at breakfast with her sister, while we began a tour of trailer camps in the Toronto area. When we returned to the house in late afternoon, success was shining on my face. I had got rid of the trailer at last, for $1,000 cash, Canadian, and it was the happiest day we had known for nearly a year.

Our apartment at Camp Shanks was at one end of an army hut; the apartment next to ours was still being finished. We had a living room with kitchenette, a bathroom, storeroom, two bedrooms, four army bunks, and four chairs. We had a gas stove and gas space heater, and were warned to get out quickly in case of fire, as a hut would burn to the ground in three minutes. I joined the volunteer fire department, spent a whole evening being fingerprinted and documented, and took part in weed-burning practice on Saturdays. I responded to two or three night alarms but never found the place until it was too late. Then I received a stern letter of dismissal, with warning of legal action and a stiff fine if I did not turn in all my fireman's equipment within a short number of days. My offence was in being a Canadian, not a US citizen as set forth in the regulations. That week our fire department lost about half its members, for the same reason.

Some other Camp Shanks cooperative ventures fared better. There was a rather expensive camp store, and word got around quickly when it had any rarity such as beef or marmalade, but its prices were so high that a cooperative store was established very quickly in an old drill hall. The former officers' mess was available weekends for various religious services. Patricia taught Sunday School and helped form a cooperative library. We both helped a drug company test some kind of lotion, for $1 a visit. Our whole community was a target for study by some of our own members and by various brands of social scientists from New York City.

At Columbia's School of Library Science most of the students were in the first-year program, and there were fewer than twenty of us in the Masters program, all Americans except me. Besides my courses at the Library School I had one in Communication in the Sociology Department and one in Adult Education at the Teachers College. During the fall term the course in Library Administration was given by our dean, who retired at Christmas. He was a quiet-spoken and uninspired speaker. His first name was Ernest, and among themselves his students referred to him as Dead Ernest. The new dean was quite different and helped me find an interesting topic for my thesis. He acted as my supervisor and was very pleased with the work when it was finished; he said it was the sort of dissertation he would expect to see in the doctoral program that he was about to establish. One of my courses was in the evening, and I would get home by subway and railway. Most of the time I commuted in a carpool along with two other Canadians and a Newfoundlander. As a family we saw almost nothing of the city except for a trip to see Stravinsky's *Firebird*, from the nosebleed row of the Metropolitan Opera, to celebrate Robbie's third birthday. He slept through most of it, but at breakfast next morning he announced, "When I jump on one foot I fall down."

We drove to Toronto to have Christmas with the McEwens. I went also to meet with Stewart Wallace, Librarian of the University of Toronto, who had invited me to do so. After I had been a quarter-hour or so in his office, he walked me across the campus for a twenty-minute chat with President Sidney Smith. On the way back to his own office, he offered me a position as his Assistant Librarian at $3,500 a year, a thousand dollars more than I had expected. I asked for a month to consider the offer, and used the time to explore possibilities in Canadian public libraries, but the best offer there was $1,900, less than we could live on, so we decided to try the University of Toronto, at least for a year. It was agreed that I should start there at the beginning of September.

For my thesis at Columbia I had undertaken to explore the relationship between size and outreach of branch libraries in a large city. In New York the Fordham Branch was the biggest one when judged by its book collection, staff, and budget. After reviewing statistics and visiting several smaller branches for comparison, I chose the Huntington Square Branch in the Bronx, which was just one-quarter the size of Fordham Branch. Was its outreach to readers more than or less than one-quarter of Fordham's? I supposed it would be less.

At each of the two libraries I went through the membership files and wrote down the address and sex of every tenth cardholder. Then I plotted this information on enlarged street maps of the two districts, maps on which I had drawn concentric circles one mile apart around the branch library being studied. Then I counted the number of library cardholders, male and female, within the circles and various rings on each map. As I had expected, my dots on the Huntington Square map were concentrated fairly close to the library, while the Fordham dots were much greater in number and scattered farther into the outer rings. But to my surprise, the total number of Fordham dots was only about four times as many as those on the other map. And compared to Fordham, the Huntington Square dots had a noticeably larger percentage of women. So for librarians who were planning to plant new branches in their cities, my message was that dollar for dollar, a small branch could have about equal power to attract members, compared to a large branch with more varied collections and services, but a small branch would serve a larger proportion of women.

While coming and going by way of the Huntington Square elevated train station, I noticed a small church-like building at the edge of the square; according to its sign it was the Huntington Free Library and Reading Room. Being curious, I went in, and after looking around, spoke to the only person there, an elderly woman at the desk. She told me that her library was well endowed but had a small collection and was very little used, except by a few local office workers who came in to eat their lunches and look at the current magazines. When I mentioned the famous Huntington Library in California, she made a face, and said she knew some things about it, but would not care to see it. And she told me why.

She said that her library was one of the many benefactions of Collis P. Huntington, who had been a storekeeper in Sacramento, California, selling hardware and mining equipment at the time of the California Gold Rush. From there, he and his partner Mark Hopkins—along with some other men, including Leland Stanford—had entered the railway business and made huge fortunes. Collis Huntington had built and owned many railways and had put together the first American line across the continent. In his later years he had taken a nephew, Henry E. Huntington, into the business. As a young servant in the Collis P. Huntington mansion in the Bronx, my informant had known Henry, and made it clear to me that she had no use for him.

She went on to say that when Collis P. Huntington died in the Bronx in 1900, his fortune was divided between his second wife and his nephew "young Henry, who stopped at nothing." He consolidated the fortune by marrying his aunt. He bought the trolley lines in Los Angeles, and land near the city, and ran the lines out to his properties. In San Marino he built a mansion that is now the central part of the library that has made his name world-famous, while hardly anybody has heard of his Uncle Collis, who made him!

I would have needed much more information to compare the power of the two Huntington libraries, large and small, on a dollar-for-dollar basis, to attract readers and satisfy their needs.

On our way home to Alberta in the spring, we went by way of Toronto to look for accommodation there. Finding nothing for rent, we bought a six-room semi-detached house on Soudan Avenue, just east of Mount Pleasant Road; the price was $10,000, roughly three times my prospective salary. The McEwens were about to leave Toronto for a new job in Winnipeg, and offered to leave behind for us, in their garage, a wooden bunk bed that they were storing for mutual friends who had gone to Venezuela. We left also our winter clothing and other impedimenta that we had hauled to and from New York and that we would not be needing during the summer. While staying with my parents in Edmonton, we sold our car and I finished work on my thesis for Columbia. Robbie was nearing his fourth birthday, and we decided it was time for him to have a baby sister. We applied for permission to adopt one. Finding no girl to adopt in Edmonton, we went on to Calgary and stayed for a week with old friends of the family. One morning Patricia's father called us from one of the hospitals to say that a bonnie wee girl baby, whom he had delivered some days earlier, was now cleared for adoption. When she looked into our eyes we felt that she had chosen us, and we signed the papers that day. We named her Karen, after my Grandmother Olson.

Our new daughter was not allowed to travel for two weeks, so I took the train for Toronto alone to report for work at the university. The house we had bought was supposed to be vacant by 1 September, but the previous owners were still there. They offered to pay a good rent for use of the upstairs for a week or ten days, until their new house was completed, and I agreed to it. They had use of the kitchen; I shared the bathroom upstairs and bought a mattress to sleep on in the dining room beside their dining room suite. As our first landlord at Comox had said, people are supposed to help one another.

When our daughter Karen was allowed to travel, Patricia and the children came to join me in Toronto. Patricia had been train-sick, but fortunately our Comox friend Marnie Clay was on the same train as far as Winnipeg, where another kind woman from down the corridor took her place as helper with the children. On arrival, Patricia was dismayed to find that the previous owners were still in the house and would be with us for two more days. When they left, we were in an empty house except for the baby's basket, the mattress I had bought, plus the bunk bed and chairs that had been left for us in the McEwen garage. It was more than a week later that we received from Calgary the items of Gibson furniture that we had inherited. With a few more purchases, including kitchen furniture and a washing machine, we began to get settled. And there was time to unpack our barrel of wedding gifts, after waiting four years.

13 Beginning at the University of Toronto Library

Reporting for duty at the University Library, the stone basilica that had opened in 1892 on the east side of the central campus, I found that there was no office for an Assistant Librarian. Stewart Wallace, a former professor of history, had run the library without an assistant for twenty-five years, and spent most of his time writing and editing Canadian history. His need to hire an assistant arose out of a decree by the new Chairman of the Board, that every officer in the university should have an understudy. I was given an old desk in the already crowded Reference Room.

Exploring the building that morning, I happened to meet Jack Sword in an upstairs corridor. We had not been in touch since his departure from the RCAF station at Portage la Prairie, but here he was, exploring the library on his first day at the university as Assistant Secretary in the School of Graduate Studies. From then on we met often, sometimes on university business but always as lifelong friends. After years as Secretary of Graduate Studies, during the vast expansion of the university's emphasis on research, he became Assistant to the President, and for two separate years was Acting President. Even after his retirement he continued to serve the university in various official capacities, in the last of which I appointed him Director of the Oral History Project that I had initiated in the library. Thus our last working relationship resembled our first, nearly forty years earlier at Portage la Prairie.

At the library, Stewart Wallace introduced me rather gradually to the routines and problems. My first assignment was to write a guide to the library. This had to include such things as library hours, lending regulations, and use of the card catalogue, and also the fact that there was a separate reading room for women and a separate wicket for them at

Jack Sword, jack of all trades: school principal, RCAF navigation instructor, Secretary of the University of Toronto's School of Graduate Studies, Acting President, and so on. Photo by Eric Singer circa 1960. Jack Sword Family Archives.

the loan desk. My draft included some light-hearted stick drawings as illustrations. Wallace was not sure the president would approve, but as it turned out, he was delighted, and a thousand copies were printed.

My second assignment, much larger, was to sort the papers of Edward Blake. Blake was the first Premier of Ontario when Ontario came into being in 1867. At the same time he won a seat in the new federal Parliament, where he served for eight years as leader of the Liberal opposition, exposing his inflated oratory to the piercing wit of Prime Minister John A. Macdonald, who boasted that Canadians preferred Macdonald drunk to Blake sober. From 1876 to 1900 he was Chancellor of the University of Toronto, where he was known as a cold, humourless man, but also as one who played a key role in renewal of the university after its great fire in 1890. In 1892 he became a member of the Irish Nationalist party in the British House of Commons, and for fourteen years commuted by ship between Toronto and London.

Blake's papers filled dozens of boxes and consisted mainly of political pamphlets and correspondence. More interesting to me were some packets of personal letters. Among the earliest of these is a letter to his mother soon after his arrival at the university as a student, asking her to please send him some bear grease for his hair so that he could be like the other boys. Her letters to him are fascinating to read, each one on a single sheet written with a very fine pen across the page, then overwritten from bottom to top, and sometimes over-written again diagonally, but with family news and motherly advice still fairly easy to read. His personal correspondence in London includes invitations to tea parties with Thomas Hardy and some friends of Kenneth Grahame, author of *Wind in the Willows*, the book I was then reading to our young son.

For my work on the Blake papers, my old desk had been moved to a small storage cupboard upstairs in the library, and that continued to be my office. There was a window at my elbow, but no telephone. Wallace sent for me from time to time when he thought there was an incident or task that might be instructive. He had learned discipline and administration in the army. With the rank of major he had been with the Third Canadian Division for two months at Vimy Ridge, and was wounded there. In 1917, before being sent home for discharge, he was president of one section of the Canadian Khaki University. One of the small paperweights on his desk was a piece of shrapnel that had been in his leg.

One day he called me to his office to say he had heard that the head of our Periodicals Department and her assistant who shared the room with her (but with separate duties) were not on speaking terms. Their

Stewart Wallace, Librarian of the University of Toronto, 1923–54. Courtesy of the University of Toronto Archives.

only communication was by way of their one clerk, thus: "Mary, you may tell Miss Todd that I will be taking early lunch today." After telling me the circumstances, he asked his secretary to bring the two women in. He told them what he had heard, asked them whether it was true, and told them that this silliness was to stop. If there was any more of it he would put them out on their ears. And they knew he would do it.

As an old soldier, he believed in commissioning in the field. One morning he called me in to say that he had just heard that one of our department heads had died during the night. He wanted to replace her immediately, to forestall needless speculation and expectations. After going over the short list of possible candidates, he decided on one, called her in, told her the circumstances, and told her that she was the new head of the department. After a few sleepless nights she asked permission to go back to her old position. He agreed, and without hesitation appointed the next in line.

Wallace relied heavily on his secretary, Julia Jarvis, a descendant of Judge Jarvis who had hanged two unfortunate rebel leaders who were captured after Mackenzie's Upper Canada Rebellion in 1838. Miss Jarvis was a handsome, brisk, efficient woman, a historian herself, who had been at the library for twenty-five years. Besides looking after all the secretarial work and the accounts, she did much of the collating and editing in support of Wallace's work. She also brought him his brandy out of the vault whenever he was about to cross the campus to Simcoe Hall for a meeting of the Senate Library Committee.

Wallace was fond of reminding me that according to the University of Toronto Act, the duties of the librarian were prescribed by the Senate, not by the president as were the duties of all other officers of the university. He would rehearse the story of a former president who came to the library to inspect the page that recorded all the books that had been borrowed by a certain professor who was suspected of being a rank socialist. Wallace was no friend of socialists but refused the request on the basis of principle: loan records were confidential information. And when the president insisted, he was turned away with this response: "Mr President, you can hire me and you can fire me, but you cannot tell me how to run the Library."

Wallace was not a person to be imposed upon. More than once he told me about a dean who had stormed into his office with a complaint, and had begun speaking in an officious and offensive manner. Wallace had risen from his chair and said calmly, "That is not the sort of language permitted between one officer of the university and another."

Then to complete the story, he would step to the side door, open it, and with a sweep of the hand, indicate the way out.

But Wallace also enjoyed a good joke, even on himself. Just before he retired, I happened to be with him one day when his old friend, Joe Evans the Registrar, dropped in to wish him well. Evans noticed the official framed retirement portrait standing on the bookshelf, and admired it. Wallace turned the compliment aside by saying that his wife didn't like the picture, because she thought it showed a spot of egg on his tie. Evans, nearly blind, stepped up close to the picture, peered at it through his special glasses with the magnifying lens hinged down, and said, "No, I don't see any egg, more like gravy!" And we all had a great laugh.

Wallace had little time for library associations and their meetings. Toronto had been (perhaps by courtesy) one of the forty-two founding members of the Association of Research Libraries (ARL) that met annually. He sometimes read their reports and correspondence, but he never attended meetings. He explained these things to me sometime before Christmas, in my first year, 1947, and mentioned that he had received notice of ARL's next meeting, to be held in Chicago in January. At previous meetings there had been discussion of a proposal they called the Farmington Plan, which was a plan for cooperative acquisition to ensure that all important new publications would be available somewhere in North America. Each ARL library would accept responsibility for acquiring and preserving all publications on particular subjects or from particular regions. Wallace had agreed tentatively to do this for all publications from Quebec, in French. The plan was to be launched officially at the Chicago meeting, and he wanted me to be there to confirm Toronto's part in it. Our president had agreed to pay my way. So it was that I, after less than six months at the library, represented Toronto, as the only Canadian there among the library directors of the principal universities and other research institutions in the United States. I had met two or three of these men during my time at Columbia, but in Chicago I met many more. And I put Toronto on the map for at least one of them, the one who asked whether I was from Upper or Lower Canada.

The morning after Newfoundland voted in 1948 to join Canada as a province, Wallace called me in to say that he wanted me to learn how a book is put together. His own six-volume *Encylopedia of Canada* would become obsolete on the new Confederation Day, 1 April 1949, unless it had a Newfoundland supplement by that time. His publisher had agreed to publish a hundred-page supplement and would pay me $100 to prepare a fully edited text. So I spent several months, including weekends and vacation time, on that job.

I knew nothing about Newfoundland and found little about it in the library. The most recent and extensive bit was in two quarto volumes, *The Book of Newfoundland*, by Joseph Smallwood. I wrote to him for advice and help. After waiting a few weeks I heard that Smallwood, a journalist and broadcaster, was fully occupied in a campaign to become the first premier of the new province, and I could not expect him to answer my letter. Meanwhile I had written to the librarian at Newfoundland Memorial College with a list of the topics that needed to be covered, and she gave me a fruitful list of possible authors.

The first to send me the sort of thing I asked for was the president of the Law Society of Newfoundland, with an article covering Newfoundland law. With my letter of thanks I sent him a cheque for about $15, for about 4,500 words. He sent the cheque back, saying he did not need it. I returned it, explaining that it was not my money, but the publisher's allowance, and if he did not wish to keep it, he could give it to a charity. He sent it back, saying that he would keep it only if I sent him my hat size. So it was that I received my first Newfoundland seal wedge-cap, which I have replaced twice. On cold days it could be pulled down to cover my ears.

Other topics were less fun. Our own Dean of Graduate Studies, author of the standard text on cod fisheries, agreed to give me an article on that subject. When it finally arrived, long after my first deadline, it was an almost unreadable scribble, mostly headings and brief notes, that I had to rewrite by referring to his book. The full text for the Newfoundland Supplement was delivered on time, however, and by Confederation Day was issued with 104 pages in firm red Morocco binding, to match the first six volumes of Wallace's set.

My next book was just an editorial job, the 602-page *List of Serials in Toronto Libraries,* which was finally published in 1953. The information had already been gathered on cards or lists from many different libraries in the city, and had only to be put together in proper form and order; it was dry work, but later I had the pleasure of seeing it listed in the catalogue of the Moscow University Library.

My first self-initiated project was one that Wallace had doubts about, so he sent me to the head of the Circulation Department to see whether she would adopt it. From my first desk in the Reference Room there was a clear view down the long hallway to the loan desk. In the afternoons I had seen a double line (one side male, the other not) of students waiting to get "reserve" books. The back of the line curved around the corner into the lobby and back through the Men's Reading Room. Enrolment had suddenly doubled after the war, which meant that there were not nearly enough books, and competition for them was keen. When the books were returned next morning, I saw them piled high on the desk and on the floor for hours, even till next day, waiting there to be checked against the loan file before being reshelved for further use.

One of my classmates at Columbia, librarian of the Yonkers Public Library, had invited me to see a commercial demonstration of numbered "keysort" cards with a row of holes and slots across the top, and one tab on each card. They could be sorted with a long needle. The system was apparently being used in some offices. To meet our problem I designed six sets of numbered keysort cards, colour-coded for workdays of the week. A card was slipped into the pocket of each book before it went out, its number having been copied onto the loan slip. When the books returned next morning, the cards could be taken out quickly and the books shelved without delay. Later in the day the cards would be sorted by a few passes of the needle. With the cards in order, their tabs made solid lines across the top of the deck, and any gap in the line indicated a missing book. Only the missing numbers had to be checked in the loan file before it was discarded. The system worked very well, saved a great deal of time, and gave us better mileage out of the books. It was used for years.

Our Move to Streetsville

In the spring of 1949 my parents and my father-in-law surprised us with the gift of a small car, an Austin 40, and our horizons were widened. We began a series of weekend drives, looking for a country place that we could afford. We started by looking east of Toronto, so that the sun would be at my back as I drove to and from work. As far east as Whitby, and as far north as King, we found nothing. We ended up buying a house on an acre and a half, on the bank of the Credit River, twenty-five miles west of the university. The price was $9,000, and the house was unfinished, although it had been lived in for one winter. The main floor had only rough underflooring, and sweepings fell through the cracks. There were no finished partitions, no trim, and no doors except two storm doors, front and side. There was no concrete floor in the basement, only mud and an inch or two of water. Being a farm boy acquainted with hammer and saw, I thought I would be able to do the finishing myself.

The water supply was an eight-foot dug well near the house, but the owner told us that a four-foot well at the end of the road had supplied two houses and 2,000 chickens without ever going dry. When I said I would like some guarantee of water, he said, "Mister, I wouldn't guarantee you water if you was hooked up to Lake Ontario." When I told Wallace we were moving to Streetsville, he said, "Well, I guess we won't see much of you in the wintertime." And so, after the move, I was careful to be at the library every morning before he was, even when roads were blocked and I had to wade a mile through snowdrifts in the dark to get to the train station.

We sold the Toronto house for what we had paid for it, plus fees, and moved on 1 June 1950, bringing with us Ralph and Edna King and their two small boys. Ralph and Edna had been our Air Force friends at Portage la Prairie. He had come to Toronto to work on a doctorate in English Literature, and they had been living in a rat-infested basement near the university. So there were eight of us, including two children in diapers, and two mothers who were used to having city water. On the third day the well went dry, and for some months we had a water tank on wheels in the driveway. Some evenings I took our children down to the river to bathe.

I hired a well digger, who brought his tripod, hand winch, buckets, and short-handled spades, and we spent evenings digging a hole near the corner of the house. We got down to twenty-nine feet through blue clay and shale that required blasting, but found no water, so we bricked up the sides and turned the eavestroughs into the hole for a cistern. My digger thought there would be plenty of water in the old hole farther from the house, if we could get down below the layer of quicksand, but he did not want to do the job himself—maybe his younger brother would do it—they had once dropped a bucket on his head.

The brother agreed to do it if there was cribbing in place to hold the quicksand out. I formed a rough cribbing out of some old planks I found beside the abandoned chicken house at the end of the road, and somehow worked it down to the bottom of the quicksand. I went down inside on a small ladder. By carrying muck out of the thirty-inch concrete tile that was already in place, I slowly shut the quicksand out. (Ralph King was upstairs working on his thesis, but came out every hour to see that I was safe.) Then I got help from the bucket-on-head brother, with winch and bucket, to cut away at the bottom of the tile while standing inside it, and adding new tiles on top as the first one sank. We got down to eighteen feet, to where the man digging was up to his ankles in water. There we stopped, lowered a pipe with a valve on it, and ran a second pipe to the water pump in the basement. Our new well was not a great provider, but it was something. We often had to fill it with water by the truckload until years later when our district got city water.

Another nasty problem was the need to dig down to the footings on all sides of the house to lay weeping tiles and re-tar the foundation walls. After I had made a brave start at it myself, Jack Sword and Frank Rooke came out with picks and spades to help. They were both good workers at whatever they did. Frank retired as a Vice-President of the Canada Life Assurance Company, and Jack had an illustrious career at the university. Ralph King would have helped too, but they had moved back to the city; he eventually became a dean and acting president at Brandon University.

In August 1950 we left the Kings in charge while we drove to Alberta to visit our families. While we were gone, our main floor rooms were plastered, and a concrete floor was poured in the basement. After that, many things remained to be done. My own lack of time and skill meant that progress was very slow, so slow that Patricia, in desperation, finally hired professional help to finish the house.

So it was that after eight years of marriage and ten moves of residence, we settled into our house overlooking the Credit River, raised our children, and spent more than half our lives together there. As I write this, I am in my sixty-third year in the same house.

14 Abraham Flexner and His Gift of Travel

In early June of 1950, Stewart Wallace had begun his usual summer vacation on the St Lawrence River in Quebec, and I was occupying his office. President Sidney Smith called to say that he had just received a request from Dr Abraham Flexner. He was sending it over to me, and said I should act on it as quickly as possible. I had no idea who Flexner was or why our president should be so eager to please him.

When the request arrived a few minutes later, it was for our complete file of the annual reports of the Carnegie Corporation of New York, to be sent to Dr Flexner at Magnetawan, a remote spot in the woods of Northern Ontario. He planned to arrive at his camp there the following week and was finishing his work on the history of that corporation. This was a most unusual request, one that went far beyond our rules for lending, but I went into the stacks and found the reports, thin bound volumes taking up about two feet of shelf space. We packed them up and sent them by express that afternoon, and sent a confirming letter.

A week later Flexner wrote from Magnetawan, rejoicing to have found the reports waiting for him at his camp and asking for us to send him Hendricks's two-volume biography of Andrew Carnegie. On receiving that, he sent another handwritten letter of glowing thanks on 20 June:

> Dear President Smith:
> I do not usually hesitate for lack of words, but the promptness and courtesy of your reply to my note, requesting the further loan of Hendricks's *Carnegie*, finds me at a loss for words that will convey to you my appreciation of your kindness. For I have not only the books, but the addressed wrapping paper in which to return them!

What would this mad world of ours be like, if human conduct could be motivated by such principles; we should not require the United Nations!

Will you communicate to the Librarian of the University my grateful thanks!

With every good wish, very sincerely, Abraham Flexner

The whole business was so unusual that I wondered who Abraham Flexner could be, and decided to look him up. I found he had been born in Louisville, Kentucky, in 1866, and at age fifteen had his first "part-time" job, forty-five hours a week at $16 a month, in the Louisville Public Library. At Johns Hopkins University he could not afford the three-year degree course, so he completed it in two. He taught high school, established his own school, and became renowned as an educator in Louisville and then in Boston. In 1909 he was hired by the Carnegie Foundation for the Advancement of Teaching to make a study of North American medical schools. He visited all 155 medical schools then in the United States and Canada, and in 1910 published a 346-page report on what he had found. His report brought about a revolution in medical teaching. His rating of the eight Canadian schools varied from two that were "excellent" down to one "as bad as anything to be found on this [south] side of the line," but he saw some encouraging signs, and all eight of those schools are still thriving. South of the border a great many of the schools collapsed; in Louisville, for instance, seven schools were reduced to one. Among all that survived, there was a general raising of entrance requirements, teaching standards, and equipment.

In 1913 Flexner became a key member of the General Education Board of the Rockefeller Foundation, and through its grants continued to advance medical and other schools from coast to coast. His quest for the optimum level of teaching and research led to the founding of the Institute for Advanced Study at Princeton in 1930. He spent the last nine years of his official career as its founding director, and brought Albert Einstein across the Atlantic to be a Fellow of the Institute. Back at the camp, in June 1950, he was working on his last book.

His "camp," I learned later, was a two-storey house about two miles across the lake from Magnetawan, inaccessible by road. There were three or four guest cottages, a kitchen, and a large boathouse. According to Lucy Merritt, his neighbour at Magnetawan, the Flexners had bought the place in 1921. She wrote that Dr Flexner was "very poor in a rowboat or canoe" and that Mrs Flexner (a playwright with productions on Broadway) had "once upset a canoe with a dinner guest who came in a new outfit." Most summers the cottages were full of guests from near and far: academics, including Oxford dons, and musicians, such as Jascha Heifetz. When there were two or more musicians they ran into conflicts of practising time. Some were young people. Flexner depended on Ben Merritt (the husband of my informant) to take charge of guests when they wanted to go fishing, and Ben had to "do the hooks." Twice a week in good weather there were sailboat races from the Flexner dock, started by Professor Webb of Columbia, who was an official of the New York Yacht Club.

Imagine my surprise, later that summer in the library office, when the secretary came in to say that Dr Flexner had come to see me! He was a small man, slim, straight, and smiling, very alert and full of vitality at age eighty-four. He was coming in to thank me in person for the promptness and generosity of our service to him. He also gave me a copy of his own most recent book, a biography of his mentor Daniel Coit Gilman, whose first job had been as a librarian of Yale University, from which he resigned because he was expected to stoke the stove. He later became president of the University of California, and in 1876 was the founding president of Johns Hopkins University in Baltimore. Flexner was on his way home to New York and could not stay for a cup of tea, because his taxi was waiting outside to take him to the railway station. His detour to see me and his gift were gestures of appreciation, gestures that are of very rare occurrence in libraries. When his book *Funds and Foundations* was published in 1952, it included thanks to President Sidney Smith, Stewart Wallace, and me for our help.

Two months later, we drove to Edmonton on vacation, and when we got there, waiting for me was a letter from Stewart Wallace. He had received a letter from the Carnegie Corporation's Commonwealth Fund, inviting me to apply for a study grant to visit American and European libraries, if I could be spared from my duties at Toronto. Wallace himself, when he was appointed as assistant to Langton in 1920, had been given a tour of several American university libraries. Now he had consulted with Sidney Smith and they were both delighted to spare me for a reasonable period, if I was interested. Of course I was interested, and accepted the invitation. This was just a few weeks after Flexner's visit.

Back at Toronto I received a letter from Stephen Stackpole, of the Carnegie Commonwealth Fund, asking me to draft an outline for a study tour, and then to discuss it with him in New York. I outlined a three-month tour of important European libraries, writing that I had no other prospect of seeing them, but that I had already met many of the most important American librarians at meetings of the Association of Research Libraries, and would probably have opportunities to see some of them on their home turf.

When I met Stackpole in his office, he accepted my itinerary for three months in Europe, but only on the condition that I first spend that much time visiting American libraries; he did not want to send me to Europe before I had a good grasp of what there was on this side of the water. I needed to send him an American itinerary as well, before the grant could be estimated and made. He said also that he did not want me to spend all my time on libraries: I should also see cathedrals, castles, museums, art galleries, operas, orchestras, and famous sights to broaden my experience; that had been Andrew Carnegie's way of developing officers for his company. Once my itinerary was set, Stackpole's office would give me a list of reasonable hotels, and a supply of form letters on Carnegie letterhead that I could send ahead to open doors and make appointments. He then said that Abraham Flexner had invited the two of us to have lunch with him at his club.

Flexner was waiting for us at the club, greeted me kindly, and congratulated me on my successful application for a study tour. I could only guess, and would never know, how he learned that I was going to be in New York that day. He gave me his card and invited me and my wife to be guests at his camp some summer when we were free; I thanked him but never found the freedom or the nerve to accept the invitation.

The two study tours that followed were a great formative experience in my life and in my career as a library administrator. They gave me a visual acquaintance with the principal libraries and librarians on both sides of the Atlantic, so that I was able to read their reports and articles with greater interest and understanding than I could have done otherwise. The tours also opened the way for me to consult with colleagues quickly and widely, by letter or telephone, concerning important questions and problems as they arose. To whom should I give most credit for this wonderful opportunity, if not to Abraham Flexner?

My American Tour, 1951

In mid-May I travelled to points in New England, then worked my way south as far as Georgia, then across to the West Coast and back through the Midwest and home by mid-August. I had seen about sixty libraries in more than thirty cities. I stopped at least two days in each place. The American university libraries I saw differed from one another in many things that were obvious: in size, in organization, in building layout, and in lending regulations and business procedures, but they also had several characteristics in common with one another and with our Canadian libraries.

First, an American university library received its money from the university. It usually had some endowment funds of its own, and it might receive gifts from time to time, but the cost of operating the library was carried mainly by the university. This was an obvious arrangement, but it was important in establishing the nature of the library. It established the library as a service department of the university, one that justified its existence and its budget through the services it rendered. It served the professors by providing, as money permitted, the books they considered to be important in their fields, for themselves and for their students. As a matter of course at that time, most of the book selection was being done through recommendations of the professors, although the librarian was held to be responsible for errors and omissions.

Another characteristic of these libraries was that they tried to classify their books according to subject, so as to put books on the same subject together on the shelves. Nearly every library made some exceptions to this rule and had either its own homemade scheme or else its homemade improvements on a standard scheme of classification. Also, at that time, most American libraries had card catalogues of their books, by author and subject and by anything else that might be of help to the reader.

Emphasis on helping readers was another characteristic. There were reference departments to help people find out what to read, and circulation departments organized to find a book and produce it within a few minutes, and then retrieve it again within a few hours or a few days so that the next reader might be served.

Regarding departmental libraries in American universities, it was hard to make a general statement, because there were some very notable exceptions, but most universities had some departmental libraries housed separately from the main collection. Sometimes they were completely independent, but usually their budgets, and their acquisition and cataloguing, were centralized in the main library.

In addition to these common characteristics, there was a growing acceptance of the idea that students, in order to derive the most benefit from a library, had to have direct access to the bookshelves. Old stacks that had been designed mainly for storage were being opened to readers, and some of the new buildings had books and reading spaces intermingled. At the universities of Pennsylvania and Virginia, the stacks had been opened to undergraduates, without any noticeable new strain on the library, and self-paging of books by all readers at Northwestern University was being introduced not only as a benefit but as an economy. Except at particularly blessed places such as the Rice Institute and the University of Virginia, general open access required a door check to be maintained. Although open access resulted in some loss of books, the librarians considered the losses to be outweighed by the benefits derived by the students.

While open access was becoming more widely embraced and practised, there were also some developments that favoured closed stacks. At Michigan, for example, most of the open shelves had been closed and the remainder were about to be closed. Even in what seemed to be the ultimate in open access libraries, the new Princeton building in which the resources of a million-volume collection were open to all members of the university from dawn till midnight, I heard an opinion that at first seemed opposed to open access. Dr Boyd of Princeton told me that he believed open shelves offered only a limited advantage in a medium-sized library, and that the advantage would diminish as the collection grew. He thought that in a really large library, open access was a disadvantage, not only to undergraduates but also to research scholars, and that a large library, in order to give good service, must turn eventually to closed shelves and more efficient shelving. He did not mean, of course, that he disapproved of his own Princeton library; he meant only that a large book collection is different from a small or medium-sized one and needed to be used differently.

A compromise between the open shelf library and the closed stack had been made in many places, most notably at Harvard. Harvard's new Lamont Library for undergraduates was an open shelf collection of fewer than 100,000 volumes, a teaching collection working alongside the large research collections. Other undergraduate libraries were in use, or were being planned in various forms, at Columbia, Illinois, UCLA, Pennsylvania, Chicago, and elsewhere. These libraries were not simply browsing rooms; they provided students with an opportunity for browsing, but they also provided most of the materials that had been handled previously as "reserve reading." Their formation was important because it demonstrated that the distinction between teaching and research materials, however difficult theoretically, could be made;

once it had been made, it became simpler to process, house, and use the two sorts of materials according to the particular purposes they were meant to serve.

Along with the idea that students needed direct access to the shelves of a comparatively small teaching library, then, came the idea that scholars did not need direct access to the bulk of the research collection. This idea was arrived at either by logic or by expediency: Dr Boyd of Princeton argued that a sound scholar does not and cannot depend on what books happen to be on a particular shelf on a particular day, but depends rather on references and bibliographies, and should not have to waste time fetching his own books from the stacks. Dr Metcalf of Harvard argued that if a book was called for only infrequently – say, once in twenty years – then it didn't much matter if the reader had to wait a day for it to be delivered - twenty years and a day is not much longer than twenty years.

Once the idea was accepted that a scholar does not need access to the shelves, there was no longer any reason to shelve research collections according to subject. To save space, books could be shelved by size, as Harvard and Yale were doing with some of their books. To save money, some collections could be sent out into comparatively inexpensive storage buildings, as was already being done in Boston and elsewhere.

While every research collection is too small to do its job unaided, many of them were at that time becoming too large to be housed in their own buildings. Of course, much research material is used very infrequently – some of it never – so it seemed a pity that several libraries in a region should all buy and catalogue and store the same materials. In order to prevent this waste of money and space, a number of large libraries around Chicago had obtained foundation grants (Carnegie and Ford) to build what they called the Midwest Inter-Library Center (MILC). MILC began as a cooperative storage warehouse, in which much duplication of material could be eliminated. But it soon became a centre for cooperative acquisition and use of little-used materials. When I was there toward the end of my tour I noticed, for instance, that two of its newest cooperative acquisitions were subscriptions to the *Tokyo Times* and the *Globe and Mail*. The idea seemed to be catching on: there was a brand new Hampshire Inter-Library Center (HILC), and in the west some talk of one in southern California; I supposed it would be named SCILC and that there would be others of the same ilk, though I was thinking that one such centre, properly financed and organized, would be enough for this continent.

In many places I saw large backlogs of uncatalogued material, books by the thousands and tens of thousands, waiting to go on the shelves. In some places the uncatalogued collection was so large that a skimpy job called pre-cataloguing was being done. At Illinois it was done by the Order Department, and at Yale this kind of cataloguing was being accepted as the final job on some sorts of material. For instance, for its whole collection of German fiction published during the war, Yale had only one card in its catalogue. At Indiana the amount of cataloguing was being cut down in another way: subject work was confined to those books for which the Reference Department wanted subject cards.

There were places where various innovations were being tried, to get various parts of the work done more quickly and economically by the use of mechanical systems. At Johns Hopkins the librarian was very pleased with a new notched-card system for managing book orders, the same system that had just been discontinued when I was at Illinois. The most promising machine was the "photo-clerk," a small sort of photostat machine that Ralph Shaw at the US Department of Agriculture had invented to do much of his clerical work. The Carnegie Corporation was underwriting a two-year test of it in libraries of various sizes, but I never heard any report of the test. Shaw had also invented a "rapid selector" that was to revolutionize library research. When I spoke to Donald Coney, librarian of the University of California at Berkeley, about Ralph Shaw and his inventions, about Fremont Rider's way of saving shelf space at Wesleyan University in Connecticut by using a guillotine to cut off the margins of his books, and about Ralph Ellsworth's new kind of "modular" building at the University of Iowa, Coney said "Yes, we need innovators like them in our profession, but we don't need more than three."

Many of the libraries I saw were in new buildings. Those that were not, like Toronto, were badly overcrowded but had hopes or plans for new construction. At Wayne State University in Detroit the inside walls were of painted cinder block. At Houston the reading room walls were finished in green cowhide decorated with Texas cattle brands. At the University of Iowa the inside walls and one of the outside walls were considered to be temporary and had not been finished at all. These examples suggest the variety I saw among the new library buildings in the United States.

For the whole tour I had travelled by train except for one short flight. I had planned to stop on my way from Lincoln, Nebraska, to spend a day with my Columbia classmate from Texas, who had become librarian at Marysville College in Missouri. But in Lincoln I found there was no way to go eastward, either by rail or by bus, because of a great flood of the Missouri River. Waiting for the flood to subside would have led to serious delays in all my remaining appointments, so I located a local flier who agreed to take me to Marysville for $50. His plane was a Piper Cub, a small two-seater. As we flew at a low altitude over a watery landscape he held a map on his knee. When he noticed me map reading our way along, and heard that I had been a navigator, he offered to let me take the controls, which I did until it was time for him to land us in the grassy field that was Marysville's airport. There was nobody there but we found a telephone in the shack, and my friend drove out to pick me up.

During the tour I had taken two short side trips. On Memorial Day in May, a young Pennsylvania cousin picked me up in Baltimore and drove me home to where his great-grandfather and mine had large stone houses on adjoining farms. Along the way we stopped at Kennett Square, where my great-uncle Oliver Cromwell Blackburn was buried. It was a beautiful morning, and as I stood beside the grave it happened that a trumpeter, just within my hearing, sounded his call.

In San Francisco I called cousin Dan Beebe to ask whether I might spend a weekend with his family in Oroville. He replied that as president of the California Trail Riders he would be leading a two-day ride in the Sierras that weekend, and if I wanted to go along with him, he would find me a horse. I had not been in a saddle for fifteen years, but I went along and enjoyed it.

At the end of the three-month tour I got home in mid-August, three weeks before our son Harry was to be born. That turned out to be a very anxious event. We barely made it to the hospital in Toronto in time, even with a police escort for the last two miles. When I went to drive home after seeing mother and child in good health, I found that the frantic journey had ruined the clutch on our Austin, leaving it with a top speed of about thirty miles an hour. Early next morning the hospital called to say there was a conflict of blood types: Patricia was Rh negative, and Harry was using up his own red blood cells at the rate of 10 percent per hour. My signature was needed as consent to do a complete replacement of his blood by transfusion at a different hospital. I got in as quickly as I could, signed the form, and delivered Harry to the Sick Childrens' Hospital in the arms of a nurse, for a procedure that would take about twelve hours. After spending some time with Patricia, I went to the Volkswagen agency nearby to trade the Austin for a new Bug and went to the library for a few hours. Our friend Margaret Avison, who was on our staff, came to me to say that her own blood was Rh negative and that she would be glad to donate some if it were needed at the hospital. That evening the doctor told me that the transfusion had gone well and that Harry had a fifty–fifty chance of surviving. We prayed for his recovery, a prayer that was granted fully.

About two weeks later, when Harry was ready to leave hospital, I had a bad cold, so the nurse gave me a surgeon's mask to wear, to protect the baby. Halfway home on the highway I was stopped by a policeman on account of the mask. When he looked into the back seat and saw the baby in a laundry basket, he was doubly suspicious, and had to see documents before he allowed me to drive on.

By the end of the month the whole family seemed to be in reasonably good health, and we had arranged to have a young woman come from Holland to help out during my next absence.

My European Tour, 1951–52

For the second three months, November to January, I flew to Prestwick in Scotland, then went to more than thirty cities in Britain, Norway, Sweden, Denmark, Germany, Holland, Belgium, France, Switzerland, and Italy. Again I went by train except for a flight from London to Norway, and flights in and out of Berlin because at that time it was still in the Russian-occupied part of Germany.

Again there were certain characteristics common to most of Europe's university libraries, some of them quite different from what I had seen in North America. First, the European university library did not receive its money from the university, but directly from the government. This was not true in Britain, but it seemed to be the rule on the continent.

Accordingly, the library was not a service department but instead was a research centre quite independent of the university. For instance, the science division of the University of Copenhagen library received its money directly from the state, and its director reported not to the university but to the national librarian. It offered telephone and lending services not just to members of the university, but to all citizens of the kingdom, on equal terms, and the general public accounted for a large part of the library's use. In fact, any citizen of the state except a student could borrow a book on his own signature. A university student could borrow a book from the university library only if his signature was backed up by that of a responsible citizen or a professor.

There were some advantages, administratively, in a library not being responsible to a university, but there were serious disadvantages as well—for instance, when it came to appointing staff. At Marseille, the science library was obviously understaffed, but in order to get another cataloguer, the librarian had to send his request to the Director of Libraries in the Ministry of Education in Paris. The ministry, which conducted an annual inspection of all libraries, would consider the request, and if it seemed to be justified might appoint a cataloguer and send him or her down to Marseille, where the librarian would have to accept the ministry's choice.

Where the library did not depend on the university for its money or its readers, it was also independent of the professors when it came to selecting books. Usually, book selection was done by subject specialists on the library staff; Göttingen had ten specialists, Amsterdam fifteen, and so on. In some places, a professor who ventured to suggest the purchase of a book was considered a meddler; elsewhere there was more leniency. At Marseille, for instance, a faculty committee met twice a year to approve the list of books that had been bought and to make suggestions. At Genoa, the university contributed 100,000 lire (about $150) to the library's income of something over 2,000,000 lire, and the professors had some interest in how the money was spent. Of course the point was that the library, being independent of the university, was not intended to reflect the range of subjects being taught, or the particular interests of the professors; it was intended rather to be a sort of ideal library, an end in itself.

Since a library was considered to be mainly a research collection, classification by subject was generally considered to be of small importance. But since few of the libraries occupied more than part of a building, and very few had buildings that had been built specifically as libraries, space was at a premium and the size of a book was very important in determining where the book would stand on the shelves. In the Bodleian Library at Oxford, there was a decimal classification of subjects, but within subjects, books were shelved according to date of accession. At the Sorbonne in Paris, the system was much the same except that the subject classification had been simplified to the point where only two classes remained: letters and science. Science went to one side of the light court, letters to the other, and books were shelved by size and accession. At Cambridge there had been at least ten different systems of subject classification, and they had followed one another not by one replacing another, but by new systems being added on to whatever came before. Thus, depending on when it had been received, a book could be classed according to any one of ten different systems (it has been said that finding a book in the Cambridge library is one way to qualify for an MA degree).

Books classified at Cambridge when I was there, according to the tenth system, received a shelf mark comprising four different parts. First came a capital letter and three or four digits, for the subject; then a small letter, for the size of the book; then two more digits, for the decade of publication – 93 showed that the book had been published in the 1930s, and so on. Finally came the book's serial number, within its date, size, and subject. Then as a further aid to the aspiring reader, shelving was done not from the top shelf down, but from the bottom shelf up. With such a system, Cambridge could open her two-million-volume book stack to all readers and not be troubled by heavy traffic in the stack.

Since a research collection is approached mainly through the catalogue, catalogues were very important in European libraries, and different from what I had seen before. The first difference was in the physical form. Card catalogues in European university libraries were few and far between. My introduction to European catalogues was at Glasgow, where the catalogue consisted of a series of ledgers with printed strips pasted across the pages. The printer was about three years behind with his work, so there had to be a temporary catalogue of order slips, in boxes. In some places, especially in Italy, printing costs and delays were avoided by the entries being made directly into the ledgers in longhand, but that method was conceded to be less tidy and less flexible than the printed slips. Within the printed-strip school there was some disagreement over methods of pasting, and methods of expanding a page, but the ledger was handy to use and was thought to be vastly superior to any other sort.

There were, however, many librarians who thought the ledger unhandy, both to maintain and to use, and they preferred the sheaf catalogue. The sheaf was a small, loose-leaf booklet of about two hundred slips, with each entry on a separate slip. The advantages were thought to be obvious. A person consulting the catalogue could monopolize only one small sheaf of it at a time, and could use it quickly because it was so easy to flip through to the required entry. And then, when inserting a new entry, the filer had no cutting or pasting to do, but only taking up a screwdriver, taking out two small bolts, inserting the slip, and doing the bolts up again. There was some disagreement whether the slips should be fastened at the left end or the right end; apparently the answer depended on whether the librarian was right-handed or not, but there was no disagreement in such libraries about the superiority of the sheaf over other forms of catalogue.

But there were a few card catalogues, too, here and there in Europe. The card catalogue at the Sorbonne justified itself as an improvement on the standard American form. Each section of drawers had been painted a distinctive colour – red, green, orange, and so on; then, for instance in the red section, the colour was shaded from a pale pink in the top row down to maroon in the bottom row. Within each row of drawers was an ingenious arrangement of grooves and metal clips so that it was quite impossible to slide a drawer into any place except its own.

Catalogues vary in form, but the content is what really counts. In Europe the main catalogue always went by author, and as often as not there *was* no other catalogue. If there was another, it was a classified catalogue, accompanied by an index to the classification. At the Bodleian at Oxford, it was considered unnecessary to make a subject catalogue because the British Museum made one, and published it. At the British Museum, I was shown around first by the junior cataloguer, who apparently had qualified for his job simply by passing a civil service examination as a clerk. He showed me the main entry he was writing, in longhand, for a book on his desk, and when I asked whether the book would be passed right along to the subject cataloguers, he said, "Oh no, except in rare instances the book will go straight along to the shelf, and the subject cataloguer will use only the slip I have written."

One of the few alphabetic subject catalogues I saw was at the Sorbonne, and the importance attached to it could be judged by the fact that of sixteen cataloguers on the staff, one of them alone did all the subject work. More typical was Glasgow, where the ordering and cataloguing of an intake of about 7,000 volumes a year was looked after by three people. These people worked longer hours than American cataloguers, but most of the difference in staff size was explained by the difference in the catalogues produced. The difference in attitude was expressed in a remark made by Sir Frank Francis of the British Museum about the Library of Congress: he thought the LC was a great library but that there might be a bit too much virtuosity in its work.

American libraries put great stress on perfection of service to readers. In contrast, the emphasis in Europe was on perfection of the book collection, and readers were expected to fend for themselves. For instance, in the very large and modern library of the University of Cologne, the public catalogue room was open only eleven-and-a-half hours a week, or about two hours a day, and the lending room was open only twelve hours a week. When I inquired of Dr Juchoff, the Assistant Librarian, whether those hours were long enough, whether the readers were satisfied to have access to the catalogue for only two hours a day, he said, "Why, they have to be satisfied. That is when the catalogue is open!" And when I asked the librarian at Cambridge about subject catalogues and other help to readers, my host replied, "Well, if a student does not know what book to read, what's the use of him coming to the library? He'd better go ask his professor!" And when I asked what sort of system was used to keep track of books that were borrowed, he said, "Oh, I can't really say. That sort of thing is looked after by the porter at the door." And it was.

I found the typical European university library to be rather like the research collections that were beginning to be recognized in American universities. But where, then, was the teaching library? The teaching library had to be apart from the university library. As a rule, every department or institute or seminar, or whatever a subject division of the university was called, had its own library, which was supported by the department's own budget and administered quite independently of any other library. This was an expensive arrangement, since it led to a great deal of duplication of books, but it was handy for the professor, since he could buy the books he most wanted and keep them right at his elbow. It could be convenient for his students, too, although some faculty libraries I saw – for instance, the Letters and Philosophy library at Bologna – were very cramped, and arranged mainly to serve the teaching staff.

Clearly, it was assumed that a university student would buy for himself most of the books he wanted to read. But just as clearly, most students were no longer doing so. At Cambridge this fact was blamed on the Labour Party, at Bologna it was blamed on the Communist influence, in Berlin it was blamed on the cost of living; but whatever the case, students were not buying their own books as they used to do. As a result, there was a great new demand for books in all libraries. There were some attempts to meet the demand. At Cologne the university library was buying two or even three copies of certain kinds of books; the economics library at Cambridge was duplicating some titles and restricting some book loans to overnight; at Liverpool there was some thought of opening an undergraduate library in the American style. Mostly, however, the new demand was being ignored.

Still, the new demand existed, and coupled with the rising cost of books, it was creating financial problems. There was beginning to be talk of economizing by centralizing the budgets of the departmental libraries. Dr Luther at Göttingen thought that the resources of all libraries in that university would have to be combined eventually. Two years earlier in Italy, a conference of government librarians (and that would include the university librarians) had asked for coordination of the faculty libraries with the Italian university libraries. But the tradition of faculty libraries was strong and would not change quickly.

There were some other schemes for coordinating collections, in some countries. In Germany there was the *Notgemeinschaft der Wissenschaft*, an emergency committee formed in 1919 to help supply the needs of scholarship. The library committee of the *Notgemeinschaft* administered grants for the purpose of making sure that at least one copy of every important foreign book or journal was brought into Germany. Certain general periodicals were placed in each region of the country, but of most material only one copy was supplied, and placed according to a recognized subject specialization among the libraries. This arrangement was much like the Farmington Plan, which had been operating in the United States since 1948, except that the Farmington Plan was a cooperative scheme in which libraries agreed not only to buy all new publications in a particular subject, but also to make them readily available to others within the plan. The *Notgemeinschaft*, in contrast, operated with government grants and corporate donations.

European library salaries were low. At Newcastle the beginning rate for graduates was £400 (or about $1,120), compared to $1,800 at Toronto. In London the figure was a bit higher, and in Scotland a bit lower. In Norway, graduates received the same salary as high school teachers, or about $1,000. The national librarian was paid according to the twenty-second grade of the civil service, in which the twenty-eighth and ultimate grade – attained only by such people as bishops and railway executives – was about $4,000 a year. After doing some window shopping in Oslo, I asked Dr Munthe how his assistants could live on $1,000 a year – many of them were men with families – and he said he didn't know himself, but in the previous very hard times there had been a great demand for overtime work, and in 1951 he could hardly get anybody to work overtime. So he had to think his people were able to live well enough.

There were two curious books I saw along the way, both victims of military action. In the librarian's office in Copenhagen was a large volume badly bent in the middle, but still intact; it had been struck by a cannonball from one of the British ships commanded by Admiral Nelson at the Battle of Copenhagen in 1801. The other was in the office of Marburg's public librarian; it had been part of Germany's national library collection, which had been stored rather hastily for safekeeping in a salt mine during the Second World War. This particular volume must have fallen to the floor and become impregnated with salt, for it was a solid block gleaming with salt crystals.

Many of the European libraries I saw were in old buildings that had not been planned as libraries. Some of these buildings were very old – palaces, monasteries, and such – but there were also some quite new buildings. One in Liverpool had plenty of big windows and blond wood and bright floor coverings; one in Copenhagen had an air-conditioned stack closed by an electric-eye door; a new city-and-university library was under construction at Gothenburg, Sweden. The newest library I visited on either side of the Atlantic was in Berlin, where I had a long evening session with Dr Wieland Schmidt over library plans for the new Free University.

In every library that I visited during my grand tour, on both sides of the Atlantic, I was treated by the director as a welcome guest. Even where the name of Toronto was not well known, apparently the name Carnegie was. Usually when I arrived, the director chatted with me for half an hour or so. Then he or one of his minions showed me all through the main building, answering questions and introducing me to some of the key people. Then I was taken back to the director's office for an hour or two. Often he then took me to lunch or dinner.

At Göttingen, just before Christmas, I was invited to accompany Martin Luther and his wife to a University Fest, a traditional annual celebration that had been interrupted by the war and was just then being revived. The dining hall was filled with long tables of people in formal evening dress. One of the professors at our table told me he was a Toronto graduate, having taken courses of lectures from Toronto professors at the POW camp at Gravenhurst, north of Toronto. After dinner and an entertainment given by all the foreign students performing their national dances and songs, the evening closed with a promenade or *conversazione* in which all the guests walked in pairs around the room and through the hallways. My partner had no English and I only limited German, so our conversation was not profound. As the Luthers walked me back to my hotel, Frau Luther remarked, "There are many Martin Luthers in Germany. Mine is the poor one."

The academic library scene reported above constituted the background against which tremendous changes would be wrought in the ensuing sixty years, changes arising out of the expansion of universities in number and scope, the expansion in student enrolment and in graduate studies, and an unimaginable revolution in communication technology. Tools and procedures have changed, and the workshop has grown, but for librarians the basic responsibility remains: the acquisition, organization, preservation, and presentation of recorded information and ideas.

15 Working with Wallace

Although Stewart Wallace had never been active in the Canadian Library Association (CLA), he rather reluctantly agreed to serve as its president in 1950–51, when the annual conference was to be in Toronto. When I returned from my Carnegie tour the following spring, he told me that the next meeting was to be in Banff. Although he, as past president, might be expected to attend, he hoped that I would be willing to go instead, to represent him there. I replied that I should be very happy to go, but because I had too many unpaid bills, I really could not afford it. He drew a $50 bill out of his wallet (a goodly amount in those days) and said it was worth that much to him not to have to go. I could hardly refuse.

The annual conference met, and was housed and fed, at the Banff School of Fine Arts. At the last general session, just before the farewell luncheon, Elizabeth Morton summed up all the good things that had been accomplished. Her one regret was that the total cost of the conference had exceeded the budget by some $200. I stood up at the back of the room, and said how pleased I was to have represented Stewart Wallace at such a good conference, and that I would be sorry to tell him that it had ended in the red. I moved therefore that the treasurer be instructed to find a suitable basket immediately, and to hold it just inside the door when the meeting adjourned, for the convenience of members who had enjoyed the conference and would like to make donations of folding money. The motion was passed with cheers. As we gathered for lunch I was told that a place had been set for me at the head table. After the blessing, Elizabeth Morton announced that the conference fund was well into the black. More cheers.

After lunch there was to be an executive meeting. A few of us, including Earle Birney who had been our speaker that day, waited outside in the parking lot to catch a ride to Calgary. A message was sent out to me that I had been nominated as the CLA's new treasurer, if I would accept. And so it was that Wallace's shyness about meetings set me on a path to several years on the executive of the CLA, and its presidency in 1958-59, when the conference was on the university campus in Edmonton.

For years, Wallace had lectured on Canadian Literature at the Library School. When the school prepared to offer a Masters program, he was invited to lecture to the MLS candidates on Library Administration but nominated me for the task. For $300 a year I lectured to small classes for several years, until I realized that I had time only to speak from stale notes. My largest and best class, the one I remember, had seven students. We started with a map of the University of Saskatchewan campus, where a new library was being planned. My students drew up their own plans for it. They began with the names of the faculties, the size and growth rates of the library collection and the student body, budget, and so on. They decided on the site and orientation of the building. Each student worked on a particular aspect of the scheme. They decided on a reasonable number of years to plan for, and on ways to provide for expansion. They decided on the amount and kind of space needed for each aspect of administration and use. They agreed on the levels of access and security, and on how the physical spaces would relate to one another. Eventually they drew up floor plans and sketches of elevations, and wrote a building program incorporating what they had agreed on.

Before the last session I wrote to Saskatchewan and received a set of preliminary drawings by the architect there. We were gratified to find them fairly similar to what we had done. Later on, nearly all the members of that class were responsible for planning academic library buildings of their own.

When Wallace was invited to become the Canadian consultant to *Collier's Encyclopedia*, which was being revived in 1950 after a lapse of twenty years, he offered my name instead. There was a modest honorarium attached, plus travel expenses for a two-day meeting in New York at least once a year. I usually drove and took Patricia along. We would be given dinner in some posh place and tickets to a play on Broadway. One time they apologized for not being able to get us tickets to *Camelot*, and we were pleased to say that we had already seen it in Toronto, with the same cast. Another time Jack Sword happened to be in New York on university business; his wife Connie drove down with us and there were tickets for all four.

We became very accustomed to the drive to New York, and sometimes stopped overnight at Corning to have another look at the glass factory and the museums. Boston was about the same distance, and we drove there for a few meetings. Chicago was also about the same distance, but usually I went there by air, because executive meetings of the Midwest Centre were held in the airport, and I could go and come home the same day. Washington, too, was a day's drive, but on the way down we usually broke the journey to visit my cousin near Oxford, Pennsylvania, where my father and grandfather were born.

Wallace nominated me for membership in the Faculty Club. The club occupied the upper dining room at Hart House, a building for men only; female faculty members had their own dining room in the Women's Union. He explained that it was important for me to be a member, to uphold the prestige of the library. But he advised me never to go there, because "you will find yourself at table between a professor of Greek and a professor of Thermodynamics, and their only interest in common will be the shortcomings of the library." Actually I went there often, and made a point of sitting with men I had not met. Many of them did have complaints against the library, most of them based on ancient lore or misunderstandings that could be cleared away easily. But there were some valid complaints that had to be considered and dealt with if possible.

For the first few years, however, I usually had lunch with Jack Sword in his Graduate Studies office. We had our brown bag lunches. One of us would read aloud while the other ate. We went through many books that way, mostly history or biography, including two or three that I needed for a radio drama that I was planning to write, and that was produced eventually on *CBC Wednesday Night*.

For Wallace, preparation of an annual budget request was a matter of minutes only. With the current salary list in hand, he added a fixed amount beside each name, usually $50. The year I was away on study leave he drove out to Streetsville to tell Patricia that he had succeeded in raising my salary by $100. For equipment and supplies he would add small amounts, and for the book fund something like $5,000 or even $10,000. Then he made a few appropriate changes in the supporting paragraph, or wrote a new one, and gave his new budget to his secretary to type for his signature, for presentation to the president. Some time after that, he would be invited to discuss it with the president, before it was passed on to the Board of Governors for approval.

In 1950, when Sidney Smith appointed Claude Bissell as his first vice-president, he sent out a letter assuring the deans and directors that the appointment was meant only to relieve himself of routine administrative duties, and to allow him to give more time to the problems of his senior officers. When the president's secretary called to set a date for Wallace to go over and discuss his budget request with the new vice-president, Wallace was furious. For nearly thirty years he had made his presentation to the president of the university, and he was certainly not about to deal with any young whippersnapper vice-president! He sent me instead.

Instead of waiting for Wallace to prepare the next year's request, I presented him with my own draft; it included a doubling of the book budget. He was shocked. He said we could not possibly get it. The university was always short of money. He knew that some of the faculty deans had been going hog-wild in their demands, but he valued his own reputation for making reasonable requests. And he had never been turned down. I argued that it was our duty to say what was needed, and the duty of the president and board to decide what was possible. He would not sign my proposal, but if I wanted to risk my own signature, I was free to do it. I did, and Claude Bissell was pleased to present it to the board.

The following winter, somewhere in Europe, I received a letter from Wallace, with two pieces of bad news. First, another of our department heads had died. Second, the university had received the first instalment of a new federal grant, and the board had used part of it to grant the whole of the request I had made. It was "more money than the Library could possibly spend wisely before the end of the year"!

I was able to work with Bissell on library problems for a few years before he became President of Carleton University in Ottawa. Carleton was getting ready to move to a new campus, where the first building to be completed was the library. Fortunately, Bissell returned to Toronto to preside from 1958 till 1971, key years in the great expansion in our whole library system.

The Sigmund Samuel Library

In Stewart Wallace's first annual report, in 1923, he had emphasized the urgent need for new library construction at Toronto. During the years

Claude Bissell, President of the University of Toronto, 1958–71. Courtesy of the University of Toronto Archives.

that followed there were two false starts at planning for more space, but no action. When planning was authorized again in 1949, for construction of a new wing to the old building, he put me in charge of it. The authorization was limited to a budget of $2 million, and "that didn't mean $2 million and ten cents." A small advisory subcommittee of the Library Committee met once to discuss a short paper I had written setting forth my ideas of what was needed. We sat in a half-circle in front of Wallace's desk, and when he asked me to present my ideas, I began with a deep breath that popped the button of my jacket right out to the middle of the floor. But the committee proceeded solemnly to accept my outline and forward it to the architect.

Some months later, the university's Superintendent of Works invited me to his office one afternoon to see a set of preliminary plans drawn by Shy Mathers, the chosen architect, whom we were to see in his office next morning, presumably to accept what he had done. What he had done showed no sign of what I had written. The drawings were quite unworkable, but showed me approximately what area might be got within the budget. The Superintendent was most reluctant to let me borrow the plans overnight, but yielded to my urging. I bought some sheets of squared paper and tracing paper, and worked at home all night on a sketch of three levels that would be workable. It was a modular plan with columns centred 18 feet apart, making an exact fit in either direction for standard steel shelving.

At the meeting next morning, the superintendent was shocked when I presumed to explain to Mathers why his plan would not work for us, and then to bring out my own sketches. Mathers looked at my sheets for five or ten minutes without saying anything, then asked whether he might make blueprints of what I had brought in. After that, I worked closely with him and the superintendent's office. Eventually my sketches, with one corner rounded, and a slice taken off one end because of rising prices, turned out to be the plan of the Sigmund Samuel Library. The superintendent wanted to take one more slice off the end, to be sure there would be money enough left for all the steel shelving, a big item. I argued that I would rather open the building at full size with only half its shelving, than open a smaller building with shelving complete; it would be easier to add shelving later than to add a bit to the building later. So he agreed not to take another slice off the plan. Then a lull in the Korean War brought steel prices down to a point at which we could order and install a full set of shelving.

When construction began, a crew of Scottish stonemasons set up their benches under a canvas roof beside the front walk and began applying their chisels and hammers to load after load of building stone. The clerk of works hired to be sure that all construction followed the working drawings was the same man who had performed that duty for the earlier addition in 1910; he was no longer very nimble and spent most of his time in the construction shack. When the building began to take shape I made my own daily tours of inspection and was able to forestall at least one serious error: wooden forms were ready to be filled with concrete to create a heavy reinforced beam that would have blocked entry from the loading dock into the receiving room.

The moving of books from the old, overcrowded stacks began in August 1954, with President Smith and my ten-year-old son Robert pushing the first load up the ramp into the new wing. And so the Sigmund Samuel wing opened in September, two months after Wallace retired and thirty years after he had asked officially for an addition to the library.

The university took Wallace's retirement, and my appointment to succeed him, as routine matters that did not need any special attention. My appointment was a simple matter of the president calling me to his office one morning in January to offer me the position, and me accepting. In March, Wallace decided to trade offices with me; he moved up the winding steel stairway to my room at the top of the tower, to get on with his writing, and I moved down to his desk where I had a secretary to help me recruit more staff and make other preparations for moving into the Samuel wing. And I now had the advantage of a telephone; at that time there were only two lines into the building: one to the secretary's desk with an extension to mine, and one to a wall phone out in the busy corridor, for use by staff members in case of emergency.

Wallace's retirement party was a staff picnic on a Sunday at the end of May, beside the farmhouse where his secretary Julia Jarvis lived with her brother. There was a punchbowl and a toast to which Wallace responded briefly, ending with a public announcement of my appointment, and his best wishes for me. He said he was passing along to me the gift he had received from his predecessor Hugh Langton: a promise never to come to the office again without an invitation. It was a gift I have given my own successors without mentioning it until now. In my impromptu reply I thanked him for the interesting seven years he had given me, and said I would try to maintain the high standard of pulchritude that he had maintained in his choice of ladies for the staff.

* * *

The Sigmund Samuel wing opened in 1954, attached to the University of Toronto's first library building (1892) and the 1910 addition. Courtesy of the University of Toronto Archives.

The office I inherited from Stewart Wallace contained at least two things that he had inherited from Hugh Langton. The largest was the old oaken partners' desk, designed with plenty of space for two people to face each other across it while they worked. The other, sitting beside the clock on the mantel over the brick fireplace, was Sir Daniel Wilson's skull.

Sir Daniel was the president of the university who died of pneumonia after spending a very cold December afternoon in our cold library structure that was almost ready to be opened in January 1892. He was not only the president but also the professor of English, a talented painter and engraver, and a sometime archaeologist. The skull indeed belonged to him; he had dug it up somewhere near Lake Simcoe. I did not care to have it watching me at work in the office, so passed it on to a more appropriate home in the University College Archives.

The Sigmund Samuel Library, named after a donor, was a plain bit of construction compared to what I had been seeing elsewhere, but I was allowed to plan a rather ambitious celebration of its official opening. It began in the afternoon, with a special convocation and the award of honorary degrees to Stewart Wallace, the Librarians of Harvard and Oxford universities, the National Librarian of Canada, and Wihelm Munthe, National Librarian of Norway and Librarian of the University of Oslo. Munthe gave the address, in which the key word was *Feliciter*, which soon became the title of the CLA magazine.

At this point I digress for a brief look into the near future, at a really unique set of coincidences. Our present Chief Librarian Larry Alford is planning a celebration of the fortieth anniversary of the Robarts Library, to be held in November 2013 in the new conference room that has been named for me. He has invited his friend Sarah Thomas to be the principal speaker. She was the first American to be Librarian of the Bodleian Library at Oxford and is now Librarian at Harvard. November 2013 happens to be also the fifty-ninth anniversary of the Sigmund Samuel Library, and after fifty-nine years both Oxford and Harvard will be represented here for the second time. Moreover, Sarah Thomas, just before moving to Oxford, was the Librarian at Cornell University, a library that has had close links to Toronto for well over a century. The Olin Library at Cornell and the Robarts at Toronto were designed by the same architect. I was at the opening of the Olin, and at our double anniversary here this November, Sarah Thomas will count as a representative of Cornell as well as Oxford and Harvard.

The special convocation here fifty-nine years ago was followed by a reception in the Stewart Wallace Room of the new library, a room of 10,000 square feet, our version of Harvard's new undergraduate library. Next morning there was a university-wide colloquium in the same room, on the topic of preserving our Western heritage, with the five new graduands as a panel of speakers. It happened to be on the day of that year's Grey Cup football game; Edmonton was in town to compete with Montreal. Torontonians had been shocked the previous evening by an Alberta cowboy riding his horse into the lobby of the Royal York Hotel. Just as our colloquium was winding down, it was interrupted by the Grey Cup parade passing close by our front window, complete with leggy cheerleaders, bands, and cowboys on horseback. All eyes and ears were turned to the parade. I remarked that our Western heritage seemed to have overtaken us, and adjourned the meeting for lunch.

16 Staffing the Library

When I succeeded Stewart Wallace in 1954, I insisted on having the new title of Chief Librarian, to make room for other staff members to be called librarians. Since 1892, all other staff members had been called Library Assistants, whatever their duties were. Graduates of the university's own Library School were hired elsewhere as librarians, but at Toronto they were only assistants.

In the existing staff of seventy-five, the only men were Wallace himself, the caretaker, two "stack boys" who did the shelving, and myself. Actually, the caretaker had been placed there and was paid by the superintendent's office; he supervised the work of the cleaning woman, ran the receiving room, went back and forth to the post office and bank, and in his spare time sauntered through the public areas in jacket and tie, maintaining order. A sizeable dent in his forehead, probably a war wound, gave him a certain aura of authority, and probably most of the students thought he was the librarian. He and his wife lived in a small apartment directly under the library office, and when she had a roast in the oven its aroma drifted upstairs.

Nearly all of the seventy women on staff were unmarried; the university had had a rule against employing married women. Most of them were the daughters of professors or other professional people near the campus, daughters who had not wished to be teachers or nurses. Most of those who had university degrees were graduates of University College, Wallace's own college, except for one who was a graduate of one of the federated colleges, and she was the only one who had a Library School degree. The staff were organized into four departments, plus the bindery.

Since 1892, the official workweek at the library had been five-and-a-half six-hour days, thirty-three hours a week. Each division of the university set its own rules about such things. But in 1954 the university had just had a survey of non-teaching positions, and the surveyor's report, if adopted by the board, would establish a university-wide norm of five seven-hour days, a total of thirty-five hours. To have a defensible budget, my first task was to adjust my staff to longer hours. Some of my people objected strongly, but they had to accept the change. At the same time, with the Sigmund Samuel wing due to open in a few weeks, I needed to hire some trained librarians. The first one I hired was Ritvars Bregzis, newly minted from the Toronto Library School, a man who eventually played a vital role in our library and far beyond it.

The surveyor put little value on education. The point system he used in evaluating positions gave up to 30 points for physical labour, 90 for experience, and 10 for a degree in librarianship (which had to follow another university degree). He classed librarians somewhere in the university's mid-clerical grades, well below the going rate for librarians in other Canadian libraries. When I went to his office to explain that his report, if accepted by the university, would make it impossible for me to hire any librarians, he simply advised me to "get used to the idea that the woman who cleans under a desk earns more than the woman who sits at the desk." As I left him I thought about the message that had come to me through the grapevine, that somebody named Daisy Duncan who worked at the library had bought the $7,000 mortgage on my house; she was our cleaning woman.

In a meeting the next day with Vice-President Bissell, I was able to have librarians exempted from the recommendations of the consultant's report, and to have them placed in a separate category of staff with its own graded salary scale. The basic annual rate began at $2,400, the same as at the Toronto Public Library. My own salary that year was $6,000. I think Stewart Wallace's salary in the year of his retirement, after thirty-two years, had been only $7,000; his annual pension after more than forty years in the university was only about $2,000. In that context, $2,400 seemed a reasonable beginning rate for librarians.

It took longer to reach a suitable scale for our clerical staff, whose work required strict accuracy and stricter hours than in most other parts of the university.

The long-time head of our Catalogue Department came in to ask me to speak to her new typist – she could not bring herself to do so. The problem was that the young woman, a recent immigrant to Canada, continued to wear the same wool sweater and wool skirt every day; in the crowded office her odour was offensive to the ladies working beside her. When I had the young woman come to my office along with my secretary, she explained tearfully that the only wash basin in her rooming house was in a hallway. She could not bathe there, or even wash her clothes there, because she had no other clothes and could not afford to buy any. We gave her some funds out of petty cash, had her taken to a thrift shop, and sent her to the YWCA where she might be directed to better housing.

Most of our assistants were grandmothered into the new category of librarians, but there was one who could be classed only as a clerk; I had to tell her so, and there were more tears. Among the others were three women who were notorious slackers. Wallace knew of them, but had told me that the university had to carry its dead wood. I could not accept that dictum, and called each of the three in to be told that she would not receive any further salary increases until she began to pull her share of the load. Two of them resigned as I had hoped; one of them came in later to thank me, saying she had always been unhappy at the university and had found much more satisfying work in a law library downtown. The third woman said she would pray for my soul, and slugged along at her old pace for three or four years before she retired.

It was not long before our new clerical staff outnumbered the librarians. Many were Hungarian refugees after the revolution in 1956. One of them, in filling out his application for employment, wrote that his former employment had been "looking after my family estates." Another, a Hungarian major general who took charge of our History reading room, had begun his life in Toronto as dishwasher in a hotel. We had both men out to Streetsville, along with a Ukrainian refugee, for Christmas dinner.

For the first Christmas in the new Sigmund Samuel Library we had a dinner in the staff lounge. Patricia roasted two thirty-pound turkeys, and the department heads brought all the fixings. Wearing a chef's cap, I served the turkey, and we had live music by one of our new cataloguers, who had brought his harpsichord. The same pattern was repeated for two or three years until the staff became too numerous for the size of the room. We moved the party to the Great Hall at Hart House for a year or two, but the hall was too big and the cost too high to manage. I continued to deliver a Christmas turkey to our caretaker, as Wallace had always done, for as long as he lived.

The rapid growth in the number and size of academic libraries in North America during the 1950s created a great shortage of professional librarians, especially those with leadership experience. There were still only two library schools in Canada, Toronto and McGill. I made recruiting trips to some of the American schools as well; after I had interviewed their students, some of those schools allowed me to search through their lists of former graduates for Canadians who were employed in the United States. I wrote to those I found, and at least two of them returned to Canada and became directors of libraries, although not in Toronto. I advertised in the library association newsletters of other countries, and hired at least four librarians sight unseen. Two of them returned home (to New Zealand and South Africa) to become chief librarians; the other two stayed in Canada and became heads of academic libraries here.

The demand for experienced librarians reached into my staff. My first Assistant Librarian, David Foley, became chief at the University of Manitoba, then a professor at the new Library School at the University of Alberta, and then, after a siege of medical problems, moved to an American college where eventually a new library building was named after him. My next Assistant Librarian, Brian Land, was given leave to take a one-year appointment as Executive Assistant to the Minister of Finance in Ottawa, and returned to the university as Director of the Library School. My third Assistant Librarian, Gerald Proderick, moved to the new Library School at the University of Western Ontario, and the fourth, Peter Steckl, went to Ottawa as head librarian in a federal department. Other members of my staff left for senior positions elsewhere.

For a few years I opened a position of Administrative Assistant, to which I appointed promising young librarians for one year only, on the understanding that at the end of the year they would move either up or out. One dropped out at the end of her year to be married, two had promotions that led to headships in college libraries, and one was promoted to department head and went on to become librarian of a large American university.

For the first twenty years I interviewed all applicants myself, and if they were hired I followed their progress and problems, but in 1974 I shifted that load of work to a Library Personnel Officer, who took the reins firmly, with instructions that he should not tell me anything that I did not need to know. Eventually, as the library grew, the staff reached a peak of 639 full-time positions, plus 100 or more students as part-time help.

In the early 1960s, when we began to experiment with the use of computers, we needed to find computer programmers. Programming was a new profession with few practitioners, and there was a strong demand for them in the financial and commercial marketplace. The university's Personnel Office had no category for them and wanted to accommodate them somewhere in its prescribed list of clerical positions, far below the going rate for programmers. In earlier days, before there was a Personnel Office, I had solved a similar problem by getting a presidential decree that moved librarians into a separate category of staff, but that kind of solution was no longer available. We had already trained some members of our own staff who were interested, but as our mechanization schemes developed we managed somehow to attract other programmers from outside the university. At one point I had to meet with the whole group, a dozen or so, who were threatening to leave unless there was more money for them. With an explanation of the international importance of the work they were doing, and of my efforts to reward them in the next budget, I somehow managed to hold them temporarily. And I must have skated around the official impediment in order to keep them.

In the late 1960s and early 1970s, Toronto was caught up in the student revolt that was sweeping the continent. In its most violent forms, it was a revolt against authority of any kind, especially against what was characterized as a combination of military, financial, and academic powers. The general name for the movement was "Students for a Democratic Society," but its leadership and activities took different forms, mostly negative.

Universities were obvious authorities to attack, for they were inhabited by the attackers. And libraries, by their nature, were a favourite target across the country. Columbia University was shut down briefly by militant students in the spring of 1968. The following spring the library at Cornell was occupied by armed students and some of the card catalogues were frozen with white glue. Other places suffered various disruptions and damages. In the summer of 1971 some Toronto students declared the area between Hart House and our library to be a free campground for itinerant students; the resulting loud noise and trash reached a point at which my friend Jack Sword, as acting president, had to have the police remove it. One drawer of our catalogue cards disappeared, to be replaced at great cost. Two fires were set in our book stacks, but were caught in time. I received two or three bomb threats, but ignored them on the advice of the university's security officer, who maintained that bomb threats in Ireland had often led to bombs being detonated near the exits where crowds were hurrying to get out. We did not give these events any publicity, for we did not want to advertise the library as a target. There was a sit-in in my office, demanding that I reinstate a student helper who had refused a task and cursed his department head, but the gang went away after I left them there for a few hours and took my work downstairs.

In the autumn of 1971 a student leader declared to one of our vice-presidents, "We'll get you this year, on the issue of access to the new library." They invented the issue by announcing falsely that undergraduates would not be allowed to use the research library that was then under construction. Their announcement in the student newspaper spread to the city papers and to the floor of the Ontario Legislature, and defied my efforts to correct it. There was a sit-in with loud music and speeches in our main reading room, followed by a sleep-in while a few of our staff guarded the locked entrance to the book stacks. The "no access" issue led to a public meeting of the Senate's Library Committee, in a large amphitheatre near Convocation Hall, attended by students in force. When the meeting appeared to be going against them, the students bolted and ran to Simcoe Hall, where they occupied the president's office and the Senate Chamber. After some days the occupants were removed by the police. There was a large, noisy demonstration on the central campus, demanding the president's resignation. It was not a happy time for the university. It led fairly soon to the University Senate being abolished and the Board of Governors being replaced by a Governing Council that included some elected members of the faculty and a few students. And the research library, when it opened, had lost the degree of control that had been planned for the long-range security of its unique collection. Outside the universities, the student revolution of those days put a chill on the public's enthusiasm for higher education, and on public support.

During the 1970s most university budgets were frozen or even cut. The rising cost of books, and especially of journals, could not be met without reducing library staff, while the university's program of teaching and research kept calling for the library to do more and more, faster and faster. By 1980 more than one-fifth of our full-time positions had been eliminated, and more cuts were expected. A small part of the loss was cushioned by mechanization, but many of the services and programs I had initiated had to be reduced or dropped. I lost the heart to go on tearing down what I had built, and began to think that somebody else could do it with less regret.

Patricia was still recovering from a cancer operation, and while the operation appeared to have been a success, it reminded me that time was fleeting. With these thoughts pressing on me, I decided to take early retirement at the end of December 1981, ninety years to the day since Stewart Wallace's predecessor, Hugh Langton, had taken charge of the University's first library building.

My three Associate Librarians – Ritvars Bregzis, Maureen Hutchinson, and David Esplin – and I had done what we could to prepare for the future. The four of us were within a very few years of being the same age. If I were to stay on three more years to age sixty-five, my successor would be faced with the task of having to replace all of his or her most senior positions in short order. Looking through the staff list, we agreed that the head of our Reference Department, Carole Moore, with thirteen years on staff, would be the most able to take charge. We decided to enlarge her experience by moving her quietly to take charge of Technical Services. This involved moving three people in a sort of merry-go-round of positions, if all three were willing, which for various reasons they were. The day after the switches were announced, a posse of reference librarians marched into my office, demanding that I resign immediately for having filled Carole's position without advertising a vacancy. There had, of course, been no vacancy, only a new deployment of staff, but the posse took the matter to the president's office, and what I had done had to be affirmed some weeks afterwards by arbitration.

This was not the first time that I felt a threat to my position as Chief Librarian. At the end of my first year, at a meeting of the Senate's Library Committee, the chairman, who was President Smith, remarked that he had heard rumblings that the new library was being run for the convenience of the library's staff, not of its users. He asked the committee whether they thought there was any substance to such a rumour. The principal of one of the colleges, and one of the deans, spoke up immediately in praise of the new regime. So ended the meeting, but I followed the president back to his office and told him that if his remark had arisen out of his having any lack of confidence in me, I had better resign. He threw back his head and laughed, saying, "Look, my friend, I was just flying a balloon, and didn't they just shoot it down in grand style!"

That, however, was not the end of it. Technically I was Chief Librarian of the university and of University College. That autumn I received a long list of complaints, with notice that I was to appear the next afternoon at the College Council, to answer them. While reading through the list I was visited by one of the professors of English at the college who was noted as a bibliographer and who, I later discovered, was gunning for my position. He handed me a supplementary list of complaints gathered from his own graduate students. Next morning I went through the complaints with my department heads, to be sure of my ground, and that afternoon I stood for a couple of hours in the witness box at University College Council.

Most of the complaints were related to the new building and new staff. A senior professor had suffered the indignity of being asked, by a new clerk, to show his library card before entering the stacks. The new Reference Room was being overrun by students, and the SILENCE sign that had stood on the table in the old room was not in sight. Books that had been placed on reserve by professors were now on open shelves in a large reading room, out of control except for that of a clerk at the door. A book that one of the professors had recommended for purchase two years ago had not been bought. Since books had been spread out in the new stacks, they were a long way off and hard to find. Cataloguing of new books was too slow. And so on, for two hours, until we got to the end of the list. I offered to go on to the supplementary list from graduate students, but by then the council was weary of the game, and the inquisition ended. The principal told me later that a young lecturer, who had helped lead the charge, had missed a promotion on that account.

In the mid-1960s our annual intake of new books and journals took a sudden upward bound in response to the urgent needs of the increasing population in the university, and the growing number and depth of subjects being covered. Dealing with the intake required more and more staff. Getting money for books was the easy part, because all the deans were howling for more books to be added more quickly – my friend Jack Sword in the president's office remarked that I was getting apples almost without shaking the tree. This in spite of the fact that in the university's budget-making process the library was in competition with all the teaching divisions, and was either second or third in size. But money for staff was not so easy, nor was it easy to find and keep staff with the necessary qualifications. For instance we took two years to find a cataloguer who could deal with books printed in Ottoman Turkish.

Toward the end of the 1960s, with plans advancing for a great new library building, a presidential advisory committee was struck (two deans and a college principal) to consider the library's future. The Dean of Arts was chairman. After having had a few meetings, they invited me to meet with them, to discuss a proposal they were considering. It was that the library, being such a large and important part of the growing university, should have an academic person as its director, overseeing a librarian who would look after the technical details. I was tempted to match my two graduate degrees against the chairman's BA, but simply said that I agreed. The library should be directed by an academic person, and I thought that I was that person. If the university thought otherwise, I would resign, and they should find somebody else. They went away and I heard nothing more about it.

In drawing up my budget, knowing the competition across the land for senior staff, I had raised the salaries of my three Associate Librarians almost to the level of my own, which was set by the central budget office; I had never asked for a raise. By 1970 my three associates were about to overtake me, even pass me. Around that time I received an invitation to visit the University of California in Berkeley, then reputed to have the second most distinguished collection in America, after Harvard. After a day of interviews in Berkeley I was given a large offer to become librarian there. On getting home I went straight to President Bissell's office, and asked to see him on a personal matter. His secretary said he was in conference with the Chancellor, but because I had said it was on a personal matter, he told her to send me in. I told him I really wanted to stay at Toronto, but had to consider a very attractive offer from Berkeley. He simply glanced at the Chancellor and sent me on my way, saying "We'll match their offer, whatever it is!" Berkeley's offer was the second one I had refused; there had been one from the Board of the Toronto Public Library when their librarian died in 1956.

I used to attend at least one convocation a year, just to show the flag, usually on the occasion at which students would be graduating from the Library School. The platform party, in caps and gowns, gathered in the Senate Chamber to be lined up for the procession into Convocation Hall. First went the mace bearer, the Chancellor, the President, and the honourary graduand, if any. Then came the vice-presidents, then the deans and principals, followed by "all others," including me. Sometime in the 1970s the Chief Librarian was moved up to be with the deans and principals. After that, to my surprise, I was placed just after the vice-presidents. I wondered who had made that decision, and why; maybe it

Retirement party in 1986 for Maureen Hutchinson, Associate Librarian for Reader Services for many years, then Acting Chief Librarian, with Carole Moore who was then the incoming Chief Librarian. Courtesy of the University of Toronto Archives.

Larry Alford, appointed Chief Librarian in 2011, when Carole Moore retired. Courtesy of the University of Toronto Archives.

was my seniority on staff, but I am sure the deans must have wondered also. Wallace would have been pleased, for the sake of the library.

My first successor as Chief Librarian was an American whom I met only once, by accident. After two Toronto winters, she moved to California. I was delighted when her successor turned out to be Carole Moore, the person my associates and I had thought would be equal to the task. I was sorry that the university had adopted term appointments for all senior officers. Deans, principals, and even presidents, at the end of a term appointment, could go back to their full-time teaching and research quite comfortably unless they were offered wider opportunities. But the task of directing a large library is wholly administrative, and I could not imagine a Chief Librarian, myself for example, being able to drop back comfortably to a place behind the counter in the Reference Department, or somewhere behind the scenes in my own library system.

Carole's appointment was for seven years, but she was well prepared and did so well that the term was renewed twice and then extended to a total of twenty-five years. She did a magnificent job locally, nationally, and internationally, during a time in which the world of libraries and cooperation among them was transformed beyond anything I could have imagined. She too was a builder: she refurbished buildings and added to them, built the first two modules of an off-campus storage centre in which the three-million-volume capacity is already more than half full, and had plans ready for an addition to the Robarts Library that would provide 1,100 additional study spaces. When she retired at the end of June 2011, I was glad to be around to say that I was proud of what she had accomplished. And I have met several times with her successor, Larry Alford, who seems very well fitted for the job and has made an impressive beginning. The university has named Carole its Librarian Emerita, so now there are two of us carrying that honour.

17 Promoting the Library in the University

In the autumn of our first year in Toronto, Patricia and I were invited, along with all new members of the teaching staff, to a reception at the president's residence. Soon after we arrived, President Sidney Smith went from room to room, starting conversations by asking each of us to say where we had been at that time last year. He prided himself on being able to remember all our names, and each of us got to know a few other newcomers.

By the mid-1950s, the academic staff was growing so rapidly that the president was having to hold several such receptions, in quick order, every autumn. I suggested that his purpose could be served more easily by having just one reception each autumn, on a Sunday afternoon, in the Stewart Wallace Room of the new library. There would be room to invite not only the newcomers but also the deans and directors, members of the Board of Governors, and retired professors. Newcomers would have a glimpse not only of one another, but also of an important layer of the university community (and all would have seen the library and been welcomed there). The president was delighted and would pay for the catering. And so it began, and continued for many years. The president and I and our wives stood in line just inside the door, receiving guests as their names were announced. Tea was poured by Patricia and the president's wife and a few other ladies of our choice, usually our department heads and the wives of deans and principals, while volunteer members of the library staff passed the trays.

To celebrate the millionth item being added to our library, in 1962 the annual tea party was combined with seven other events. The president of Macmillan of Canada, the publisher, opened an exhibition of the manuscripts of Mazo de la Roche, our first such item, which he had helped us acquire. An engineer from the National Research Council, designer of the *Alouette I*, Canada's first space satellite, opened an exhibit that included a full-sized model of the satellite's nose cone. It stood in the middle of our Science Reading Room. Next morning, in the university's boardroom, the National Librarian Kaye Lamb presided at a conference during which senior members of our teaching staff, Ed Williams of Harvard who had made a survey of twelve Canadian university libraries, and the librarians of all those universities, discussed the Williams Report.

That afternoon there were two public lectures, well advertised in advance. At University College the editor of *Atlantic Monthly*, who had "discovered" Mazo de la Roche as a Canadian novelist, spoke about her work. In the Physics Building the designer of *Alouette I* spoke about the satellite. That evening, in the Great Hall at Hart House, there was a banquet, President Bissell presiding. After the chairman of the Varsity Fund had presented the millionth volume, our National Librarian introduced Ed Williams of Harvard, who delivered a short address that concluded with congratulations and warnings on our entry into the Million Volume Club.

Thus our annual tea party had bloomed as an event that reached into all parts of the university, including the scientists, and also into the City of Toronto and the community of Canadian universities.

Wallace's annual report to the chairman of the Senate's Library Committee (the President) had been as short and easily written as his budget requests – just a matter of crossing out the old figures and putting in the new ones given him by the department heads, and then perhaps altering a sentence or two. My own early reports too were fairly short and simple until 1960, when I received a copy of Steve McCarthy's report from Cornell. He had sent copies to all his friends in the ARL. It was informative about the work of each of his departments, and about new projects and plans, and it was attractive. My own report for 1960–61 was, by comparison, a rather homemade job of twenty pages, beginning thus:

> *In the arms of the university, which adorn our letterhead, are depicted two open books and a beaver, couchant. Last November, with the eagerness of readers who pushed the library's circulation of books some 36 percent higher than it had ever been before, it was suggested that the arms might appropriately be altered so as to depict one book and two beavers, rampant.*

Soon the length of my reports more than doubled. Copies were available to all our library staff, and they were sent to all our deans and principals, to all Canadian academic libraries, and to other librarians who might be interested. They went also to Canadian and American library schools before I visited them to recruit staff. Some of the heads of Toronto's teaching departments asked for extra copies for use in their own recruiting campaigns. I think those reports helped boost morale in my own staff, and to spread word within the university and beyond about what we were doing and what we needed.

Other Libraries in the University

The other libraries on campus, apart from the Central Library, were many and varied, and it was the Chief Librarian's explicit responsibility to coordinate them all into an efficient system. There were the libraries of the federated colleges and universities, some of them older than the central collection and quite outside the budget and control of the university. Within the university there were many faculty and departmental libraries, one dating as far back as 1893. Some were financed by departmental funds; some were collections transferred from the central collection. My annual report for 1969–70 listed forty-four departmental libraries with holdings of nearly 250,000 volumes.

A university's budget officers and the Chief Librarian should always be eager to avoid unnecessary duplication of books, equipment, space, and staff. Naturally they favour centralization; they have done so at Toronto from the beginning. Their efforts, however, had long been subject to exigencies of space, and to the decisions of university library committees composed of professors – or at least dominated by professors. These committees were usually sympathetic to any request for the creation of a new departmental library. Wallace, given the shortage of space in the library, had not been averse to transfers out of the central collection, and the Senate's Library Committee seldom refused a request for a new departmental library. But I felt it was my duty to build and maintain as strong a central collection as possible, and in some quarters I was cast as an ogre, or at least a miser, guarding the library's hoard against inroads by faculties and departments. Two or three examples will indicate the sorts of forces that were at work.

Caesar Wright and the Law Library

When our first undergraduate reserve-reading collection was moved to University College in 1934, the space it had occupied in the basement of the apse became the Law Reading Room. Statutes and law reports were shelved there to relieve crowding in the stacks. When the School of Law moved into Baldwin House on St George Street in 1952, the space made there for a library was filled immediately with the contents of the Law Reading Room plus a liberal sprinkling of other materials that Wallace had allowed the lawyers to select from the central stacks. When the university inherited Glendon Hall, a property some miles from the campus, in 1956, the Faculty of Law took over the hall itself, and Dean Cecil Augustus (Caesar) Wright devoted a good deal of his time to building up the collection his faculty would need in that isolated location. The fact that his efforts were severely limited by the size of the Law allotment in my budget created a good deal of frustration on both sides. Relations were not improved when the University Library refused to pay for a large and expensive set of books that the Dean himself had ordered directly from a dealer, a set he had asked us to buy for him and that we had already ordered from another source at a much lower price. The Dean's complaints grew louder and more frequent, about cataloguing, binding, and other things besides acquisitions, until it became apparent that we could not hope to satisfy him no matter how much time we spent in the attempt. I therefore recommended to the president that the book fund allotment for Law be transferred to the Dean's budget and administered by him. Perhaps the prevalence of separate law libraries in universities is related to the fact that contention is cultivated as a skill in that profession.

While Caesar Wright had been applying relentless pressure on the library for new acquisitions for his library, he had pressed also for wholesale transfer from the central stacks of everything classed as law. This was a residue of about 7,500 volumes, about one-quarter as much as he had already received, and consisted of subsections such as Constitutional Law, which our historians and political scientists considered to be their meat. When I refused the transfer except for a few distinctly legal titles, the dean pursued his request and the Library Committee struck a subcommittee to consider it. In the subcommittee, which was chaired by President Sidney Smith, Caesar Wright came up against Donald Creighton (History) and Vincent Bladen (Chairman of Political Science and Economics), who defended the existing policies and their own interests in the central collection. The resulting stalemate allowed me to ignore the whole issue for a time.

The president then asked me to arrange a tour with Vincent Bladen and Bora Laskin, Wright's deputy (and future Chief Justice of the Supreme Court of Canada), to see how such matters were handled in certain well-known American universities. Vincent, Bora, and I made a three-day tour of the University of Michigan, Northwestern University, and the University of Chicago. After visiting the central library and law library at each place, we usually separated to have lunch or dinner with friends in our various specialities. In our railway compartment on the way home, it was evident that Bladen and Laskin were no closer to agreement about what they had seen than were the proverbial blind men who went to see the elephant. Our report to the president was a large compromise, recommending special funds for duplication in both the law library and central library. It was not a compromise likely to appeal to the president.

Since it was evident that no consensus could be reached in principle to resolve the conflicting claims based on our old classification scheme, it was suggested that an accommodation might be reached by inspection of the shelves within the contested area, book by book. At the next meeting of the Library Committee, I was asked to invite a small representative committee to work out a reasonable distribution in this manner. Soon afterwards I spent three bleak afternoons in the stacks with Laskin and Jim Eayrs, Bladen's representative. Each came to the task with opposite assumptions: Laskin's was that anything that smelt of law should be transferred to Glendon Hall, while Eayrs assumed that anything of possible interest to non-lawyers should stay where it was. During the first two days we went through twenty or thirty shelves and agreed on a handful of books that could be transferred, but on the third day we stalled at the first shelf, and the subcommittee ended in a minor explosion.

Dean Wright, having crossed the Rubicon, was not prepared to turn back. He launched a spirited attack on the positions taken by the departments of History and Political Science, and proposed that an arbitrator be engaged to settle the dispute. His letter was addressed to me, copied to Donald Creighton, Bladen, and the president. I responded as politely and firmly as I could in five single-spaced pages, with copies all round. Creighton's reply to Wright was sharper, especially the middle paragraph:

> I cannot, however, let your communication to the Chief Librarian pass without comment. Its tone is quite exceptional, so far as my experience goes, in the inter-faculty and inter-departmental correspondence of this university. In your letter you resort freely to intemperate language and you employ adjectives such as "irrational" "extravagant", "fantastic" and "absurd" to describe the representations

made by the Department of History and the principles approved by the Library Committee of the Senate upon which the Chief Librarian has based his decision. You thus cast reflections upon the scholarly judgement and integrity of your colleagues in the Department of History, reflections which are mere impertinences on your part; and you make assumptions and statements about the problem under discussion which are incorrect and inadmissible.

Wright's reply to Creighton, with copies all round, reached new heights of intemperance and invective. I did not see what he expected to gain by it unless he was relying on President Smith to call a halt and give him the victory. Wright and Smith were close friends. In their youth they had been fellow lecturers at Osgoode Hall Law School in Toronto; more recently they had worked together to break Osgoode Hall's monopoly on professional education of lawyers in Ontario. They enjoyed fishing trips together. It would be embarrassing for Smith to refuse him. But clearly my duty was not to render unto Caesar everything he was trying to rend from me.

To save the president the embarrassment of ruling either for or against Caesar, I invoked my authority as Chief Librarian responsible to the Senate, to end the struggle. I wrote, with copies all round, that the controversy had already cost the university too much time and energy. I ruled that the existing division of material, with some minor adjustments to be made at my discretion, would stand. And it did. Apparently the dean shared my guess that he could not win his point by having it referred back to the Senate. That was the end of the matter.

So it was that a large portion (but not all) of the central library's material classed as law – most of it acquired for the use of other departments before law become an active part of the curriculum – became the nucleus of a separate library administered by the Faculty of Law. Once the boundaries were settled, the dean and I and our separate libraries settled down to a reasonable working relationship. After the Law Faculty, in the summer of 1961, swapped quarters with York University, which had begun its career in Flavelle House on the Toronto campus, a special wing was added to house the faculty's library. When we established a union catalogue of all collections in the university, the Law Library was, of course, included.

The East Asian Library

The East Asian Library also has a unique history, beginning with William C. White, the Anglican bishop of Honan province in China, whose skill as a collector of antiquities helped Toronto's Royal Ontario Museum accumulate one of the largest Chinese art collections in North America. In 1932, White was preparing to return to Toronto to take up a position as the university's first professor of Chinese Studies. At the invitation of his old friend President H.J. Cody, he bought the library of a Professor Mu of Beijing and had it shipped to the University of Toronto. After various adventures the Mu collection arrived and was housed at the Royal Ontario Museum, along with other books that were there on transfer from the University Library. Clearly it had been bought for the university, and presumably it was to be used by Professor White and his successor L.C. Walmsley and their staff in the course of their duties. The question of ownership, however, became clouded, even though the museum had begun as a joint institution of the university and the Province of Ontario, and became an integral part of the university in 1947. While White held a senior appointment at the university, he held an appointment also as Assistant Director of the ROM and keeper of its East Asiatic collection. Sigmund Samuel, a member of the Museum Board, had contributed toward the purchase of the Mu collection and construction of the gallery in which it was housed. Moreover, the museum, as well as the University Library, had added many volumes over the years to the Far Eastern Library, which was administered as a part of the museum's Division of Art and Archaeology.

Soon after Bill Dobson was appointed in 1952 to succeed Walmsley as head of the university's Department of East Asian Studies, he spent several months in Hong Kong buying books with a Carnegie grant of $42,000 and shipping them to the East Asian Library at the museum, where his department had its offices. The museum, however, was in the throes of a planning review, and refused to accept the shipments. The crates piled up in the basement of the University Library, in the former Law Reading Room, until Dobson could appoint somebody to unpack them and begin organizing a second Chinese library.

When the new Arts Building, Sidney Smith Hall, opened in 1961, it provided quarters for the Department of East Asian Studies and its library, including the Mu collection. Professor Tushingham, head of the Museum's Division of Art and Archaeology, contended, however, that the Mu collection belonged to the museum, and he did not wish to give it up. Vincent Bladen, then Dean of Arts and Sciences, called me up one afternoon and asked me to move the whole East Asian Library, including the Mu collection, to Sidney Smith Hall immediately. I had seen some rather inconclusive correspondence between Bladen and the museum's director, and was not prepared to take action without having a note from the president, who alone had the authority to break the impasse. Bladen said the president was out of town and that he himself, as Dean of Arts, was therefore Acting President and would send me a presidential note within the hour.

Next morning I arrived at the museum with three experienced packers and several hundred cartons, showed my warrant to the museum's Far Eastern Librarian, and went to work. Tushingham arrived on the scene and said that as director of the museum he had instructions to retain everything related only to art and archaeology and fine printing, and a small proportion of the English-language books that bore the University Library stamp but were in daily use in his department. Packing and transport were completed on the second day with the help of professional movers, leaving behind about 150 shelves of books and journals to be sorted out later when various key people would be available. Bill Dobson, with the bulk of the Mu collection safely in his domain, used to take some pleasure in calling its acquisition "the Rape of Tushingham." I preferred to think of it as the unforeseen but crucial play in a game of Chinese checkers. Dobson's East Asian Library was one for which we recruited a librarian and supervised him, at least in theory. We agreed also to look after the purchasing and cataloguing of future additions. Eventually, when the occupants of Sidney Smith Hall outgrew their building, the whole Department of East Asian Studies moved into the top floor of the old warehouse in which Borden's Dairy used to keep its wagons and horses. In that location, too, the Chinese and Japanese collections soon outgrew their space and stood two-deep on the shelves. That library's final move, in my time, was to greatly enlarged quarters on the eighth floor of the Robarts Library, where its administration came fully into the hands of the central library. At a library reception for retired staff early in 2010, to show what had been completed so far in a renewal program for the thirty-six-year-old Robarts building, the showpiece was the renovated East Asian Library.

A Test of Library Records

Another incident, related to the Museum Library, illustrates the sort of misunderstanding that could arise between the University Library and individual professors. William P. Wallace, no relation to my predecessor, was a respected Professor of Greek and Latin. I knew him as a formidable but generous opponent across the chessboard. If an opponent made a move that would sacrifice an important piece, either by mistake or perhaps as bait for a trap, he would mutter, "Beware the Greeks bearing gifts!" And he was an idealist, and an unquenchable quoter of limericks.

In the spring of 1962, while preparing to renew his study of Greek coinage, specifically the coins of Chios, he borrowed one volume of the *Numismatic Chronicle* from Series 4 in the large file of it in the University Library. Along with other numbers, it contained three that he needed, but on looking at them he was amazed and annoyed to find his own annotations in them. He had been unable to find his own copies at home, and now thought he must have left them in the library, and that we had found them and bound them, along with other numbers, into the volume he had in hand. He had taken the problem to somebody on my staff, who said she would look into it, but before hearing from her he was aggravated further by receiving notice to return the volume to the Library. When he came in to protest against the notice, he had a rather acrimonious discussion with the head of our Circulation Department, who explained that the standard loan period of one month had expired, that it could be renewed if he simply brought the book in for that purpose, but if parts of the volume had really been his own property, he had lost ownership by leaving them in the Library. He wrote all this story to me in a carefully civil tone, remarking that the question of ownership could be tested in a court of law, but that he thought it could be settled otherwise. He suggested that the library should try to buy a replacement for the volume, so that he could have his own with annotations, but otherwise he would be willing to accept new copies of the three numbers he needed. He said that since he had bought the numbers in question and that he needed them, he was not very willing to return them.

On looking into the matter I found that our library had begun its subscription to *Numismatic Chronicle* in 1924, and for thirteen years had transferred each issue to the Museum Library, where there were earlier files of it. In 1956, at Professor Wallace's own suggestion, the museum had given its whole file, going back 124 years, to the University Library, all in bound volumes, except for a few numbers in Series 4. At the time of the gift, according to loan records still in the Museum Library, several numbers had been out on loan to Wallace for many years, long enough for him to think of them as his own. But in the spring of 1958, Wallace had delivered those numbers to our Order Department, and binding of the whole set was then completed. Wallace had to accept the recorded facts, and wrote that he had "survived the emotional stress of this crisis by the simple device of composing scurrilous limericks."

Here are a few of them:

What's the use of a private collection?
I'll come and extract a selection.
You can see them again
From five until ten
If you pass the Librarian's inspection.

It's too bad that you wanted to use them.
But to read books is just to abuse them;
You can go to the stacks
And look at their backs.
If we let them out people just lose them.

I replied that we had just rented a Xerox copy machine, and would like to test it by making him copies of all the articles in question. I then closed my letter with another limerick:

By a curious and gift-giving quirk, these
Greeks have entangled our work. Seize
the day! Now apply us
to coinage of Chios
and Xerox may yet redress Xerxes!

Wallace replied with thanks, but doubted that the machine could make useable copies of the essential photographs of coins. If it could do so, he would be glad to pay for the copying. But he had already written to *Numismatic Chronicle* to see whether they had extra copies for sale. And so his complaint was dealt with, at some cost of time and energy on both sides.

The Engineering Library

The Engineering Library had its own set of adventures. When I took office there were seven separate libraries scattered through the two buildings on campus that were occupied by departments of the Faculty of Engineering and Applied Science. Most of them had some books and journals transferred from the University Library and listed in the central catalogue. But all seven had some other material acquired independently, with catalogues concocted by the departmental secretaries who supervised the libraries.

When a new Engineering wing was added to the west of the old Physics Building, the two Engineering departments that occupied it put their libraries into the same room and were surprised to find how handy it was to have the two side by side. They had room to spare and there was talk of bringing in the libraries of other Engineering departments as well, but the other departments resisted. One of the department heads, who kept his departmental library locked behind glass, told his daughter (who was on my staff) that his library would never be moved during his lifetime. And so it came to pass.

When the Physics Department moved into a large new building, its former space was inherited by Engineering. While planning expansion into the inherited space, the Dean of Engineering discussed with me the possibility of moving all his libraries together into a large space on the second floor in the Engineering wing. As a result, the seven libraries were consolidated in the early 1970s, inter-shelved, with a single catalogue, and professionally staffed by the University Library. There was ample room for expansion of the collection, and seating for 125 readers.

The university's first library had been destroyed by fire on Valentine's Day, 14 February 1890. I thought about that as I drove to work on 11 February 1977, having received word early that morning that the Engineering Building was on fire. When I arrived, the Toronto Fire Department had closed off the south end of the campus, and our own emergency squad was already gathering in my office with copies of our emergency plan. The plan had been brewing for some time and had been completed only a few days before it was needed.

A few of us were allowed into the Engineering Building that afternoon. It was without heat or light or elevators. The old Physics Building had been gutted by the fire, and water had carried from there into the Engineering Library. Water was inches deep on the floor. Books shelved on the wall had been drenched, and some of the wood shelving had collapsed, throwing their contents to the floor. There were icicles. We were surprised and pleased to see that the firemen had been able to cover the free-standing shelves with tarpaulins that protected most of the collection, though the tarps were not long enough to cover the lower shelves.

Early next morning our emergency plan went into action. Our Science and Medicine collection had been located temporarily in the stacks of the Sigmund Samuel wing, awaiting renovation of its place in the old part of the building; the renovation had just been completed and the collection was to have been moved the following week. Instead of waiting, we began the move immediately, to make room for the Engineering books. At the same time we had a team in hard hats in the Engineering Library, putting dry books into hundreds of plastic milk crates supplied by a local dairy, wheeling them to a window, sliding them down an improvised chute to a platform below, and loading them into vans that took them to the front door of the Sigmund Samuel Library, whence they were trundled to the newly vacated shelves.

When the dry books had been looked after, the others followed the same route, but could not be shelved. Those that were dry enough to be opened were fanned out and stood in rows on the floor, facing a battery of electric fans. Most of them were saved, although some needed rebinding. Altogether about 55,000 books and journals were saved. About 8,000 were waterlogged and beyond rescue. About 600 unique items were frozen and dried later in a large vacuum chamber at the Canadian Forces base at Downsview. The card catalogue was ruined, but fortunately was no longer needed, its contents being available on computer.

The whole process attracted extensive coverage in the Toronto news media, and we received many queries from other institutions about our emergency plan. Dr Merrill Distad, then a member of our staff, was principal author of the plan and an active worker at the wet end of its application. He is now completing a remarkable career at the University of Alberta as Associate Librarian (Research and Special Collections Services) and University Archivist, and at the School of Library and Information Services as the lecturer in a special course called "Administering Library Preservation, Security, and Risk Management," a topic grown out of his experience in restoring our Engineering Library after the fire.

18 Catalogues and Computers

Our library catalogue, when I began at Toronto, included some cards that had been handwritten by H.H. Langton, the librarian when our first separate library building was opened in 1892. Our classification system, which determined the order in which books were placed on the shelves, was inherited from the same period. It had begun as a very simple mnemonic system, but as new subjects arose and old subjects were renamed or subdivided, the system had been altered and corrected by so many hands that it had gradually tied itself in knots. It was expensive to maintain. It also prevented us from saving the time and money we could have saved by ordering readymade sets of cards from the Library of Congress for many of the books being added to our collection. When anybody talked about the possibility of switching to the Library of Congress system, professors who knew their section of the stacks did not like the idea of having to go to a new place to find new acquisitions, and many of our cataloguers thought it would be too difficult to make the change.

After President Smith resigned in 1958, I had a long talk with the Acting President, and he appointed an advisory committee on planning for the future of the library. Chairman of the committee was my friend Roly McLaughlin, Dean of Engineering, a man who liked getting things done. He brought Steve McCarthy from Cornell for a three-day assessment of the library, and McCarthy's advice was evident in the McLaughlin Report dated 1 January 1959. Its first recommendation was that we adopt the Library of Congress classification scheme. Claude Bissell had just returned to Toronto as our president, and at his first meeting of the Senate's Library Committee he obtained agreement that the new scheme would be adopted for all future acquisitions and that necessary reclassification of existing material would be carried out as quickly as possible.

We knew that Cornell had made the switch to Library of Congress classification and was in the middle of the largest reclassification project we had heard about. Our Chief Cataloguer spent two months at Cornell learning what had to be done, and after she got back the change was made. We pushed the old book collection, in its old classes, as far back as possible in the stacks, to make room for what was to come. On May Day, President Bissell walked across the lawn to shelve the first book in the new order, so that we had a buffer against murmurs of protest.

Campus Union Catalogue

Another recommendation of the McLaughlin Report was that we have a Campus Union Catalogue. When Canada's National Library began to compile a National Union Catalogue, it began by microfilming the catalogues at the five affiliated college libraries at the University of Toronto. Then it lent its camera to us and we filmed our main catalogue. Then we brought in the catalogues of all other collections in the university to be filmed. In this way we obtained about one-quarter of a million new entries for a University Union Catalogue as a by-product of the national project. We had those microfilms printed on five-inch rolls of photographic paper, and the rolls were cut by hand into the traditional size for filing. I rigged a three-inch stop on the cutting board, and a small chute into which the cards dropped and were flipped over so as to end up in proper filing order. The first card in our new union catalogue was filed at our millionth-volume celebration in November 1962.

Of course the honour of being the first (and largest) collection represented in the National Union Catalogue was a mixed blessing; it exposed us to thousands of interlibrary loan requests that might otherwise have been sent elsewhere. But it also made it possible for us to have a second copy of our catalogue, so that our Catalogue Department could be moved away from the central file. In fact, contingencies of space caused it to move three times within the next few years: it went first to occupy what until then had been the Women's Reading Room, then to a rented office building just south of the campus, then to a rented factory building a mile north of the campus.

The existence of a Campus Union Catalogue had an interesting effect on the five theological colleges on campus. They all had their own libraries and knew there was quite a bit of duplication among their collections. Their joint committees of principals and librarians sometimes invited me to their meetings, trying to find some way to economize. A consultant from the United States had told them that their total expenditure on materials was equal to that of Princeton Seminary, yet their own collections were not very good; they should find some way to cooperate. But how? The five colleges had begun sharing classes within a new federation they called the Toronto School of Theology, and surely there was some way to solve their library problem.

They were shocked when the Campus Union Catalogue showed how heavy their overlapping really was, and wanted to meet with me again. They were agreed, in principle, that they should cut down the cost of their journals by eliminating duplication and by creating a joint fund to cover the cost of buying and binding one set only; they were also agreed that all journals should be in one of their libraries. Each of the colleges agreed, as long as the journals could be in its own library.

I broke the deadlock by proposing that each college should limit its purchases to those books related to the teaching of their students, and that their joint fund should be large enough to cover all other purchases, as well as the salary of a book selector appointed by them, who could have a desk in our Acquisition Department. The University Library would buy, catalogue, and bind all the research material their selector chose, within the available fund, and inter-shelve it with the central university collection after identifying each volume with a Toronto School of Theology bookplate. In this way each college would have its own teaching collection, and there would be a single research collection centrally located to share with the whole university. The system seemed to work very well.

Introduction of Computers: The ONULP Project

At the beginning of the 1960s, many university presidents had been infected by the notion that computers were soon to make books and libraries obsolete, thereby relieving their institutions of the growing burden of library costs. Librarians, for their part, saw that computers might reduce costs and improve efficiency when it came to producing and maintaining library records of many kinds. Ritvars Bregzis, one of the first fledgling librarians I had hired in 1954, had become our Chief Cataloguer and then my Associate Librarian for Technical Services. He was an up-to-date promoter of the idea of developing uses for computers. Some of the people he was in touch with were aiming to begin with their subscription lists or order files or loan records, but he was convinced that those operations were only spokes of the wheel; for him the centre of the wheel, the axle on which everything turned, was the catalogue. He was working on a format for mechanizing catalogue records, and there were many problems. In those days data were entered into computers through punched cards, stored internally on tapes, and printed out with mechanical print-chains. Ordinary print-chains did not have all the characters needed for printing catalogue entries, so Bregzis, along with his contacts at the Yale Medical Library and Florida Atlantic University, designed and ordered the first library print-chain. We shared the cost of having it made, and tested it in 1963.

German libraries had designated the University of Bochum as their centre for developing uses for the computer, so we invited its librarian to come to Toronto for a few days to exchange ideas. We applied for a foundation grant to help finance our experiments, but were refused, and had to build those costs into our own library budget. This turned out to be an advantage, for we watched other libraries, which *had* received foundation grants, having to spend time producing reports and waiting for grants to be renewed.

In 1963 we had a chance to test what Bregzis had been thinking and doing. The Ontario government had announced plans to establish about a dozen new universities in the province, to open within two years. I saw that if these new institutions started to assemble their own libraries after they had acquired their initial staff and space, and opened for business, they would put a tremendous load on Toronto's resources. Bregzis and I went to the office of the Minister of University Affairs and offered to assemble, within two years, a start-up library for each of the new institutions that was interested. Our offer was to assemble libraries of 30,000 volumes each, based on what we had in our own undergraduate collection in the Stewart Wallace Room. They would be identical collections, bought, fully catalogued, stamped, labelled, and ready for the shelves, thus gaining a great economy in labour as well as time. The minister agreed to the idea and to our estimated price and gave us a contract for the five institutions that were interested.

Our estimated price was $1,847,000. The Ontario New University Libraries Project (ONULP) began in September, even before we had the money in hand, and was to be completed within two years.

Bregzis pounced on the chance to create five mechanized catalogues from scratch, using the university's Computer Centre, with no old back-

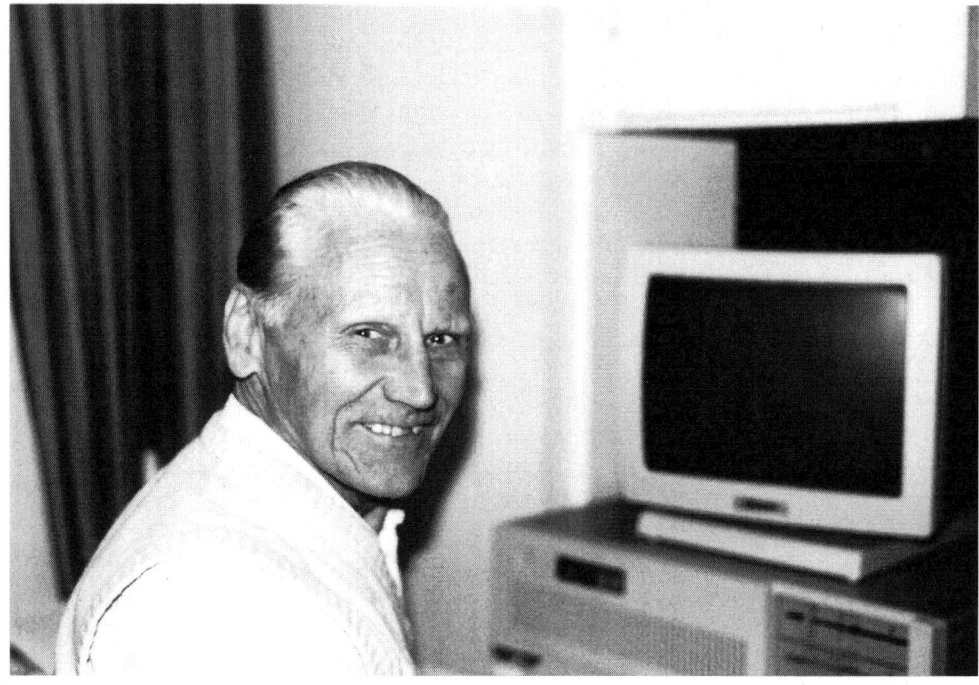

Ritvars Bregzis, Associate Librarian for Bibliographic Systems and Technical Services, creator of the MARC format.

log of existing catalogue records to match or worry about. The project was completed before the two-year deadline and below the estimated cost. The ministry allowed us to use part of the balance to show what we had done, by sending fifty sets of the completed catalogue, in eight or nine quarto volumes, printed three columns to a page, to selected libraries in Canada and other countries. At that point each of the five new universities receiving its ready-made library could choose to receive its catalogues as printed cards in proper order, or to have its catalogue in book form and carry on with its own mechanized additions.

Publication of the ONULP catalogue in 1965 brought us a flood of visitors, and not only from this continent. My report for 1965–66 mentions that there had been visitors from Canada, the United States, Britain, Germany, Holland, Africa, South America, Australia, and New Zealand. My staff and I published some articles and were invited to speak at conferences on aspects of what we were doing.

A Challenge to the Library of Congress

In November 1964 the Midwest Interlibrary Center held a special two-day retreat for all its members. The hot topic was the need for cooperative mechanized cataloguing. All in attendance were feeling pressure from their presidents to take advantage of the new technology and save money. Two or three of the members had obtained foundation grants for their experiments but were not making much progress. Most were waiting for the Library of Congress to break trail. But the Library of Congress, having published a consultant's report on possibilities and large costs, seemed to have put the whole matter on the shelf. As the only foreigner at the conference (and perhaps the only one who did not have a secret yearning to become Librarian of Congress), I made a proposal. I moved that the Library of Congress be informed that unless it announced, within a year, a plan to become a computerized centre for cooperative cataloguing, the Midwest Center would take on that task. The motion was adopted, and sent on to Washington that day, with copies to the ARL and the ALA, both due to have their annual conferences in January.

Most of us expected to see the Librarian of Congress at the ARL meeting in January, and wondered what he would have to say about the challenge we had sent him. Shortly before Christmas he called me on the phone, inviting me to a meeting on mechanized cataloguing in the first week of January, at the Library of Congress. I accepted on condition that I could take Bregzis there with me.

At home on Sunday, in the late afternoon before the meeting was to take place, I noticed that it had begun to snow. Bregzis phoned to say that he had called a friend in the Washington area, who said they had seven inches of snow there, and more coming, and that the airports were closed down. I found that all airports on the northeastern seaboard were shut down and that there was no rail or bus connection that could get us to Washington in time for the meeting. The only chance of getting there was to drive. Bregzis came out from Toronto, and Patricia insisted on going along even though she had just recovered from a bout of pneumonia. There was heavy snow all the way, but I knew the road and we got to a hotel near the Library of Congress about five o'clock the next morning, in time for a short nap before breakfast. Bregzis and I were among the first to arrive at the great library, and when the Librarian of Congress got there he was amazed to see us. Taxis were not running in Washington, and delegates who had stayed at downtown hotels overnight had had to wade up the hill through deep snow. The meeting was rather small because of the weather, but large enough to establish an Automation Planning Committee, with Bregzis as a member. Thus we helped the Librarian of Congress have an answer ready for the ARL three weeks later, to the question posed two months earlier by the Midwest Center. The ultimate decision arrived at by his committee was for a cooperative scheme using a machine-readable format (MARC) very much like the one Bregzis had designed and used in our five-library project, and it became the worldwide standard.

In 1966, Basil Stuart-Stubbs, the librarian at the University of British Columbia, suggested that he and I sponsor a Canadian conference on automation in libraries, to explore what was happening, to create interest, and to discuss what might be possible. Basil did most of the work, beating the bushes to find out which Canadian libraries were adopting computers in any way. We arranged for a two-day conference; Laval University in Quebec agreed to host it. We met with thirty people, librarians and a few of their systems analysts, from fourteen libraries. The chairman was head of the computer centre at Laval, and Stuart-Stubbs took minutes. We heard about computer applications being tried in six areas of work, although only British Columbia and Toronto were working on catalogues. Three UTL staff accompanied me from Toronto, and of course Bregzis made an important contribution. At the close of the meeting we adopted a resolution to ask the Canadian Association of College and University Libraries to establish a working group in the area of automation. I think that one important outcome was that our own National Librarian began to have an inkling that computers might some day be applied somehow to the mission of his library.

When the Library of Congress had its scheme ready to be tested, it invited Toronto and thirteen other libraries to participate in a pilot project by a regular exchange of their newly created catalogue tapes. In 1967 the Library of Congress delegate to the International Federation of Library Associations, in Toronto, reported that Toronto had been the most active participant. By that time our university's Computer Centre could not allow us the time or flexibility we needed, and this helped me convince the Board of Governors that we had to acquire our own mainframe. Bregzis had ascertained that the only computer with the built-in flexibility he would need was the Sigma 7, made in California. In making my presentation to the board, I was faced with the fact that the president of IBM Canada was not only a member of the board, but also a friend of our Vice-President (Administration), and had given urgent assurances that IBM was ready to work with us in developing the necessary flexibility. I left the meeting with very uncertain feelings, but that evening at dinner with the board (my only such experience), I was congratulated by the chairman for my plan and told to "go for it."

The Sigma 7, a huge affair with rows and rows of large cabinets that required special air conditioning and a false floor to contain their cables, was installed in our Technical Services Department in the old factory building already occupied by our technical services, in January 1969. As far as I know, our library was the first anywhere to have its own computer, but it took nearly two years to became fully operational. One serious problem was a shortage of qualified staff to operate it, with skills for which the university's salary structure made no provision and for which there was high demand in downtown Toronto.

UTL Automated Systems (UTLAS)

Our new president, John Evans, former Dean of Medicine at McMaster, was eager for us to extend machine-readable catalogue service (MARC) to other libraries, especially to justify Toronto's good fortune in the eyes of other Ontario university presidents, but also to begin repaying our investment. We were not yet fully ready, but in May 1970 we began providing other academic libraries in Ontario with weekly searches and printouts of card sets from MARC tapes that we received regularly from the Library of Congress and the British National Bibliography. The service was still geared to the production of library cards, but the rapid sharing of the work of cataloguing was a great boon.

The following year, at the behest of our president, I separated the administration of the computer and its staff from Technical Services, creating a new division that came to be known as UTLAS (UTL Automated Systems). The idea was to give UTLAS a computer expert as full-time director. The best director I could find knew little about libraries and thought their problems were simple; I had to meet with him and Bregzis together regularly, trying to keep them in step with each other.

When technology developed to the point at which computers could exchange data by telecommunication rather than the exchange of plastic tapes, MARC service to other libraries developed rapidly across the country and beyond, and the UTLAS equipment ran day and night. When our customer libraries on the Atlantic seaboard were closing for the night, our customers in Japan were just opening. I did not realize at the time how important our service was to the development of many academic libraries in Japan, although I knew it brought us visitors from there. Apparently it resulted in many visits in both directions, as well as staff exchanges that are still going on forty years later.

Closing the Card Catalogue

Our objective from the beginning was to replace the old card catalogues with a fully automated catalogue. By 1975 the conversion project had reached a stage at which the computer file covered the content of both the old catalogue and the new one. For our current additions we were still producing MARC records and also printing sets of cards for the catalogue. The cost of maintaining a card catalogue for the public and an automated one behind the scenes was more than we could afford. Closing the card catalogue and switching to the computer would be a very complicated operation, technically, and might easily become snarled in campus politics if we asked permission to begin. So I simply made a management decision to go ahead and do it.

We were not ready to go straight to fully automated service; there had to be an intermediate step, in the form of printout on microfiche (small sheets of microfilm). We made three sets, arranged by author, title, and subject, to sit in a box beside each microfiche reader. We placed about sixty of these readers with our first edition of the COM (catalogue on microfiche) in our reading rooms, on every floor of the stacks, and in all faculty and departmental libraries for which I was responsible. We offered free microfiche readers to other departmental libraries or faculty offices on condition that they pay the cost of producing sets of microfiche, which we would make for them. Soon there were more than one hundred microfiche sets and readers around the university. We froze the card catalogues on 30 June 1976. Of course we expected some trouble and had prepared posters and many other forms of information and explanation, but hardly any objections were raised; instead, people were very pleased to have such convenient new access to the catalogue, even without coming to the library. Of course the card catalogues were still in place, and would be for some time, without any additions being made, but use of them declined rapidly.

Toronto was the first large library anywhere to have its whole catalogue in machine-readable form. Again we had visitors from all over the world to see our COM innovation, and within two years UTLAS was producing COM catalogues for fifteen other library systems. Again there were many visitors, articles for us to publish, and talks to be given at conferences. Bregzis spent a week or more at the University of North Carolina as a consultant, helping establish a joint automated catalogue among three institutions in that state. Their catalogue was envisioned as a research tool that would be on microfiche as long as microfiche was needed. One of the people who worked on implementing the plan at North Carolina was a young man named Larry Alford, who was just beginning his library career; he is now Chief Librarian at Toronto. I had the pleasure of bringing Alford and Bregzis together to discuss old times. Bregzis was still alert but in poor health, and died in February 2013. In due course, when we were ready at Toronto, our COM catalogues were all replaced by direct access, without cards or microfiche, so that our catalogue could be consulted at computer consoles in the library, on the campus, or anywhere in the world.

Cataloguing Rules

There have been many efforts to arrive at standard rules for descriptive cataloguing, so that a given book will be described in the same way by all libraries that adopt the rules. The objective is to make life easier for readers who use more than one library and to promote the easy exchange of information among libraries. Attempts to create an international standard led to publication in the mid-1960s of a set of *Anglo-American Cataloguing Rules*. In the 1970s the ALA formed a committee to review those rules. I was so accustomed to the announcement of new studies, surveys, and assessments every second day that I paid little attention to what looked to be just another routine exercise. But when the committee's report was published in 1978, I was shocked to learn that the international committee had produced what it thought would be an ideal set of rules, without giving any thought to the high cost of adopting them and using them in conjunction with existing catalogues. It was really distressing to hear that the proposed rules were to be implemented in January 1980 by the Library of Congress, the principal source of ready-made cataloguing.

I had hoped the plans could be derailed by discussion at an ARL meeting in May 1978. There was serious concern expressed at that meeting, but the Associate Librarian of Congress told us flatly that his library was going ahead as planned, in agreement with the British Library and the national libraries of Australia and Canada – nothing could be done to change it. My three associate librarians and I thought we should at least try to do something. By telephone I found that many of our colleagues agreed, in Canada and beyond. When the Canadian Association of Research Libraries met the next month, with our National Librarian present, I proposed a motion calling for the cost implications of the new rules to be studied, and for implementation to be delayed. Within an hour of the motion being adopted it had gone by wire to the national libraries and library associations of the four countries involved, and a chain reaction set in. The upshot was that implementation of the new rules was postponed for a year, and application of them by the Library of Congress was modified in several ways that reduced the cost.

UTLAS Moved Out

In 1979, when our automated services to other libraries were bringing in enough income to begin paying for our original investment in hardware, the university decided to take UTLAS out of my hands and put it in the hands of the Vice-President (Administration) as one of his "ancillary services." He invited me to join his advisory committee, but his meetings were not very useful. He was in declining health and seemed unable to make decisions, so the UTLAS operation began to decline. At a crucial meeting that was to decide on an urgent update of UTLAS hardware, our chairman fell asleep twice, and no decision could be made. Fortunately his successor was a wise and strong administrator (and book collector) who was able to get UTLAS back on track. He

My wife Patricia with our children Karen and Harry on a camping trip to the Maritimes and Newfoundland, 1963.

Gradation photo of our son Robert, 1965.

moved it out of the library to the basement of a large commercial building in the city, where my son Harry visited it often as supervisor of the maintenance of Xerox equipment in that district.

But in 1984 the university sold UTLAS to a large business corporation, where it died. In its prime, the only serious competition UTLAS had as a worldwide library utility was the Ohio College Library Center (OCLC), which is now called the Online Computer Library Center. That organization has flourished and now serves more than 74,000 libraries in 170 countries around the world, including Toronto. When Larry Alford came to Toronto as Chief Librarian, he was Chairman of the Board of OCLC.

19 Fireworks, 1959 to 1969

In the period from 1959 to 1969 there was an explosion of other important new events in our library system, besides the beginning of computerization of catalogues and its export to other parts of the world. They were being lighted one after another but going off at the same time or during the same decade; the best way to describe them seems to be to take one theme at a time and follow it through to some sort of conclusion.

Delivery Systems

Early in 1959 I read of a scheme being tried at the University of Virginia, with the backing of a large grant from a foundation. The objective was to make it possible for professors to use the library while sitting in their own departments, thereby reducing the need for departmental libraries; it might even allow departmental collections to be centralized. The method involved putting a television receiver in each department, connected by coaxial cable to a camera in the library. A professor could telephone a special number and ask to see a particular book or issue of a journal; a person at the library would set the item up in a sort of cradle that was equipped with an automatic page turner that could be operated by the professor, who could then read at leisure.

On that Easter weekend, Patricia and I drove to Virginia to see the thing in action. The library there had two cameras near the reference desk; they were not in use just then, but the system was explained to us. The page turners available at the time had been designed only to turn pages of magazines for patients in hospital, and did not work well with books, especially for a professor who wanted to flip from title page or contents to index or to a certain chapter or page. Therefore the person at the library would have to sit beside the camera and turn pages as requested by the professor on the telephone. Almost every professor who tried the scheme was satisfied just to see that the item in hand was the one he wanted; he could then ask to have it sent over to him in the van, which had been added to the operation.

After getting home, I told President Smith what we had seen, and watched the dollar signs wrinkle his forehead as I spoke about television equipment and coaxial cables. But then I told him we could have the equivalent of Virginia's expensive project merely by adding a small van and its driver to the library budget. By September our van was making a daily circuit of thirty-two departmental stations on campus, thus reducing unnecessary traffic in the library, saving professorial shoe leather, and relieving some professorial frustration at having to compete with students in the Reference Room and at the catalogue. By 1972 we were using three special telephones and four vans; the latter, besides picking up fifty or sixty bags of mail a day and carrying material between far-flung locations of the central library, were making twice-daily calls at more than sixty delivery stations, and handling about 100,000 loans and returns a year to and from and among the stations.

In the mid-1960s I proposed a system of van delivery among Ontario university libraries. It began as the Inter-University Transit system in 1967, centred at York University close to the big east-west highway. It called five days a week at twelve university libraries along a route of six hundred miles, and provided airmail service to two in Northern Ontario. In Ottawa it called at the National Library and the National Science Library; eventually it also linked up with a similar service in Quebec. Other university departments, besides the libraries, found the scheme so useful in exchanging mail and equipment that the organization of presidents took it over from their librarians. My idea thus developed far beyond my early attempt at the Calgary Public Library to start a home delivery service.

International Federation of Library Associations

In the spring of 1959 the Canadian Library Association (CLA) held its annual conference on the campus of the University of Alberta, and I was ending my year as president of the association. One of the decisions made was to invite the International Federation of Library Associations (IFLA), which was holding that year's conference in Warsaw that autumn and had never met outside Europe, to hold its next conference in Canada.

That August, Patricia and I left our car in Montreal to be picked up by friends who were already in Europe, and sailed to Calais, where we picked up the Volkswagen they had left there for us. It was our first time on a ship, and Patricia's first time in Europe. We flew from Vienna to Warsaw with some misgivings after the porter at our hotel asked us whom she should notify if we did not come back at the appointed time; she knew of people who had gone there and never returned.

At the Warsaw airport we were met by Waclaw Slabczynski, a senior librarian at the Polish National Library, who was our guide and protector for the week, and became our friend. He and his wife had us to dinner in their tiny two-room apartment. On the final evening we took him and his wife to dinner and they took us to an operetta; his wife wept at parting. Next morning they saw us off at the airport and she wept again; he told us it was "old Polish custom." On our way home from a later IFLA conference in Moscow we stopped at Warsaw long enough to take them to breakfast. His doctoral thesis had been on Polish explorers in North America. I invited him later on to attend a CLA conference in Halifax, as prelude to an exploration of Slavic book collections from Halifax to Vancouver, to help us plan Toronto's policy on building our Slavic book collection. Years later their son (using some material I had been able to send him) wrote his Master's thesis on Canadian geography. Afterwards the son was our guest for a month at Streetsville, travelled to Edmonton with our son Harry and his wife, and then with a one-month bus ticket continued his exploration as far as Vancouver and Mexico City.

In our hotel in Warsaw, Martin Luther recognized me at breakfast on the first morning and joined us at our table. He had travelled from Göttingen by rail, third class so as to be with the people, and was marvelling at the generosity of the Polish people he had met on the train, who had paid for his dinner when they found that he had no Polish money. As a former officer in the German air force, he dropped a few tears in telling us about it. Patricia and I spent a good part of that day with him, walking around the city. Warsaw was observing the twentieth anniversary of the invasion by Germany. In every square and at many street corners there were framed lists of names and some photographs of citizens who had been killed at those spots by German forces. These memorials had an increasing impact on our friend, so we had an early supper and went back to the hotel. We did not see Luther again during the week, and were too busy to miss him. In years that followed he and I had some correspondence on library matters, until I received a letter edged in black that said he had died of a sudden severe sickness. I learned later that he had thrown himself into the stairwell just outside his office.

At the conference in Warsaw some days were taken up with committee meetings, in which I had no part. The general sessions were very large, with reports and discussion in the three official languages, and with delays while the important parts were interpreted by the multilingual secretary Joachim Wieder. In due course I spoke my two minutes' worth of invitation for the IFLA to meet in Canada, but I was beginning to wonder how Canada could accommodate such a complicated affair.

Guest of the German Government

In the summer of 1964 I had a chance to become better acquainted with Joachim Wieder. I was one of eight Canadian librarians invited on a three-week tour of German libraries, sponsored by Germany's foreign guest program, with all expenses paid and even some pocket money. Three of the eight were university librarians, and for most of the time we had our own itinerary that allowed a few side trips of our choice. Beginning at Bonn, where the library was in a new building, we visited twelve cities, including West Berlin. In most libraries, after an orientation tour, we would have a long session with the librarian and some members of his staff. In Munich we spent time at the Technical University, where Wieder was librarian. At Marburg we walked up the hill to visit the room in which Luther and Zwingli had conducted their famous debate. On the first afternoon at Stuttgart, we were given a tour of the countryside, followed by dinner at a famous rural restaurant. The next evening I was given tickets to take Wolfgang Brockhaus and his wife and their daughter Christine to the opera. As we settled into the Royal Box he exclaimed, "Last time I was in this building, the King sat in this chair!" Christine Brockhaus had already spent a month as our guest at Streetsville, and was about to spend a year on the staff of our Order Department at Toronto.

At the Johann Gutenberg University, newly revived after being interrupted by Napoleon, we were met by the Past Rector, who envied the strength of North American university presidents with their open-ended appointments, compared to that of a German Rector Magnificus, who was elected for one year by the deans from among themselves, and then before he had time to do anything, had to step down to the position of Past Rector, whose duty was to receive visitors.

A New System of Book Selection

When I began at Toronto, Stewart Wallace looked after the selection of books and journals related to Canadian history, but for all other subjects the job was left to departments of the university, as in most other North American universities. The Library Committee, following the advice of the librarian, approved an annual set of allotments of the book budget for the various departments, and each department appointed a selector, who received order requests ("green slips") from his colleagues and passed them to the Library. Our Order Department then placed the orders, until the department's allotment ran out. The system was traditional but was full of bottlenecks and frustration. Some professors did not bother with it, and those who did would often wait to go through book reviews and dealers' catalogues until after their classwork was well under way in the autumn. Green slips would pile up in the Order Department when the allotment ran out, and when orders were finally placed, the work was very often wasted because the books were no longer available.

In the late 1950s and early 1960s, with the number of new professors in all departments growing by leaps and bounds, we found that our book collection was very spotty, clustered around the particular interests of the old teaching staff. Something had to be done about it. A larger book budget and larger Order Department were not the answer.

I saw a book by Periam Danton about the German system of book selection, which basically involved libraries having their own teams of bibliographers. This system was being adopted by the University of California at Berkeley, the first American university to do so. I had seen the system in Germany and thought of it as an extravagance, but now I realized that it was the way we should go. I invited Danton to come to Toronto for a few days and arranged for him to talk to my senior staff and to several key professors. In 1966 I hired David Esplin, who had been deeply involved in setting up the new system at Berkeley, as head of our new Book Selection Department. We assembled a corps of book selectors, some of them from my existing staff.

We began contracting with selected book dealers in various countries; they would send us all important new publications within carefully defined fields as soon as they were published, on approval. Selections by the dealers were monitored and supplemented by our own bibliographers. In the first year about 10 per cent of the "dealer selection orders" had to be sent back, but after that only a very few. Within two years we had dealer selection contracts with dealers in thirty-six countries, including the Brockhaus firm in Stuttgart for German-language publications in Germany and Switzerland. The system worked very smoothly. Esplin and his staff travelled to at least eight countries to inspect and negotiate the purchase or donation of special collections. Esplin went to India for the Indo-Canadian Shastri Institute to set up an office that selected and bought Indian publications for Toronto and a few other Canadian research libraries, paid for out of a block fund that had been established in lieu of payment for Canadian wheat. He returned to Delhi twice to sort out problems at that office, and of course he visited some of our other agents along the way.

At first some of our professors were unhappy about the library taking over book selection, but they soon found they had no reason to complain, because we continued to accept any green slips they brought in. After a time, they found that things they were asking for were already in our stacks, and the green slips gradually vanished. For a while we invited the teaching staff to inspect the dealer-selected material, which we placed on shelves for a week after it was received; there were a few visitors and then no more.

To strengthen our whole collection we had a lot of catching up to do; in the four years between 1965 and 1969 our annual intake rose from 218,000 volumes to 284,000 into the central library collection, more than any other university library on this continent, probably in the world. I don't know how many other libraries on this continent adopted in-house selection plus a dealer selection plan, but certainly we were the first in Canada.

IFLA Conference in Toronto

The IFLA chose Canada for its 1967 annual meeting, its first meeting outside Europe. The CLA decided it should be held in Toronto on our campus, and asked me to chair the local planning committee. Based on experience, I envisioned a large, unwieldy committee that would be expected to include representatives from every library constituency in the CLA, that would be difficult to convene and slow to make decisions. I was too busy with other things to be involved in such a task.

David Esplin, Associate Librarian for Book Selection and Acquisition.

Among other things, we were in the final stages of planning for a large new building. I agreed to be chairman of planning for the IFLA conference if it could be a one-man committee with authority to enlist help as necessary, and that condition was accepted.

Also that year I was Chairman of the Board of the Midwest Interlibrary Center in Chicago. Our library had become the nineteenth member of the center, and for several years was the first and only member from outside the US Midwest. Libraries outside the center's membership were by then pressing to use its resources, and because the whole operation was growing and had to be supported by fees levied on the members, it was running into financial problems. By 1967 two other universities had joined; I think they were Harvard and the University of British Columbia. As Chairman of the Board I was pushing for a new constitution that would welcome universities from across the continent and that would set a scale of fees for occasional use by various categories of non-members. This change required, among other things, shedding the word Midwest and becoming the Center for Research Libraries, a change from MILC to CRL. But for my presence, it would have been the American Center for Research Libraries, ACRL. There were many details to be dealt with, and I was having to hold monthly executive meetings in Chicago. I am glad to know that the center is still flourishing and has hundreds of universities and other research institutions as members, including several in Canada.

To prepare for the IFLA meeting that autumn, I had to keep in close touch with the CLA office in Ottawa and recruit local help in Toronto to do what was needed. Bundles of IFLA committee reports were received from Ottawa (after anxious delays and some threats made to the managers of a transport company) and arranged neatly on tables in the biggest room at Victoria College, which was to be the headquarters. The lists of delegates from thirty-two countries were received, rooms assigned, name tags made, folders of agendas and other information assembled, and so on.

When the great day arrived, we were ready. Three hundred delegates from thirty-one countries were met at the airport, driven to the campus, shown to their billets in the Victoria residences, and guided to dining rooms. They had maps of the committee meeting places in Victoria classrooms. For their large general sessions they would have to cross University Avenue to one of the concert halls in our Music Building, where there were microphones and we had arranged for simultaneous translation in three languages. One morning at that crossing I heard a loud screech of brakes and saw a car shuddering to a stop just in front of a large woman in a blue dress; for a moment I thought the woman was Elizabeth Morton, Executive Director of the Canadian Library Association, who had been in a blue dress at breakfast; but it was not Elizabeth and luckily there was no accident. And the whole week's agenda ran smoothly, with hardly a hitch.

The only serious hitch was almost an international incident, averted only by the ingenuity of my secretary. I pause here to say a word about my secretary. Wallace's secretary, Julia Jarvis, had stayed to see me safely through my first year in office, and then left to help Wallace manage Dora Hood's Bookroom, which he had bought after retiring from the university. My next secretary, Betty How, had been secretary to Lester Pearson when he was High Commissioner at Canada House in London during the war. Her husband, lately deceased, had been a collector of sterling silver; she often provided the urn and some other pieces when arranging social events at the library, or staff parties on the lawn at her own home in a stylish part of Toronto. She took prizes in ballroom dancing. She told me she did twenty push-ups every morning. She took her holidays in winter at a famous resort in the Alps and had been carried on shoulders in a torchlight parade after winning the Gold Trophy for mastering every ski run at that resort. And she was a first-rate secretary. One time when I opened the door between our offices to give her some wonderful news about the approval of a budget item that we had been worried about, she was so delighted that I thought to celebrate my own elation by doing something special: standing in the doorway, I reached up, hooked my fingers over the door lintel, raised my knees slowly, leaned my head and shoulders back, brought my knees and feet up through the gap between my arms and on back until my shoes were just above the floor — a sort of backwards somersault that is called "skinning the cat."

Betty How took charge of the seating plan for the dinner that the university had agreed to sponsor in a downtown hotel on the first evening of the IFLA conference. There was to be a very long head table, and many large round tables throughout the room. We had names of the delegates from the various countries, and other guests, including all the librarians on our staff. Betty How placed at least one of our own librarians at each table, facing me at the head table, along with a mixture of nationalities. There were about thirty Russian delegates, to be at thirty tables. Their leader, according to the list, had a hyphenated name, Rudomino-something; I was surprised to see a hyphenated name on the Russian list, but remembered Rimski-Korsakov and thought no more about it. I had met the lady herself after breakfast on the first morning and she said to call her simply Rudomino. I gave her one of our Canadian Centennial lapel pins and she gave me a similar pin marking the fiftieth anniversary of the Soviet Union.

That evening at the hotel, Betty How had posted the seating plans and placed the name cards; everything seemed to be in order. The head table guests, including Rudomino, were all assembled in a separate room, and the kilted piper was puffing up his bagpipes to lead us into the dining room, when Betty How rushed in to tell me that the leader of the Russian delegation was insulted and ready to take all his people home because his name was nowhere on the seating plan. *His* people? We had been misled by the hyphenated name; there were two leaders, one professional and one political, and the second one was very angry. But it was an easy thing to send Betty How back to the angry one and conduct him graciously to his place at the table just below the centre of the head table and facing it, the place that was being "saved" for him by one of our librarians. He was mollified, and did not take his people home.

Other social events that I had arranged went smoothly, with only a few anxious moments. There were tours to various sorts of libraries in the city. There was a roast beef luncheon sponsored by the Province of Ontario, and a play at the Shakespeare Festival Theatre in Stratford, sponsored by the National Library. There was also a trip to Niagara Falls, followed by a picnic in a Niagara vineyard. At the picnic, Patricia and I shared our blanket with my friend the Librarian of the University of Uppsala; he had a son Henrick the same age as our Harry. Henrick came to live with us for a year and attended school in Streetsville.

At the IFLA meeting the next year, in Frankfurt am Main, there was another Russian incident. Steve McCarthy (Cornell) and I had taken an early morning train to Cologne, to see a new conveyor system. In newspapers on the train we read that Russian tanks had invaded Czechoslovakia during the night. When we got back to the IFLA meeting during the coffee break that afternoon, we saw the Russian and Bulgarian delegations gathered in one corner, and everyone else gathered around the Czechs. My Czech cataloguer was in tears, saying she had thought that all the younger people had been lost to the Soviet system, but there they were throwing Molotov cocktails at the tanks!

Library Openings

After the Second World War the great surge in university enrolments across the continent was accompanied by a surge in the construction of new libraries. There were many invitations to formal openings of new buildings; I attended as many as I could, to see the latest designs and equipment, to talk to colleagues, and to see and enjoy the celebrations. At Cornell the celebration included a stadium concert where the Boston Symphony performed Beethoven's Ninth Symphony, with Schiller's *Ode to Joy* finale, sung by four renowned singers and a chorus of four hundred students.

At Notre Dame, Patricia and I were met by a student who conducted us to our room in residence and who would be our personal guide for the next two days. In the library we noticed that practically every room and every bit of furniture bore the name plate of a donor. The building's most amazing feature was its front elevation, which faced the stadium across a very long reflecting pool; its front wall was entirely covered by a huge Christian mosaic in strong colours, said to be larger than the pagan mosaic on the front of the National Library of Mexico.

Next morning, High Mass was celebrated on a platform in front of the Library, by the Dean of the College of Cardinals (flown in from Europe for the occasion), supported by about ten other cardinals. That afternoon, in the same setting, there was a special convocation. Visiting directors of libraries, in academic caps and gowns, walked in the academic procession between two rows of honour guards, Knights of Columbus in uniform. Then, with everybody sweltering in the sun, at least twenty honorary degrees were granted, mostly to the presidents of Indiana universities and colleges.

In the evening there was a banquet for about eight hundred guests. There were two head tables, one higher than the other; they seated the new graduands, university officials, principal donors, and other dignitaries, each one introduced in some detail. Each of the contributing trades (excavators, carpenters, artists, and so on – but no librarians!) had a table and was thanked warmly. Finally, about eleven o'clock, the chairman introduced the evening's speaker, the president of Indiana University. After thanking Notre Dame on behalf of his fellow graduands, he spoke only to them, congratulating them on not having been asked to sing for their supper, and advising them to attend every such occasion in order to enjoy the benefits, and to know that while they were away from their offices, no mistakes would be made!

Stewart Wallace had an MA from Oxford University and in 1952 received an honorary doctorate at the opening of a new library at McMaster University; in his early years he had lectured in History at the

University of Toronto and also at McMaster when that institution was in Toronto; on his appointment as Librarian at Toronto he was required to give up both lectureships. At the opening of the library at Waterloo University in 1966 I received an honorary doctorate along with two friends: Jack Brown, a classmate of mine at Alberta who had become Librarian of the National Research Council in Ottawa, and Bertha Bassam, the Director of Toronto's Library School. Some years later I was doctored again by McGill University and the University of Toronto, so now I hold seven degrees from five universities, probably enough to have satisfied my grandfather.

I attended many other library celebrations in Canada and elsewhere, but none that were more grand than Notre Dame's, except for two to which I received personal invitations: the 350th anniversary of the University of Uppsala in Sweden, in 1965, and the opening of the new Royal and National Library in Brussels in 1969; both events were attended by their respective kings, and my way was paid in full out of foundation grants those libraries had obtained. I was the only Canadian librarian there.

When it came time for us at Toronto to open the largest academic library building in the world, the opening ceremony was quite different.

There were three libraries at which I was an official visitor. In the early 1970s I was the only librarian at a two-day meeting of the external advisory board appointed by the president of the Massachusetts Institute of Technology to advise him concerning the organization and operation of his library. And for three years in the mid-1980s I was the librarian on an advisory committee that met at least once a year, appointed by the president of the University of British Columbia for the same purpose. In the early 1990s I spent ten days or so in Ottawa as consultant to the National Research Council, assessing the policies and operations of the NRC Library. Since then I have approached libraries only as an occasional visitor or user.

Steps Leading to New Library Construction at Toronto

At the opening of the Sigmund Samuel wing in 1954 I said that it was a forty-year expansion thirty years too late, and that more would be needed within ten years. President Smith was taken aback at the time, although by then the maximum student enrolment for which we had been told to plan had already been exceeded. Actually a new library building committee was formed in 1960. I wrote a program for another extension to the old building, but the cost estimated in 1961 was $4 million: the committee was told to find ways of cutting the cost, but could not.

Meanwhile some other space was becoming available and provided some relief. In 1962 Victoria College opened its first library building, for which I had been engaged to write the architectural program. University College obtained a Canada Council grant and a private donation for a library wing that would close the quadrangle of the college's U-shaped building; the principal asked me to chair a planning committee, and I wrote the program for what opened as the Laidlaw Library in 1964. Of course the stone walls of the new wing were too clean to match the three old wings, which dated back to 1850, but the new walls had some features of their own; the faces of four well-known university officials looked down in stone from near the top of the north wall. Another feature was in the windows of the north wall, which looked out over the back campus soccer field; I placed them four feet above the floor, so that readers would not be distracted by what went on there.

In that same period, other college libraries sprang up on the campus. Massey College, an endowed postgraduate residential college, opened in 1963 and had space for a sizeable library. New College, one of the two new undergraduate colleges spawned on the campus by the university, opened in 1964; it had space for a library, for which we had a book collection ready. Trinity College expanded its library space and appointed its first full-time librarian. St Michael's College also expanded its library space, and began drawing plans for a separate library building. And two suburban extensions of the university, Scarborough and Erindale Colleges, a few miles east and west of our campus respectively, opened in 1965, their libraries supplied with collections ready-made as part of our five libraries project, ONULP. Meanwhile the university had appointed a new library planning committee in 1963 and acquired a large building site at the corner of Harbord and St George Streets. This was to be a Humanities and Social Sciences research library, and headquarters of our library system. With instructions to plan for the next quarter-century, I wrote a new program, and Shy Mathers the architect went to work again. Just after finishing his preliminary drawings, he died suddenly and left his son to present them to our committee. The plan presented by Andy Mathers was estimated at $10 million; fortunately it was rejected out of hand by the board, and we were sent back to the drawing board.

Our planning committee was enlarged to include some professors and students, and had new instructions. We were to plan for fifty years, at the energetic insistence of Ernest Sirluck who had just arrived to become Dean of Graduate Studies, after being on the library planning committee at the University of Chicago. Our project was to include space for the Library School, which was operating in rented space off-campus under the direction of Brian Land, one of my former Assistant Librarians. Brian and I wrote a new program, and with the Library School program included the document came to seventy pages. Design architects in New York were appointed to collaborate with Andy Mathers, who would make the working drawings in Toronto (because working drawings, if imported, would have been taxed at the estimated value of the completed building). The whole project, estimated at $41 million, was approved by our Board of Governors in June 1968.

One unique feature of our program was its call for one thousand lockable study carrels in the book stack, so that a doctoral student could leave his or her books and papers spread out and come back to them day after day. This number of carrels was far beyond what I had seen or heard of anywhere else, but our building was conceived as a laboratory for advanced study, not just a filling station. So the carrels were very important, and we hoped that each one could have at least an illusion of daylight.

After studying our program, our design architect (designer of the Olin Library at Cornell) brought us five small models of different shapes. One was round, one square, one triangular, one a hollow rectangle, and one crowned with a high tower. He said that the space we needed could be arranged in various ways, and before beginning serious work he wanted to know which general shape we might prefer. President Bissell, who was suffering from comments being made about the row of cracker-box buildings that had sprung up along St George Street, asked whether the triangular model might have any advantages. The architect replied that for a given floor area, a triangle had considerably more perimeter than a square or a circle; if we chose that shape, and allowed for three levels of carrels in every two levels of book stack, we could have a thousand carrels with a small window in every one. And that is why the main structure is triangular, with hexagonal wings for the Library School and the Rare Book Library.

During the planning period we built a plywood mock-up of a pair of carrels and had them tested by many people; I have been told by those who use them that they are the best part of the building. The lack of large windows in the upper storeys, and the windowless walls in the rare book wing, have been lampooned by some critics who do not understand the need to protect books from damage by sunlight.

All during the planning period there was continuous participation by the library staff. My assistant Hugh Smith worked closely with my department heads, the architects, and the university's project manager Howard Milne, and kept me posted.

About eighteen months into the process, when the detailed drawings were far advanced, the Ontario government began to see the project as a provincial resource and asked for three storeys to be added. I called the design architect in New York to ask what three additional floors would do to the design; he replied that they would "improve the hell out if it." With costs rising every day, it was too late to redesign the whole thing, so we just had to insert one storey at ground level and add two more to the top without altering the rest of the design. The cost of the extra floors was included in the $41 million estimate.

At the time we were planning, there was much speculation about computers and how they would be used in libraries. I had seen plans for the new Madison Building at the Library of Congress, where they were planning floors that were almost hollow to accommodate cables for future computers; this feature was adding about 10 per cent to the construction costs. We wondered whether such provision was really necessary, so we brought in two consultants who had never met each other, one a specialist in computers and the other in information handling. After a two-day session with them, we decided to use only the normal sort of duct work in the floor slabs, and so far that has proved to be sufficient.

The architects in New York made a large half-model of their design, mounted against a mirror that gave it the impression of being a full model, and trucked it to Toronto just in time for a crucial meeting in 1966. Kept on public display, it attracted much attention in the university and was an object to amaze the international delegates to the IFLA conference in 1967.

In 1968 our project received final approval from the Ontario government, and bids were called for. Unfortunately the lowest bid was $7 million beyond our budget; we had to trim that much out of the plans, starting with the things that were least essential to the basic operations of the library. The auditorium was postponed. And we lost the terracing that would have improved the approaches to the building, as well as the allowance for artwork that would have enhanced the interior. Floor coverings and wall finishes were downgraded. Switching systems and some walls were deleted, only to be restored later at greater cost. Every possible deletion was priced. Deletion of the tower at the end of the rare-book wing would have saved $10,000, but the design architect explained that it was needed simply as an architectural feature to close the vista on Harbord Street; anyone approaching it from the east would see it on the centre line of the street where it curved to go around the building; without the tower that part of the building would look like the big end of an elephant backing out of its stall. Our Board Chairman sighed and said that for $10,000 he liked the tower, and it stands as a puzzle to people who have speculated that it was meant for a clock tower, a ventilation duct, a lucky symbol, even a gun emplacement.

The final layer of provincial approval was received in November 1968, and construction finally began. It took four-and-a-half years.

Our large and expensive building plan had raised eyebrows at other Ontario universities. The provincial Council of Presidents of Universities had asked for and received a showing of our plans, and were criticizing Premier John Robarts for giving so much more to the City of Toronto than to their own cities: the Ontario Science Centre, the Art Gallery of Ontario, and now this great library building. Our new president did not want to make a great show of the share we had received. He did not want even a formal sod-turning ceremony for our new library, so I bought a new spade with which Stewart Wallace and I (assisted by Brian Land, Director of the Library School, and his predecessor Bertha Bassam) churned the sod on a snowy morning, with a few of our staff taking their turns. Next morning I found the spade beside my desk, cleaned and gilded by our caretaker.

The president did allow for a small, poorly advertised ceremony to lay the cornerstone of our new building. The deed was done by Premier John P. Robarts, whose government had approved our plans, and for whom the new Humanities and Social Sciences Library had just been named. He used the occasion to point out that Toronto, as the capital of a great province, needed to have great buildings and institutions. But when our building was brought into use, and we should have had an official ceremonial opening, the president refused, and did not want to discuss the matter. Our official opening was different from anything I had seen or heard of anywhere else; there was none.

I could hardly let the matter end there, and thought of how to have an unofficial event that would not involve the president's office or the local press. I invited the Association of Research Libraries to have its two-day annual meeting in our library, its first meeting outside the United States. I had just finished my fifth year on the ARL board, and the members were eager to see the outcome of the plans they had been hearing about. We gave them an orientation lecture and guided tours, and then a banquet in Hart House. Former President Claude Bissell (a determined founder of libraries) was in the chair. Our own staff librarians and the librarians of the other Ontario universities were sprinkled among the guests. Our National Librarian, Kaye Lamb, introduced the speaker, Ed Williams from Harvard, whose survey of Canadian university library collections had helped start the ball rolling for general expansion and improvement throughout the country.

The fact that our governors had rejected a $4 million project in 1961 and then approved one of $41 million in 1965 seemed like a miracle, but could be accounted for by the tremendous new emphasis that had been placed on higher education and research in both the provincial and federal governments in the early 1960s.

From experience we knew that moving a library into new space was a very complicated business, so two years before the great move was to take place we hired an industrial engineer. The Department of Rare Books and Special Collections had to be brought in from its temporary location in rented space east of Yonge Street, a mile away; this occurred in December 1972, in time for the department to open just before Christmas. Other departments and some book collections had to be moved from various locations on and off campus, but the most complicated move, that of the public service departments, was made over a weekend in July 1973. We closed down service in the old building at 4 p.m. on Friday afternoon, and opened in the Robarts Library on Monday morning at 8:30. One of the most surprised people was a professor who had borrowed a book in the old building on Friday afternoon and tried to return it there on Monday, only to be met by workmen in hard hats, who told him that the library was gone. The Sigmund Samuel wing was being refurbished as a library for undergraduates.

Throughout the planning and building process, which covered twelve years, there were many setbacks, and many compromises made for many reasons, but the building has been very functional and adaptable to changing needs. The rare book wing, the Fisher Library, was designed not only for the preservation and use of its collections, but

The Robarts Research Library and Thomas Fisher Rare Book Library opened in 1973. At that time (and perhaps still), it was the largest academic library building in the world. Courtesy of the University of Toronto Archives

also to attract gifts. When visiting librarians, seeing it for the first time, looking up to its five-storey ceiling and down into its two large reading rooms, exclaimed at the extravagant use of space, I used to tell them that this was the most functional part of the whole building, because it paid for itself in gifts before it was even opened. And now for many years the value of gifts each year has been several times the original cost of the rare book wing; indeed, the total value of gifts received during the following forty years has been several times $41 million.

One special feature of the rare book wing was that it would have no ordinary exhibit cases, the sort in which rare materials are boxed behind glass and baked with lights. My idea was to put exhibits outside the box and the people inside. The large, hexagonal lobby has glass walls through which people see the exhibits ranged on a wide shelf in the controlled atmosphere of the great room.

Anyone approaching the Fisher Library from the west along Harbord Street may notice a small gazebo on the lawn. It was built very early, as a sample of the various gravels and finishes that were being considered, and as a test of the triangular fibreglass tubs that were to be used for the waffled floor slabs. (The tubs were in fact shown to need interior steel bracing). It was supposed to be removed before the contract was finished, but I liked it and arranged for a time capsule to be planted beneath it; I wonder what the people who open the time capsule will be thinking about this building.

The Robarts Library complex was the last building for which I wrote the program. The others were our Sigmund Samuel wing and the libraries of Victoria College, University College, and the Ryerson Institute of Technology, all in Toronto. I wrote programs also for two public libraries, one for Streetsville when I was chairman of the Library Board there, and one for a small town in Northern Ontario at the behest of a graduate student who was the wife of Roland Michener, Canada's Governor General. And I worked with Steve McCarthy of Cornell on a program for the Sir George Williams University Library in Montreal. It was a kind of task I enjoyed and thought I might do in retirement, but there were few libraries being built in the 1980s.

Preservation of Information

For several years in the 1960s I served the ARL as a member of its Preservation Committee, along with the Assistant Librarian of Congress and one or two others. We had a foundation-financed laboratory in Richmond, Virginia, where the durability of paper was studied under different conditions of heat, light, humidity, chemical content, and wear and tear due to handling. The Library of Congress had a special concern about the durability of microfilm, which had been thought for some years to be the ultimate medium for preservation of print, but some older files of it in Washington were developing mysterious red spots, measles, for which no cure had been found. Our committee met from time to time in Richmond (a long day's drive from Mississauga) to monitor progress and discuss further steps to be taken. Our work did lead to the production of acid-free paper with much better durability, and to its use by some important publishers.

For years I was chairman of the CLA's program for finding and microfilming the best existing files of older Canadian newspapers, most of them extinct papers that were not widely known and in poor condition. Most historians were grateful for our work, but one American professor of Canadian history told me it was making his work harder. He said it was easy to write Canadian history when there were only a few well-known sources, but with old papers lurking on reels and reels of microfilm he never knew when something might turn up to refute what he was writing.

For me the most interesting thing we filmed was Timothy Eaton's mail order catalogue. When I was a boy and the Canadian population was mostly rural, we received an issue of the *Eaton's Catalogue* every spring and autumn. It was at least two inches thick, fully illustrated, and offered a great range of clothing and many other kinds of merchandise in varieties and styles far beyond the range of the general stores that were available in rural areas. A few of the pictures of ladies' wear were in colour on slick paper, but all other illustrations were black and white, on newsprint. Each issue was scanned eagerly and often by all members of the family; if any item ordered turned out to be unsatisfactory, it could be returned without charge. *Eaton's Catalogue* was an important aid to rural life, but it was not the sort of thing that libraries collected, and most out-of-date copies disappeared into rural privies. Yet as historical documents the catalogues could be a unique source of designs, prices, and styles of interest to social scientists, artists, novelists, costume designers, and other breeds of historians.

Our hunt for copies of the catalogue began because of the discovery of the first issue, a small booklet dated 1884, in one of the provincial archives in the Maritimes. And we knew there was also a French version begun in 1910. We soon found that there was a complete archival file of catalogues at the T. Eaton headquarters in Toronto, but the man in charge would not consider letting us borrow them for microfilming. Finally I persuaded him that he should have a security copy on film to be kept somewhere else within his company, and I offered to give him a free copy if he would allow us to have the filming done just beside his own office. Thus the whole file from 1884 to 1964 was filmed, and bought by several libraries in Canada and a few in the States.

Sometime in 1967, Canada's centennial year, I was invited to a small luncheon in Ottawa, with Kaye Lamb who was our National Librarian and Archivist, John Diefenbaker the former Prime Minister, Roland Michener the Governor General, and two American officials. The occasion was a formal exchange of historical documents between our two countries, an exchange that included a full set of the CLA microfilms.

20 A Sabbatical Year

After twenty years of work as Chief Librarian, and after a decade of exciting events, such as the beginning of delivery systems on campus and beyond; establishment of a Campus Union Catalogue; replacement of card catalogues by a computerized system; seeing our machine-readable format become an international format; being involved with the ARL and IFLA and hosting a conference for each; being involved in the evolution of the Midwest Center into the Center for Research Libraries; introducing a new system of book selection and acquisition; and planning and opening new buildings, including the largest academic library building in the world, I was granted my first and only year of sabbatical leave.

In the summer of 1974, when our new Humanities and Social Sciences Research Library was open and running, Patricia and I sailed on a Russian ship from New York to Bremerhaven, and picked up a new car at the Volvo factory in Sweden. In ten months we drove about 26,000 miles, mostly along the coastline of Europe, from Norway to Finland to Portugal to Turkey and back to Sweden to have the car shipped home. Our three children and their small families joined us at different times along the way, to share our journey for a few weeks.

Our son Robert had been married that spring; he and his bride had just begun a holiday in Europe when my mother died in Edmonton. A few weeks later my father met them in Paris, travelled with them as far as Hungary, then flew to Edinburgh for a week or two in Britain with Patricia and me. For the last week of our ten-month tour we were accompanied on a six-country trip from England to Sweden by my sister Betty, her daughter Lynne, and Peggy Field, who was an old friend from our Calgary Public Library days.

During the ten months of our journey I accepted two invitations. One was from the British Museum, the other from the association of academic librarians in Bavaria. Sir Frank Francis, Keeper of Books at the British Museum, had been president of the IFLA during the conferences at Warsaw and Toronto and had seen the model of our new building. The British Museum was in the throes of planning a library building for itself, and Sir Frank had invited me to London to look at their plans. I spent the first day going through the plans with his assistant, asking questions, and having the whole project explained to me. On the second day, Sir Frank chaired a day-long session with his senior staff, his architect and engineer, and one or two London city officials. He wanted to begin the meeting with some slides I had with me, of the floor plans and elevations of our finished building; discussion of those took up the whole morning. Toward the end of that session the architect remarked that people who moved into a new building usually saw some flaws in it, and asked me what flaws we had found so far. I replied that I could not think of any, although some might have been found during the eight months I had been away; I had told David Esplin, who had been left in charge, not to get in touch with me while I was away. Sir Frank gave me a surprised look and said, "But surely you must have heard that it burned down!" Going along with his joke, I said, "Good, then I won't have to go back to it." And on that note we adjourned for lunch.

In the afternoon we discussed my thoughts and questions concerning their own plans. After that I heard no more from them. I heard later that they had moved away from the site we had been looking at, and put up a large building, but I have never seen it.

Munich

My friend Dr Joachim Wieder, as president of the Bavarian Library Association, had invited me to spend two weeks visiting Bavarian university libraries. Patricia flew home from Frankfurt for the two weeks, to check on the house and family there, and I took the train from Frankfurt to Munich, where Wieder was Librarian of the Technical University. This was my third tour of German university libraries; I had seen their traditional emphasis on independent faculty libraries and had resisted it at Toronto, but I had heard that changes were taking place in Germany and was glad of the opportunity to see what they were.

I arrived in Munich a full day before my appointment with Wieder, to do some sightseeing. I visited the Old Picture Gallery, the Museum of Antiquities, and the Museum of Classical Sculpture, where there was a fine statue of Alexander (about whom I was then reading) stepping up toward his father's chariot; there was also a noseless head (marble portrait) of Agrippina, Nero's mother, about whom Patricia had been reading. Revisiting the Science Museum, I concentrated on the rooms of road and bridge construction, which were fascinating.

Wieder said that the Bavarian state government had recently placed all books and library funds in the hands of the university librarians. The institute libraries, run by the heads of institutes, were resisting this, and there was great excitement. The Rector of the Technical University had been persuaded (by the professors, in three secret meetings) to declare that the law did not apply at the Technical University; the ministry had countered with a letter reaffirming its new law and naming Wieder as executor of it at the Technical University. So there was a great struggle, with Wieder and the ministry against the rector and the professors, and it was unlikely to end in a happy truce. The Technical University was preparing to withdraw to the country over the next ten years and would put up a new library there when there was money, but Wieder thought the rector was unlikely to press for it.

Meanwhile the library had spread into various parts of the old building, and had installed an ingenious conveyor system: a self-propelled wagon that carried up to 10 kilos of books in a hanging basket, and that ran on horizontal rails and vertical cog tracks in response to push-button calls from many stations or according to a central address panel. The system had been invented for the library, but as "Tele-lift" was being used by the new BMW head office tower as well as by many other places. It was the thing that Steve McCarthy and I had tried (without success) to see at Cologne.

At the State Library in Munich the main innovation was a "leaf caster," which used wood pulp (tinted to match) to make a new sheet of paper incorporating old torn or fragmented pages, so that the old bits of ancient books were mounted in and surrounded by new paper. There was also a process for treating illustrated pages that needed to be strengthened but that could not be laminated between plastic or rice paper sheets without spoiling the sharpness of line and colour; each page was split by being pasted between two sheets, which were then separated, while wet, and a strengthening sheet inserted between the two halves. It was almost unbelievable.

Dinner one night with the Wieders was very interesting. She had taught German at Vassar for a year before the war. He was a survivor of the Battle of Stalingrad, and his book on it had been translated into seven languages. His study, up under the rafters, had hundreds of symphonies and quartets (on tape), dozens of picture albums arranged by city and country, thousands of slides, gift books from many countries, and a very large collection of German and French accounts of travels in Italy, his own special field. They went to Austria every Christmas to ski, went to Italy at least once a year, had a country house for summer, and so on. His energy and knowledge put me to shame, but I felt that his eagerness to show me everything in one evening was slightly pathetic. He kept repeating that he had returned from prison in Russia with nothing. The next day he was going to Wolfenbüttel to take part in a three-day literary seminar, and I was to go to the opera with his wife and daughter, as a guest of the State, to sit in the Royal box. The fact that I was there at all was, of course, due to his energy.

Wieder had been one of the three foreign librarians who had breakfast with us at Streetsville during the IFLA conference in Toronto in 1967. In 1978 he returned to Toronto at my invitation to spend a month as Visiting Librarian. He and his wife stayed in the guest rooms at Hart House. This was part of my program of bringing in outstanding people for a few days or weeks, to expose our own librarians (and sometimes some professors) to ideas from outside our own institution, and for me to profit from their comments. Over the years we had eight such visitors, three from Europe, three from the United States, and two from Canada.

Regensburg

Among the dozen or so other Bavarian libraries I visited on that trip, several of them for a second time, Regensburg (French: Ratisbon) was the most interesting. It was a very new university but already had about nine thousand students. Its librarian, Dr Pauer, had been on the scene in 1964, before any other officers or staff (or a rector!) had been appointed. In ten years he had spent $18 million on books and built up a collection of about 1.3 million volumes; that autumn, he had opened a new central library and some branch libraries – an amazing feat. He was in charge of all library services, the first academic librarian in any German university of whom that could be said. He had half his collection on open shelves. He thought that closed shelves and the arranging of books by sequence of acquisition – both of which had been standard in Germany and saved much work and money – were expensive in the long run because they made institute libraries necessary. His libraries were beautifully furnished, lighted, and ventilated; together they seated four thousand, which was more than 20 per cent of the expected maximum enrolment. His catalogues were various, all produced by computer, and seemed to work. He told me that the new universities in Bayreuth and Augsburg were following suit.

At noon I lunched in town with Pauer and two of his people, who took me for a walk around the area, and to see a baroque church. Later in the day I had tea and homemade raspberry cake at Pauer's home, where he arrived by bicycle. The house overlooked an old battlefield; Pauer pointed out a small knoll just beyond his garden, on which, so he told me, Napoleon had stood during the battle. I was reminded of a poem we learned at Victory school:

You know, we French stormed Ratisbon.
A mile or so away, on a little mound, Napoleon
stood on our storming-day,
with neck out-thrust, you fancy how, legs wide, arms locked behind,
as if to balance the stern brow
oppressive with its mind ...

Regensburg is at the northernmost bend of the Danube, on an old trade route to Asia, and claims to be the oldest city in Germany. There had been a Celtic town there, and then a Roman camp, and then fortress Castra Regina, built at the command of Marcus Aurelius. Part of the fortress wall had been incorporated into the Bishop's Palace, which had become my hotel (Bischofshof am Dom), and one route out of our courtyard was through one of the original gates (Porta Praetoria). Maybe Marcus Aurelius slept there. Surely Charlemagne did when he made this city his capital. The first German parliament was there for centuries, and Emperor Charles V (whose path we had crossed in Spain) attended three sessions there. At the last one (1546) he had changed world history by sleeping with a local lass (Barbara Blomberg), who later presented him with a son who became Don John of Austria, the Christian general whose fleet defeated the Turks at the Battle of Lepanto in 1571. Patricia and I had seen Don John's tomb in Spain, near that of his half-brother King Philip, who launched another Armada against the other infidel, Elizabeth of England.

On the second day I went back to the university library and gave an hour's lecture to about twenty staff and visitors. I showed slides of our new building, concentrating on points of organization and service that differed from theirs. From the reception and questions, I think it went rather well; two people came up afterwards to say how easily they understood Canadian speech, after having difficulty in understanding American visitors. Perhaps it was because I know only common words and speak slowly.

One piece of equipment at that library was really quite surprising: a swinging gate like a garden gate in their belt conveyor system. The conveyor ran through the stack at about waist level, but people could walk through it as necessary, because the belt stopped when a gate was opened.

That afternoon I walked through the town and took a few pictures: the Roman gate; the oldest stone bridge in Germany still in regular use; Roman square towers; the Gothic cathedral; baroque churches; Kepler's house; a Celtic portal in St Jacob's Church; and part of an old Irish monastery from about 1200. Mostly these things were the original structures; there was little restoration visible except in two piers of the Roman bridge, which had been bombed in the 1940s.

St Gallen and Santa Maria

During other parts of our sabbatical journey I saw very few libraries. The most memorable was the rococo abbey library at St Gallen, Switzerland, a World Heritage site. The ceiling and walls were covered with paintings; balconies and shelving were carved and inlaid wood, almost more than the eye could take in. My daughter Karen and her family were with us there, and she discovered that the inlaid panels between shelves hinged outward to reveal lists of contents.

Compared to St Gallen, the other two libraries we saw were barren indeed. On the acropolis at Pergamum in Greece there was a stone floor and the stubs of two walls shown on the map to have been the library. At Ephesus there were stubs of columns indicating the facade of the ancient library of Celsus; when I was there again in 2008 the building had been restored, closing the vista of the main street on which much had been restored as well.

The only other library-related part of our travels was a short holiday in Santa Maria, a small village at the eastern tip of Switzerland, where we had arranged to meet Wolfgang Brockhaus and his wife Liselotte; their family name had been firmly attached to the University of Toronto Library since 1892, when the University Senate resolved that the firm of

Brockhaus, publishers and booksellers in Weimar, should become our official agent in Germany. The university's first library, of some 30,000 volumes, had been destroyed by fire on Valentine's Day 1890, and within two years the gifts received from around the world amounted to about 30,000 volumes, of which one-third had been gathered and sent by Brockhaus.

Wolfgang Brockhaus, after being liberated from a Russian prison camp after the Second World War, had revived the book-selling part of the firm in Stuttgart, and begun to make business calls in Canada every year or two. When he stopped in Toronto I used to bring him home to dinner, and our friendship blossomed into an enduring connection between our families, a connection that continues and has given us many happy times in Germany and Switzerland, as well as in Canada and the United States.

On the road from Geneva to Santa Maria, on the first Saturday in October, we took a very secondary road through the valley of Emmenthal. At one point we had to stop to let a family (some members in local costume) drive their cows past us. The first few cows had garlands of asters on their horns, and had cup-shaped cowbells at least eighteen inches across, with a very deep tone. Others had ordinary brass bells about the size and tone of school bells. Close behind this group, another family came past with their herd. At the next village we found the annual cow fair in progress, or just beginning to break up. Just below the road, across from what seemed to be a hotel and town hall, some two or three hundred cows were tied in rows, while various people, including judges in white coats, wandered along the rows. At one end of the field, alongside a rope fence, were large piles of cowbells and swarms of children who were eager to have their pictures taken. The cows were very large, yellow with white patches, and had grazed in high pastures during the summer, up as high as 2000 metres, herded by young boys. The fair was an annual celebration held when the animals were brought back down to the valley; there would be a similar event before they went up again in the spring. We just happened to be in luck to see the celebration, which included the awarding of prizes.

Beyond Emmenthal we stopped in Altdorf. On seeing a larger-than-life statue of William Tell in the square, we recognized it immediately because its picture had been in our school readers. We decided to stop for the night, and put up at an inn named for Tell's famous shot at an apple on his son's head. Before supper, as we went out to view the town, bells were ringing and the whole town seemed to be hurrying toward the parish church. A ten-year-old whizzed past us on his bike and skidded to a stop, just in time to go in with some of his buddies; we followed them in. As Communion began we slipped out and noted that the pews were so full of young and old that dozens were standing along the back wall.

On Sunday morning as we left Altdorf the church bells were busy again and some people were on their way. At the first village uphill the bells were ringing in a smaller church, and there were dozens of families walking toward it, most of the men in blue embroidered jackets. We picked up a young hiker in a business suit, and could not understand a word of his German, but he was on his way up to the next village to join the throng of churchgoers there, in the rain. Beside the road was a large orange signboard with black hand-lettering that said NICHTE OHNE KETTEN. The first two words meant "not without," but I didn't know the meaning of KETTEN, and, thinking it was some kind of advertisement, drove on. Later we found that KETTEN is the word for CHAINS!

From there the road went steadily upwards, quite steep with fairly tight turns, and the rain turned to blinding snow. The one car-track ahead of us became less and less visible, and the mountainside on our left was invisible white. Presently we could not see anything at all except the row of stones or iron pipes spaced along the outer edge of the road, and only the next two or three were visible. There was nothing to do but keep going, just inside the markers. After what seemed a long anxious time we got to the top and a sign that said KLAUSEN PASS 1948M. We met a bus that was stopped there, with the driver and several passengers out putting on chains, and after a moment thought we should perhaps go back and ask them for advice, but found we had no traction for backing up. We decided that if the bus could make it up that far without chains, we should be able to get down safely in first gear, and we did. Near the bottom, with green valleys in sight again, we saw a few skiers. We were very glad to get down among cows and villages. We felt restored enough to laugh at a row of beehives we saw in a small pasture, each box a different colour and with its own large black number; we thought that perhaps they were colour-coded like the catalogue drawers at the Bibliotheque Nationale, for bees that could not read numbers.

We had planned a route to take in two or three other passes that day on secondary roads, but revised our plans and made two wide detours by main routes that took us over the Julier Pass (2284 m) and Ofen Pass (2149 m), both of them higher than Klausen, and both with plenty of snow in sight and wonderful sunny views of the Alps but no snow on the road. Later Mrs Brockhaus, the driver in their family and a veteran of the Swiss passes, said that Klausen was one of the worst and that she had found it so on her one trip over it in summer.

We reached Santa Maria in time for four o'clock tea with Wolfgang and Liselotte Brockhaus, and for a walk along the valley before supper. We saw two chamois in the meadow, at some distance. Next morning I took the Volvo in for its six-thousand-mile service, as prearranged, and Mrs Brockhaus drove us in their BMW for lunch at a hotel in the national park, just west over Ofen Pass, which we therefore saw twice that day.

Santa Maria itself had an elevation of about 1500 metres and was having a very late season. There were haycocks still in the field, and the innkeeper had just got his potatoes picked the day before, in a rush after the first frost. We went to the second village up the valley for dinner at a little hotel from which young Manfred Brockhaus liked to do his mountaineering, and on the way home we encountered a snowstorm. About nine o'clock, as we finished our tea in front of the fireplace, the innkeeper, Konradin, invited us to step outside "to hear the stags roaring" as they began to move down for the winter; we heard them again louder during the night.

Konradin had records of his family back to 1128 in the adjoining valley, and in the lobby of the inn had a framed family tree back to 1600. In the hotel he had an impressive collection of old carved furniture and chests and a fine carved Madonna, also very old. And on a small table by the stairs were two or three old Bibles. The newer one, an early-eighteenth-century Romanche edition printed in Chur, was missing its title page and needed some repair. Brockhaus offered to have a facsimile title page made with paper of the same vintage, and tipped in, but our host declined with thanks. Konradin explained that the title page, which was in red, had been torn out on purpose by an ancestor, to save the Bible. During the Counter-Reformation in those parts, soldiers had gone from door to door inspecting all books and destroying all Bibles (which they recognized by the red title page), because Bibles were forbidden. This copy, because of the missing page, had escaped and was an heirloom, not to be altered.

Tuesday morning there was a good six inches of wet snow on the ground and on the apples just across the road; haycocks were just bumps in the white field. The four of us spent the day on a sightseeing trip down the valley into Italy, where there was no snow and where apple orchards shone red in the sunshine. We visited an old Benedictine monastery and a church that had some wall paintings dating back to the eighth century.

The next morning when we checked out, Konradin called his wife out specially to say goodbye to us. Liselotte and Wolfgang were staying a bit longer. Wolfgang sent us off with his quaint and cherished small finger-wave and "Wiedersehen, So Long!" It was too long, and I am sorry not to have seen him again after that.

Patricia and I had enough unusual experiences during that sabbatical tour to double the length of this book. In the English Lake District we drove up and down Hard Knott Pass, where the sign warned amateur drivers away because the turns were tight and the maximum grade was one-in-three. At John O'Groats at the northern tip of Scotland we boiled water for tea in the back of our car, to keep out of the wind and rain. In Norway, at the twelfth-century Nideros cathedral in Trondheim, we saw my grandparents' marriage certificate. In Finland we slept on bare plywood beds with paper sheets in student-run hostels. At the western tip of Portugal we walked across the stone compass rose on the site of the former navigation school founded by Prince Henry the Navigator. In Split, Yugoslavia, on New Year's Eve, we had a turkey dinner while sitting on our beds because the dining rooms were full; the next morning we walked through the courtyard of Diocletian's palace, which was still in daily use. In Morocco we had camel rides. In Greece I jogged around the track at Olympia on which Nero had been allowed to win an Olympic race, and we visited the small museum at Pella, the ancient capital of Macedonia, where Aristotle was tutor to the boy Alexander who became the Great. In Turkey we drove through the triple gate into Nicaea, where Constantine presided over the first great council of the Christian Church, and at Ephesus we tested the acoustics of the great amphitheatre where the Apostle Paul was shouted down by the silversmiths; near the top row we encountered some restoration work being done by two men with a wheelbarrow. But traditionally, one who goes away on sabbatical leave is expected to bring home some creative bit of scholarly research to show for it, and all I had to show was a Van Dyke beard.

For many years I had carried a briefcase home with me every night, and often two on Fridays, but when we got home I found that the library had got along very well without me for a whole year. After that my briefcases were retired and came out only for special occasions.

21 Retirement

The week before I retired at the end of December 1981, busloads of my staff celebrated by having a banquet in the Great Hall at the Ontario Science Centre, with speeches and the presentation of a mahogany workbench and woodworking tools to go with it. My friend President Jim Ham, former Dean of Engineering and author of a report on mining safety, held a large reception for me at his residence, again with speeches and a gift set of the *Dictionary of Canadian Biography*.

I was given a six-month extension of salary to write a history of the University of Toronto Library, an extension that ended just in time for me to miss an 18 per cent salary increase across the whole university, that would have been a help to my pension. And I was given an office in the University Archives on the top floor of the Rare Book Library. For the first year I went in three days a week, before slowing down. Finally, after about four years, the text was done and then proofread by my three best friends at the university, who had helped make most of the history. Then there was a lapse of four more years until the book was published.

By the time of my retirement, Patricia had established a library in our church and in each of Streetsville's two elementary schools and had finished her part-time work in the library of Lakeshore Psychiatric Hospital; we had eight good years together without any formal employment. Together we delivered Meals on Wheels two or three mornings a week. We continued to attend meetings of the Streetsville Horticultural Society; the year I was chairman of it, we had the final meeting as a party in our garden. We continued to attend the Toronto Symphony, the concert series at the Faculty of Music, and plays at Stratford and

My retirement photo, December 1981.

Niagara-on-the-Lake. With some old Alberta friends we went to an annual series of plays in Hamilton. And we were both on the board of our church in Streetsville.

We also attended the Toronto Round Table that met for lunch in Hart House, and I was chairman of that group for two or three years. We showed some of our travel slides at the Round Table, the Faculty Club, and many other places, including several times at a small travel club in Toronto. We went to monthly lectures for retired staff at University College, and I was chairman of that series for two years. Closer to home we attended an annual series of lectures for Friends of Erindale College. And we went to lectures and other functions at the Rare Book Library. We went fairly regularly to the Faculty Club for the Thursday morning coffee-plus-lunch-plus-speaker event that Jack and Connie Sword had started, an event that continues thirty years later. We also spent time with our children and grandchildren, and drove west to see friends and relatives, in Edmonton, Vancouver, and California. On a month's tour in Europe we picked up Jack and Connie Sword south of London, where they were visiting friends, and took them to Scotland by way of southern France and Bavaria.

We found and enjoyed the Elderhostel program when it was fairly new, a program that has recently changed its name to Road Scholars. It was a program in which a group of up to forty seniors, mostly couples, met for a week at a college or retreat centre. There were three lectures a day, and free time to enjoy the surroundings and companionship. We attended fifteen such weeks, between Arizona and Newfoundland. One of the early ones, at Berea College in Kentucky, has had an important effect on my health; every morning before breakfast it offered a twenty-five-minute program of loosening-up exercises that I still follow nearly every morning, using weights. We went to one Elderhostel in New England when Patricia was wearing a cast over a broken ankle. We often took friends with us, most often the Swords. Jack and I developed a spiel-and-slide show concerning Elderhostel, that we delivered at the Faculty Club and to other groups of seniors in Toronto, and as far afield as two hundred miles. Our last Elderhostel with the Swords was in the Laurel Mountains of Pennsylvania, six months after Patricia's liver cancer had been diagnosed. She was not able to take part in the nature walks, but enjoyed the lectures and played piano as usual for a sing-song on the final evening.

In late October 1989 Patricia wanted to go to Vancouver to visit her sister there, and to go by train to have a last look at the prairies and mountains. The train was delayed for a day by a heavy snowstorm, but we had our books and the Scrabble board with us as usual. We had always enjoyed the game and often played it with the Swords at their home and ours, at their cottage in the YMCA Geneva Park (for which Jack Sword was Chairman of the Board), at our time share suite farther along the lake, and at other places on both sides of the Atlantic. But Patricia and I played it mostly by ourselves; our Scrabble notebook shows the tallies of 555 games in the eight years after my retirement. The final game, in mid-November, was interrupted by her pain.

Patricia's last time out of the house was earlier that month, to attend the formal launching of my book on the history of the University Library, the library that had taken most of my time and thought away from wife and children. Once during her last days she told me that I would have to marry again, but I could not imagine it. I asked for forgiveness of my long neglect of family, but she said only, "We both did what we had to do, and we have done our best." I promised to put each day that I had left to some good purpose. When she died I felt that my own life also had ended.

Over the years, Patricia had begun to write her own family history, going back as far as she could to the origins of her four grandparents, all born in Ontario. She began several times, and started over; there was much overlapping but something unique in each set of notes. I decided to edit the pieces into one, as a memorial volume, and bought my first computer as a flexible typewriter for the task. To fill in as many blanks as possible, and to check on discrepancies, I spent months in federal and provincial archives, church records, cemeteries, the genealogical records in several public libraries, in correspondence and visits with her family connections, and in finding certain buildings and farm sites on the back roads of eastern Ontario. The result was an illustrated book printed at the University of Toronto Press in 1992.

In the meantime there had been other things to do. About two months after Patricia's death, our Streetsville United Church congregation voted to have an every-member canvass. The aim was to raise the level of annual givings in order to change the appointment of the assistant minister from part-time to full-time, and to improve the program in various other ways. At its next meeting the board struggled with the questions of how high the financial target should be set, who should be on the committee to conduct the campaign, and who would chair it. The meeting dragged on until I volunteered to be chairman; I had the time and was the only one there who had ever chaired such a campaign. My offer was made on two conditions similar to those I had set when asked to prepare for the IFLA conference in Toronto: that I would be a one-man committee with authority to enlist help and that the campaign would finish within four weeks, because I had another appointment at the end of that time. (My other appointment was with Jack and Connie Sword, to drive them on a holiday that would give us a week with their daughter in Connecticut, and two weeks at a cottage in Florida.) Both conditions were accepted.

At the end of the first week I presented the board with a plan, in which the target was a 40 per cent increase in annual givings by every family in the church. I gave them a proposed letter of announcement, a leaflet, pledge cards, a plan of operation, and a timetable ending with a victory dinner. After some discussion the board agreed, and chose a place for the victory dinner. Within two more weeks the printing was done and mailed, the captains and visitors recruited, and a selected list of families, with addresses, drawn up for each visitor.

For the final week, in which the canvass took place, I had reserved for myself some of the visits that could be done during the day. Each evening I stayed at the church until ten o'clock, to receive the reports of visitors as they came in. At the closing celebration I was able to announce that we had exceeded the target by $200. And a group of ladies, enthused by the whole process, began planning for all our church families to receive neighbourly visits every three months.

But I was off to New England with the Swords.

The Alberta Articles and a New Life

In August that same year, the General Council of the United Church of Canada adopted a resolution that was contrary to my understanding of what the Church should be and do. I was among those who had been too busy with Church business to notice how far the denomination had wandered from the official covenant around which Canadian Presbyterians, Methodists, and Congregationalists had united in 1925. We saw the council's new resolution as the latest step in a process of secularization that had been going on for some years, based on social pressures rather than Christian doctrine, and we could not accept it. Many prominent members of the denomination had already resigned, and now many members of the Streetsville congregation, including me, were preparing to leave the Church.

I became secretary of the local chapter of the Community of Concern (COC), a national organization of individual members of the Church, formed to resist the drift into various secular byways. We heard of a new document that had been drafted by four young ministers in Alberta, a document that was becoming known as the "Alberta Articles." It was a one-page covenant proclaiming solidarity in support of the traditional Christian faith on which the denomination had been established; by adopting it a congregation could remain in the denomination with integrity and a clear conscience.

One evening with my daughter Karen at the Toronto Symphony, as I sat relaxed, not thinking, my mind simply floating on the music, I was struck by an urgent idea or inspiration. I saw that individual church members, and even their three organizations that had been formed to press in their own particular ways for reform and renewal, had no official voice in the denomination. Congregations, however, were official courts within the structure of the Church, and working together should be able to affect policy within the denomination. My idea was that there should be a national organization of congregations based on the Alberta Articles. I presented the idea to the local chapter of the Community of Concern and to its national chairman, John Trueman, who agreed to strike a planning committee (with me as secretary) to bring it about.

Meanwhile back at Streetsville, where the congregation was wondering what to do, and many of us had been preparing to leave the Church, I presented the Alberta Articles and proposed that we adopt them and become a charter member of a national association of covenanting congregations. The matter was discussed thoroughly, and was to be decided at a special congregational meeting on Sunday, 18 November 1990.

I heard that all United Church congregations in Alberta had been invited to send delegates to a meeting at Devon, just south of Edmonton, to consider the Articles, on that same weekend! I went to Alberta. The little church at Devon was filling quickly when I got there on Saturday morning. At the door, when I told somebody that I needed to speak to the person in charge, he told me to see the attractive red-haired lady in the green top. When I found her she took me to the Devon minister, who said I would be welcome to speak in the meeting, as I saw fit. Looking for an agenda, I was told to ask Verna, who turned out to be the same red-hair-green-top. And I learned later that she was the one who had signed the province-wide invitation to the meeting.

Music for the opening service of worship that morning was provided by a dozen young people singing to guitars; in thanking them the minister made special mention of their leaders being three members of the Morgan family, but I did not make any connection between that name and the green top.

The four ministers who had drafted the Articles were there, and almost forty congregations were represented. As discussion progressed, I spoke about a meeting I had attended in London, at which eighteen ministers had agreed to present the Articles to their congregations for consideration. I said I expected that my home congregation would be voting next day to adopt the Alberta Articles and that Metropolitan Church in London, the largest congregation in our whole denomination, had already done so. At that news the chairman had everybody stand to sing the chorus to "Glory, Glory Hallelujah." Then I explained a few minor alterations to the wording of the Articles that had been adopted in London, and the meeting voted to accept most of the changes.

In the summer of 1991 one of my friends was being transferred from Ottawa to Vancouver; his company would ship only one of his cars, so I offered to drive the other. In every province along the way I took a zigzag route, phoning ahead to make appointments to visit congregations and individuals who had phoned or written for information about the Alberta Articles. Most of them arranged for me to meet with their friends and neighbours in their homes or churches, and many of them gave me bed and breakfast. Through these visits I was able to contact at least forty congregations across the country, or some of their members. Friends in Manitoba arranged for me to be interviewed at the radio station in Brandon.

On 28 September 1991, the National Alliance of Covenanting Congregations (NACC) was formally established, with nearly a hundred congregational members from Vancouver Island to Newfoundland. The four originators of the Alberta Articles were staying at my house and went the hundred miles with me to London for the first general meeting of the alliance, which overflowed the sanctuary of Metropolitan Church. One of my Alberta guests, Rick Prieston, was elected Chairman of the NACC, and I became Secretary. Another of my guests, Bob Aldrich, preached a Good Samaritan sermon that brought all the listeners to their feet.

It was a glorious celebration.

The General Council of the United Church was to meet in Fredericton, New Brunswick, in August 1992. I planned to be there as an observer to help represent NACC, to meet with people from our member congregations and with potential members. I wanted to make it part of a holiday and invited my young grandson Joel to come along on a scenic tour even if it meant shortening my stay at the meeting. He became homesick, however, and flew home from Halifax, leaving me with time free.

In Fredericton the General Council met on the university campus, in the large auditorium. The Community of Concern had rented a second-floor classroom-plus-office in which about a dozen of us, representatives of the four renewal groups, could display our literature and talk with our members and prospective members. In one corner there was a glassed-in office in which John and Dawn Trueman wrote a daily issue of *Concern*, the Community of Concern newsletter, which we all helped distribute each morning to the official delegates as they approached the meeting place. Among the other COC board members there was Verna Morgan, no longer in a green top but obviously the person who had played an important role at that first meeting in Devon church. She was at this council, as she had been at previous councils, as prayer leader for reform and renewal of the Church.

COC had produced a paper banner, perhaps fifty feet long, with a message printed in large black letters. On the first evening of the conference the official delegates were to attend a rally at Fredericton's largest church. As they lined up to enter the church, our banner was held up for them to read, by friends of the COC. In the line of banner holders I happened to stand next to Verna, who was a natural target for news photographers covering the event.

The General Council's meals were not available to outsiders, so we observers went elsewhere to eat. After the COC room closed for the day we often met for supper as a group, reviewed the day's events, and enjoyed one another's company. On one such occasion I made some remark that set the whole company laughing. From her end of the table, Verna said, "Well, I thought librarians were kind of stuffy and severe, but you are quite funny!" I took it as a compliment, and thought no more about it.

When I tired of attending a session of the Council as an observer from the sidelines, I would walk back to the COC room for coffee and a cookie. One day I heard Verna say she was sorry that the conference was so early in the fall, as she had never seen the autumn colours of eastern Canada. A day or two later I noticed a very red maple leaf on the sidewalk, and took it to her, saying, "It's later than you think." I meant only to draw her attention to an autumn leaf, but years later she told me she had taken it as a profound word from God that was being given to her. I often heard her talking about her children, who were apparently numerous and all very talented. Out of curiosity, I said to her, "You talk a lot about your children but not about a husband. Are you alone?" She answered, suddenly in tears, by saying only that she was in the middle of a very painful break-up of her marriage. I was sorry.

For the last day of the council, the agenda looked very dry, and I had decided to leave for home that day. At 8:30 a.m. the day's issue of *Concern* had not arrived from the printer, so I went down from the COC office to wait in my car in case some last-minute conveyance might be needed. Verna had come down to the back door also to be ready, when the printer's courier arrived, to take word upstairs to those who were waiting to do the morning's handout. Finally the courier's van appeared in the distance, so I waved to Verna and drove away. I planned to drive until I was tired and then stop overnight, but it was a beautiful day and the roads clear, so I was home before midnight.

Back home at Streetsville I continued my usual active participation in the local church and dealt with the expanding volume of phone calls and correspondence in connection with my work as secretary-treasurer of the NACC. I was not without a fairly active social life. Old friends, couples and widows, invited me to a meal occasionally, and sometimes I returned their hospitality with invitations to my standard company lunch: oyster soup, salad, and ice cream with banana and raspberry sauce. There were at least four widows, old family friends within an hour's drive, who invited me for meals now and then; I cut down a tree for one of them, refinished a chair for one, and spent an afternoon helping another stir the makings of several fruitcakes, but these were merely friendly gestures as far as I was concerned. I felt that I was still firmly married to Patricia, and would always be so.

In September I was surprised and pleased to receive a letter from my friend Verna Morgan. She was planning to attend a meeting of the Community of Concern as the board member representing Alberta; she was coming a day earlier than usual, on a Thursday, in order to have private conversations with her old friends, our minister Victor Shepherd, and John and Dawn Trueman. She also wanted to see me, in order to apologize eye-to-eye for her insulting remark at supper in Fredericton, about librarians being a stuffy lot. She would be staying at the Shepherd house, and wondered whether she and I could have lunch together on the Friday. Of course I replied that I had taken her remark as a compliment and had thought no more about it. I told her that librarians often joke among themselves about the widespread, old-fashioned public image of their profession. For instance, there was the story of two men trying to guess the occupations of their fellow passengers on a ship; seeing two pale old ladies reading in deck chairs, one man made a small wager that they were librarians, but when they were asked they replied, "No, just seasick." I would however be pleased to have lunch with Verna at a restaurant or at my house, whichever she preferred. And if she needed a lift to Hamilton to see John Trueman I would be glad to take her there.

Thinking it over, I thought I would like to do something more to demonstrate that I really had not been hurt by her remark about librarians. I thought of taking her to see Niagara Falls, but remembered her saying that she had been to a conference there. So I thought of the other place we had often taken visitors from outside Ontario: a play in the Festival Theatre at Stratford. I found that there were tickets available on the Friday evening, but thought I would be more comfortable if I took some of her friends along for company, so that we would not be just a twosome. I thought of Victor and Maureen Shepherd and then of John and Dawn Trueman; they had all known Verna much longer than I had, but they had other plans for that evening. Having already checked with Verna to see whether she would be free for the evening, I ordered the tickets.

When the day arrived I called for Verna at the Shepherd house, in time for an early lunch, and they said the door would be open for her whatever time she got back. Her appointment with the Truemans was for early afternoon, and on the way to Hamilton I found that she had never seen Niagara Falls by daylight, but only after dark during the course of a religious conference in that area. I suggested that if her time with the Truemans could be fairly short, there would be time for Niagara that afternoon. After greeting John and Dawn Trueman at their front door, I excused myself to make a call at the McMaster University Library, which was only a fifteen-minute walk away. When I called back an hour later, Verna bade her friends a teary farewell, and we were off to Niagara. After we had had a good view of the Falls there was still plenty of time to get to Stratford for supper and a look at the Festival Theatre before the performance began. The play was an elaborate performance of *Romeo and Juliet*, with all the surprising mechanics of that theatre, and we quite enjoyed it. By the time I dropped Verna off at the Shepherd house in Streetsville, it had been a long day with much time for talk.

Verna told me that she had needed to talk with Victor Shepherd and the Truemans about the circumstances of her marriage break-up, and she gave me some of the sad details. We exchanged stories about our children, their successes and problems. She told me about the musical worship group led by her children, and the great impression they had made on various audiences in churches, youth camps, even a prison, as she had driven them in her motor home to widely scattered venues in Alberta and British Columbia, summer and winter. It was a very impressive story. She told me about the formation of her Christian faith and about groups she had led in Bible study and in prayer. She had preached in several churches, including her own. Her future was uncertain. She had decided to train for the full-time ministry, had applied to the Alberta Conference of the United Church to approve her as a candidate, and had met twice with their Discernment Committee. At the first meeting they had suggested that she take a course in self-assertiveness as a preliminary hurdle; this suggestion was a great joke among her friends, but she had to take it seriously. At the second meeting they brought out a news photo of her holding up the COC banner at the Fredericton General Council, and made it clear that she could not be admitted as a candidate to study at a United Church seminary unless she renounced her association with the views and activities of such groups as the Community of Concern. She was thinking therefore about entering the lay ministry, for which she could become qualified after two years of supervision and some short courses. The problem was to find a church where she could do this and not be too far away from her children. As far as her marriage was concerned, there was no hope of reconciliation; her friends, including professionals, were urging her to seek a divorce. I was sorry.

Early in 1992, months before the General Council in Fredericton, my young doctor, David Clarkson, had agreed to be the first chairman of a Central Ontario Association of Covenanting Congregations, to match the London Regional Association that had taken form in the western part of the province. By that time we had about twenty NACC congregations in our area. By the end of September all the paperwork had been done and notices were sent out for our first general meeting, to be held on the first Sunday in October in St Jacobs.

In writing to thank me for the day at Niagara and Stratford, Verna had said that she would be coming to Toronto for another COC board meeting the first Saturday in October. She would be spending Sunday in Toronto with old friends with whom she had stayed many times.

Hearing that Verna would be in our area, our committee agreed that it would be a good thing to have her bring greetings to the first meeting of our new regional association, greetings from Alberta and from Devon Church where the covenanting movement had begun. Verna had agreed to do it, so I picked her up in Toronto in time for the meeting.

The old church at St Jacobs was full and the meeting went well. Verna and I had been invited back to dinner with her friends in Toronto, and we had a long evening there. During the evening Verna mentioned that she would like to stay overnight with her friends again in late October on her way to an annual meeting at Guelph, a meeting of the Renewal Fellowship, another renewal group in which she was a board member from Alberta. I offered to drive her there when the time came. As I was leaving, Verna stepped forward and gave me a hug. Our host gave me a wink and said, "Don't worry, it doesn't mean a thing. She hugs everybody."

I was not a member of the Renewal Fellowship, but had already offered to drive some other people to their meeting in Guelph. The Reverend Joe Burton and his wife Carole of Twillingate, Newfoundland, had brought their own congregation into the National Alliance and had influenced several others to join. We had become good friends by mail and telephone, and I was glad to be of some service to them. When I met them at the airport on the appropriate morning they were very tired, having left Twillingate at three o'clock that morning. We picked up Verna and her luggage in Toronto and then came to my house for lunch. I took them to Guelph by a scenic route, by way of Eden Bridge so that they could see a sample of rural Ontario, and found their conference centre in the west end of Guelph. When all three had registered and we had carried the luggage up to their rooms, the Burtons were ready for a long nap. Verna wanted to walk around the property and invited me to join her.

It was mid-afternoon. The brown oaks were casting their shadows on the layer of maple leaves that filled the path around the edge of the property. Verna told me she had been offered the possibility of a two-year position at the big church in Barrie, Ontario. She had been to Vancouver for an interview for a position as youth leader and had received an offer, but as a volunteer without pay! She had been told of an opening in the church at Lac La Biche at the end of the bus line north of Edmonton, and she was thinking about it. She was suffering greatly from the break-up of her marriage and at the loss of family unity among her children. When we had completed one circuit of the grounds and got back to the parking lot, I wished her well and drove away.

But at the curve in the lane I glanced back and saw her still standing in the road, watching me go. I felt a sudden pang of loneliness, and thought to myself that I would miss her company. It was an unexpected feeling, but it would not leave me, and it grew.

When she wrote to thank me for the drive to Guelph, I replied and mentioned some of the things I was doing. We continued to write back and forth occasionally in a friendly manner, and even to telephone when there seemed to be any special news. I was busy with NACC affairs, and had got in touch with many more congregations. She had been up to Lac La Biche to preach and had been well received there; she thought there would be a decision in the new year and that she would be asked to serve there. We discussed the pros and cons of her going to Lac La Biche. I was more and more lonesome for her, but kept that to myself. Finally I decided that I wanted to marry Verna if she would have me.

There was no use in waiting to know my fate. So on the night before New Year's Eve I phoned her to ask her friendly advice on an important personal matter. I said I had decided to marry again, but there were many things to consider. I was lonesome, in a house that was too big for me alone. I needed company, somebody to share my days and nights with, to share ideas, books, music, and travel, somebody to help and advise me. But on the other hand, there were problems. There was a significant difference between our ages. I was 73 and my parents had died at age 76, but my own health seemed to be very good; I could probably expect to have at least five more good years but could not count on it. I had settled into a comfortable bachelor routine; people at my age became set in their ways, had habits that were hard to change and maybe hard to live with. I was not a tidy housekeeper; there were books and papers scattered everywhere in the house. My work as secretary-treasurer of the NACC was really a full-time job, and most days it involved hours on the phone or at the computer. Both I and the woman whom I had come to love, and whom I was hoping to marry, had grown-up children, some with their own problems that would take attention and consideration. And we both had grandchildren to be thought of. My university pension was not great and was only partly indexed to the cost of living, but supplemented by Canada Pension it was more than enough to meet my needs.

After spilling all this information, I said I did not expect her to advise me before she had some time to think about it. But if she thought it would be right for me to marry, as I wanted to do, in spite of an age difference of nearly fifteen years, would she consider doing it herself?

After what seemed a long minute she asked "You mean me?"
"Yes."
After another minute she said, "But I will likely be going to Lac La Biche!"
Having committed myself that far, I was not to be put off so easily, and said rashly that the work I was doing could be done as well in Lac La Biche as in Mississauga. "Whither thou goest, I will go also." Verna replied wisely that we hardly knew each other. She would have to come to Streetsville so we could talk about it. But first she would have to pray about it. There were more phone calls, but she did not tell me the outcome of her prayers.

She did not tell me until long afterwards what her initial reaction had been to my fateful phone call. She had serious misgivings about our difference in ages: How could she keep young herself if married to an old man? She did not want to hurt me and had asked in prayer how she could decline without hurting me? To her surprise she heard the Lord say, "Do not be afraid to marry this man. What I am doing is a good thing." She was used to being obedient to God but did make one request of Him, "that there would be excitement and strong love in our married state." And there has been.

When I saw her at the airport, I knew she had made up her mind. I had arranged for her to sleep at the house of Eleanor Ferguson, widow of a friend with whom I had worked on a new organizational structure for our local church. I called for Verna every morning, and we spent several days in talk, in visiting a few friends, in meeting with my children Karen and Harry (to whom I had already spoken), and driving to Ottawa to meet with Rob. Before flying back to Edmonton, Verna made only three stipulations before she would marry me: first, that I change my horn-rimmed glasses for gold rims; second, that I put a window in the windowless dining room; and third, that I change my Van Dyke to a full beard.

After many more phone calls and letters, I went to Edmonton. My sister Betty, with whom I stayed, invited us to dinner. I met all of Verna's children and their families who were living in Edmonton, and heard their music as they took part in an outdoor street festival. We saw friends in Devon, and drove in Verna's Honda Civic to visit her cousins in Caroline, near Rocky Mountain House. From there we went on to Calgary for the second annual meeting of the NACC. After that we did a day's journey to Vancouver and spent several days with one of Verna's aunts, visiting old friends and other relatives of Verna's and mine. From there we went to the University of Victoria, to take a two-week residential course of training for potential leaders in the two-year course of Bethel Bible Studies. On a free day we drove up to Comox to see the United Church minister there, and in the evening spoke about the NACC to a gathering of two congregations in a church at Qualicum Beach. On the way home we stayed for a couple of days with Frank and Myrt Currie in New Westminster; Frank was the dental officer who had flown with me at the RCAF station at Comox. We drove back to Edmonton in time for an evening meeting with a church group interested in the NACC. So we had given ourselves nearly a month to become better acquainted.

Our wedding date was set for the afternoon of Saturday, 23 September, and invitations were mailed. Verna came a week ahead to stay with Eleanor again, to help me get the house ready for visitors and be sure that all the details were in place. Harry and Trudy gave a family reception at their house on the Friday night, but I missed the last part of it by slipping on the top step and ending up on my back on the basement floor. My doctor was phoned; Verna and Harry drove me to his office, where we waited in the car until he arrived after jogging nearly two miles from the hospital. After making a brief inspection he thought I had not cracked my skull and would be fit for the morrow. So they took me directly to the hotel where I was to sleep that night, my house being full of visitors, before going back to the party.

Next afternoon, the church was full and Victor Shepherd married us. My sister and her daughter and granddaughter had come from Edmonton, also Verna's two sons and her daughter Susan with her family; Verna's two grandchildren were flower girl and ring bearer. My three children were there with their families, all seven of my grandchildren. That evening we had more than a hundred guests at dinner, and music, and dancing until the Rookes, the Swords, and some other guests had to leave for their long trips home. So it was, that nearly three years after I first saw Verna, and two years after we first met at Fredericton, and three-quarters of a year after an unusual kind of phone call, we started a new life together.

Having given up the idea of becoming a lay minister, Verna carried on with her ministry in various forms. The Bethel Bible Studies, for which we had taken the teachers' course at Victoria, consists of thirteen evenings on the Old Testament and another thirteen on the New. Verna led the series twice in our church at Streetsville, with some help from me, and then presented it again for those who preferred afternoon sessions. With some other people from across the continent who had taught or taken part in the Bethel Bible Studies, we had a two-week tour of Israel and Jordan, with the geographical and historical context of the Bible more clearly focused in our minds.

There was also the Alpha course, based on a series of informative and inspirational videotapes, in ten evenings plus one weekend; Verna led that five times in Streetsville, again with some help from me. While I participated in the discussions as much as possible, my main job was to set up tables, arrange for the suppers, and clear away after.

We were both on the Board of the Renewal Fellowship organization, I as treasurer and she as chairman in the year it merged with the National Alliance of Covenanting Congregations. We were both on the Board of *Fellowship Magazine*, of which I was treasurer, and its meetings were often in our dining room. We were both on the Board of the National Alliance, I still as secretary-treasurer until I recruited Geoff Wilkins, a most able layman in Vancouver, to replace me. We continued to drive to the annual meetings of the National Alliance in Newfoundland, British Columbia, and points between.

Verna preached at our church and at several others nearby, as a part of summer supply. A few churches even invited me into their pulpits to speak about the National Alliance. We also attended at least one ecumenical conference a year, one as far afield as Indianapolis, where Verna led a workshop on prayer.

We drove also to Washington, D.C., once or twice a year, to two-day conferences of the Association for Church Renewal. That was a group of leaders of renewal movements in many American denominations; they had been meeting for years to exchange useful information and ideas. We were there when the informal group decided to give itself a formal name and program. But for our presence and intervention the name would have been the American Association for Church Renewal (AACR rather than ACR).

Eventually our own congregation at Streetsville, a founding member of the National Alliance of Covenanting Congregations based on the Alberta Articles, affected by changes in membership and the constant pressures of New Age thought, voted to drop its membership in the National Alliance. Since that membership alone had enabled Verna and me to remain in the congregation with clear consciences, we could do nothing but withdraw and move to a new denomination. Our new congregation (Anglican) is one that has rejected its bishop's departure from

With my sister Betty Mullen, 1986.

With my wife Verna in the mid-1990s.

its understanding of the orthodox faith. The bishop has now forced us out of our building, and at present we meet in rented quarters. We are part of the new diocese of the Anglican Church *in* Canada (not *of* Canada) and are making new friends in a new situation. They have even adopted one of my poems as one of their songs of worship.

Meanwhile, since my retirement thirty-two years ago, my family has helped me find time to publish seven more books.

22 Gardens and Fields

Streetsville, when I moved to this area in 1950, was a country village with a few small family-owned industries. There had been half a dozen mills in the old days, but the only one left was a flour mill, straight across the river valley from our house. It had been owned by a local family for at least three generations and still generated some of its power from the river. We used to walk down into the valley to see the beds of wildflowers, or gather fossils, or watch salmon and trout trying to leap over the dam. Wild geese nested there, and sometimes we would see a beaver, and pointed stumps left with its tooth marks. The valley was an official conservation area, a natural park for the whole neighbourhood. Our boys went down to fish for shiners, and in winter the children learned to skate on the overflow pond.

The mill had six small storage silos below the mill house but was no trouble to us. Occasionally at night we would hear a squeaky pulley, but when I called for the engineer to use his oil can, the squeaks would stop within a few minutes. Then as the village began to be the centre of a large residential area in the new city of Mississauga, the mill grew out of proportion to its surroundings, and its large silos have marched across the valley's greenbelt towards us.

The mill has changed hands two or three times and is now the property of Kraft Foods International. Verna and I joined a campaign to have it moved away to a modern industrial site, but the president of Kraft Canada would not talk to us about the benefits he could gain by such a move. We bought shares in Kraft, one for each of us, and in 2011 we drove to Chicago with our neighbour Peter Orphanos, chairman of the regional chapter of the Sierra Club, to have our say at the annual meeting of Kraft shareholders. I spoke about the need for the mill to move out of the river valley, which is a greenbelt conservation area, and about the danger of a grain dust explosion that could land tons of concrete on the houses along our side of the river. When Verna went to the microphone the chairman intervened, saying that the meeting had already heard from her husband. Verna said, "But you have not heard from me," and proceeded to explain the dangers of carcinogens in the wheat dust and other particles that drift from the mill into our residential area. After the meeting, other shareholders gathered around us to hear more. Verna was interviewed by a news reporter while Peter and I had a meeting with one of the Kraft vice-presidents.

On the road homeward that same day we thought that we had accomplished something for the cause. As the back seat passenger I got to thinking about this book, and in my head composed the preface. In the two years that have passed since the meeting, Kraft Canada has acquired a new president, and our friend Peter Orphanos has died of cancer as many people along our street have done. And to date, the mill continues to run day and night in the same location.

Wherever we go, Verna and I are always on the lookout for fine gardens, and for trees and flowering plants that are new to us or of special interest. For my eightieth birthday she had a red oak planted under my old office window at the University Library. In 2011 she had two purple-leafed beech trees planted in our yard, and in 2012 we put in three more trees, one of them big enough that we needed help with the planting.

We have seen fine gardens on Vancouver Island and in Newfoundland, and points between. We have visited them in Britain and Ireland, as well as in Venezuela, the West Indies, and many parts of Europe and the United States, including on Kauai, the garden island of Hawaii. We drove to an Elderhostel in the Carolinas especially to see a garden there that we had read about. For several years we have been spending February at an island resort on the west coast of Florida; in 2012 we extended the holiday to seven weeks and with side trips covered 6000 kilometres, with Verna as navigator and me at the wheel. As we wended our homeward way, the redbud was just beginning to bloom along the highway.

In Pennsylvania we saw a large potato patch on a farm belonging to an Amish couple, that once belonged to my great-grandfather Cromwell Blackburn. They were using the best fields for their main crop, tobacco, which would have offended my devout Presbyterian great-grandfather. They showed us through Cromwell's barn with the drive-in loft,

With Verna in Norway, 2004.

and spring water still running in a trough through the mangers in his cow barn. Before giving us supper they showed us through the large stone house that he had built before being married in 1853. They even took us up into his attic to see the smoke room he had built there, with a controlled outlet from the chimney for smoking meat.

What I thought was a fine home garden here at Streetsville twenty-five years ago has been changed quite beyond recognition by Verna's talent for design. We have sold part of our lot but have one-sixth of an acre left, still enough for gardens on all sides of the house. There are new trees replacing the old ones that became firewood; new shrubs and perennials have been planted (and transplanted!), having been chosen to give an interesting contrast of leaf and flower from early spring to late fall. And every year we think the whole garden, especially our great magnolia tree, is more beautiful than ever before. Passersby, afoot or awheel, stop to look and sometimes to ask questions.

So far we have done most of the work ourselves, but are reaching a time at which we will need more help. In 2011 we started a new vegetable garden in boxes along the driveway. We have made free-standing trellises for peas and beans; they are patterned after Alberta's oil derricks. I can still use hammer and saw, but in my mid-eighties I did stop splitting up our old oak trees for firewood. At ninety-one, to calm my wife and the neighbours, I put away the extension ladder and promised not to climb up over the roof again to clean the eavestroughs. I am beginning to need a cane very occasionally, but otherwise can carry on much as usual.

In 2012, in spite of sinus problems that required Verna to undergo delicate surgery three times, we entered our front yard in the Mississauga Glorious Gardens Contest, and it ranked among the top five in the city.

Not only our garden, but also the house has changed. What was an unfinished shell in 1950 has been enlarged in half a dozen ways, and partitions have been altered. What used to be Rob's bedroom, and then Harry's, has been enlarged into what we call the library. Besides a wall of books it has a computer and file cabinets, a pull-out sofa, two work tables, a desk, half a dozen chairs of various calibre, and wide windows overlooking the river valley. As I sit here writing I am glad to recall the reply of a famous squire who, when asked whether he had lived his whole life on the same farm, replied, "Not yet!"

Two nights before Christmas in 2000 I was struck without warning by a major heart attack. Two weeks in hospital gave me time and oc-

Our front yard and house, 2011.

casion to write a new poem, as I had done during two previous stints in hospital. The cardiologist would not advise surgery for a man of my age; care and medication might give me a fairly good quality of life for several years. The way he said it gave us visions of a rocking chair in front of the television.

Before we consulted a surgeon, Verna had me write a list of the things I had been doing in the year, and in the two months, before the attack. As he read the first page, the doctor remarked that I seemed to have been functioning at the level of a fifty-year-old. At the end of the second page he raised the bar to "better than most thirty-five-year-olds." He referred me to the chief surgeon at a large Toronto hospital, who agreed to do a triple bypass if we would accept a 10 per cent chance of failure. During the operation he found a way to make a connection that turned the triple into the equivalent of a quadruple bypass. On what was to have been my last day of a week in the hospital, I got to thinking about the famous ancient library in Alexandria, Egypt. The account of its total destruction, as I had read it in the *Encyclopedia Britannica* years before, did not seem entirely plausible. Suddenly I thought of a way by which an enterprising librarian might have saved (and possibly did save) some part of that great collection, leaving it still to be found in its hiding place. In some excitement, I called for pencil and paper, and began writing an article explaining my idea.

During that night I awoke, feeling so sick that I began to think I might never be able to finish the article. Verna had been staying at or near the hospital all week but had gone home that night to prepare for my arrival. When she came next morning, expecting to take me home, she was told by medical staff that I had a severe streptococcus bacterial blood infection and could not be moved. Having been a medical laboratory technologist, she knew what serious trouble I was in. Of course she prayed, and enlisted the prayers of people in our church, and other people in Canada, the United States, England, and Australia. When I was fit to go home at the end of another week, the doctor told her that they had nearly lost me and that my survival was really a miracle.

The Alexandrian article was finished that summer and was published in a reputable journal of library history, in Britain. When the publisher wanted me to give him the copyright, I reserved the film and television rights; he agreed on condition that he be given a bit part in any such production.

There is an old saying that you can take a boy away from the farm, but you can't take the farm out of the boy. As a farm boy I keep

My son Harry, recipient of the Lifetime Achievement Award, Ontario Heritage Trust, 2011.

Gardens and Fields 287

With Verna in Florida, celebrating my ninety-fourth birthday.

watching for fields of grain. Between Streetsville and Toronto I do not see them, not anymore. But as we drive westward towards Stratford there are still many fields, mostly of corn, and still some wheat and occasionally oats, but barely any barley.

Sometimes I think about a particular field of barley in a very dry summer, long ago, the only barley my father ever planted. It was a poor-looking stand, but by a blessed miracle turned out to be more valuable than I could ever have imagined. I wonder what my life would have been without that field of barley.

Works by Robert H. Blackburn

Books

Newfoundland Supplement to the Encyclopedia of Canada. Toronto: University Associates of Canada, 1949. Compiler and editor. 104pp.
Joint List of Serials in Toronto libraries. Toronto: University of Toronto Press, 1953. 602pp. Editor.
Evolution of the Heart: A History of the University of Toronto Library up to 1981. Toronto: University of Toronto Library, 1989. 375pp.
Patricia Gibson Blackburn: Her Memoirs and Her Ancestry in the Families Chalmers, Edwards, Gibson, Godwin. Toronto: University of Toronto Press, 1992. 132pp. Private printing.
Dear Lila: Life on an Alberta Farm in 1925 as Recorded in Letters Saved by Lila Blackburn. Toronto: Thistle, 2008. 95 pp. Private printing.
Palma Olson Blackburn, 1888–1965: Her Family and Her life. Toronto: Thistle, 2009. 67pp. Private printing.
Against the Snow, and Other Stories and Poems. Toronto: Thistle, 2012. 110pp. Private printing.
Sir Francis Drake's Last Voyage: A Verse-Drama. Toronto: Thistle, 2012. 28pp Private printing.

Articles, Reports, Briefs, Architectural Programs, etc.

"A Study of Masefield's Imagery." Unpublished MA thesis, University of Alberta, 1941. 247pp.
"Branch Library Size and Geographical Range of Service; A Case Study." Unpublished MS thesis, Columbia University, 1948. 73pp.
(with May Newton) "A Punched-Card Charging System," *Canadian Library Association Bulletin,* September 1949, 40–2.

"Radio in Canada," *Food for Thought* [Canadian Association for Adult Education], March 1950, 23–7.
"Operation USA," *Canadian Library Bulletin*, May 1952, 166–7.
"Operation Europe," *Canadian Library Bulletin*, July 1952, 8–9.
"The Job So Far," *Canadian Library Bulletin*, August 1953, ii–iii.
Annual Reports of the University of Toronto Library, published annually by the Library, 1960 to 1974 and 1976–1981.
"The Sigmund Samuel Library," *University of Toronto Bulletin*, Winter 1955. Reprinted as a separate pamphlet.
(with Elizabeth Dafoe, Neal Harlow, and Edna Hunt) "Canadian documentation," *Future of Bibliography and Documentation*, Canadian Library Association Occasional Paper no. 7, 1955. 7–10.
"Pioneers! O Pioneers" (citation presenting Wilhelm Munthe with an honorary degree in November 1954), *Canadian Library Association Bulletin*, December 1955, 119.
"What Happens to My Membership Fees?" *Feliciter* (Canadian Library Association), January 1957, 3–4.
"Next Year," *Canadian Library Association Bulletin*, September 1958, 74–6.
Report prepared for the Library Expansion Committee of the Board of Regents, Victoria University, 1958. 56pp.
"Libraries in Canada Today," *Royal Architectural Institute of Canada Journal*, April 1959, 99.
"Canadian Library Association," *Stechert-Hoefner Book News*, November 1959, 29–31.
"Status of Library Development in Canada, 1962," in Canadian supplement to *Britannica Book of the Year*, 1961, 26–7.
Building program for the Centennial Public Library, Streetsville, Ontario, October 1964. 12p.
"Je suis soldat." *Proceedings of the 19th Conference, Canadian Library Association*, 1964, 21–2.
(with Brian Land and Doris Lewis) "Forecast of the Cost of Academic Library Service in Canada, 1965–1975," brief to the Bladen Commission on the Financing of Higher Education, sent by the Canadian Association of College and University Libraries, 1964. 37pp.
"On Producing Catalogues in Book Form for Five Libraries at Once," Canadian Library Association Occasional Paper no. 48, Ottawa, 1965, 20–2.
Program for the Construction of a Building to House the Humanities and Social Sciences Research Library and the School of Library Science, University of Toronto, 1965. 77p.
"Convocation Address, University of Waterloo," *Feliciter* (Canadian Library Association), November 1965, 8–15.

"Planning Academic Libraries," *Journal of the Royal Architectural Institute of Canada*, February 1966, 33.

Brief to the Spinks Commission on Higher Education in Ontario, February 1966. 4pp.

"German University Libraries," *Newsletter #5*, Canadian Association of College and University Libraries, May 1966.

Preface to *The Way of the Makers* by F.M. Salter, ed. H.V. Weekes. Edmonton: University of Alberta, 1967. lv.

"Program for Construction of a Library Resource Centre," Ryerson Polytechnical Institute, May 1968. 41pp.

"Report of the Chairman of the Board of Directors," in Nineteenth Annual Report, Center for Research Libraries, Chicago, 30 June 1968, 3.

"Elizabeth Homer Morton, on Her Retirement as Executive Director of the Canadian Library Association," *Ontario Library Review*, June 1968, 92. Also in *Canadian Library*, July 1968, 9–10.

"The Library and Its Users, a Cautionary Tale," in *Librarianship in Canada, 1946–1967: Essays in Honour of Elizabeth Homer Morton*, ed. Bruce Peel. Ottawa: Canadian Library Association, 1968. 196–202.

"University as Stimulation, Adventure, and Collection of Knowledge," *The Varsity* (University of Toronto Students' Administrative Council), 26 February 1969, 6.

"Financial Implications of the Downs Report on Canadian Academic and Research Libraries," Association of Universities and Colleges of Canada, Ottawa, 1969. 49pp.

"Automation and Building Plans," *Library Trends*, October 1969, 262–67.

Brief to the Canadian Interdepartmental Committee on Copyright, 10 April 1970. 35pp.

"Canadian Content in a Sample of Photocopying," *Canadian Library Journal*, September–October 1970. Also in *Scholarly Publishing*, October 1970, 49–58. Also in *Library Lit – the Best of 1970*, ed. Bill Katz and J. Schwarz. Washington: Scarecrow, 1971, 146–59.

"For Argument's Sake! On the Right of Libraries to Import Books," *Quill and Quire*, 23 October 1970, 5.

Brief to the Ontario Royal Commission on Book Publishing, May 1971, 16pp and 9 appendices.

"Openness of University Libraries in Ontario," *Ontario Library Review*, June 1971, 87–9.

(with M. Scott and B. Hardie) A Brief to the Royal Commission on Book Publishing, *Canadian Library Journal*, July–August 1971, 306–7.

"Wild statements" (letter to the editor), *Saturday Night*, August 1971, 2.

"Of Mice and Lions and Battleships and Interlibrary Things: A Theorem of

Inter-Loan Advantage," *IPLO Quarterly* (Institute of Professional Librarians of Ontario), October 1971, 68–79. Also in *Library Lit – the Best of 1972*. Washington: Scarecrow, 1973. 181–93.

"Interlibrary Co-operation," in *Research Librarianship: Essays in Honor of Robert B. Downs,* ed. Jerrold Orne. New York: Bowker, 1971. 51–73.

"John P. Robarts Library" (illustrated pamphlet prepared for the opening in 1973). 16pp.

"Robarts: More Than a Library," *University of Toronto Graduate* 1, no. 11 (October 1973).

"University of Toronto Library External Record Services," *Ontario Library Review,* June 1974, 90–5.

"Two Years with a Closed Catalog," in *Minutes of the Ninety-Second Meeting, 4–5 May 1978*. Washington: Association of Research Libraries, 1978. 40–9. Also in *Freezing Card Catalogs*. Washington: Association of Research Libraries, 1978. 45–64. Also in *Journal of Academic Librarianship* (January 1979): 424–9.

"Management Experience with COM Catalogs in a Large Academic Library," in *Requiem for the Card Catalog,* ed. D. Gore et al. Westport: Greenwood, 1979. 123-40

"Library Cutbacks, Blackburn Speaks Out," in *University of Toronto: How's It Doing?* University of Toronto Students Administrative Council, 1980.

"Blackburn Family," in *Vegreville in Review*. Vegreville and District Historical Society, 1980. I:333–38.

"Robarts Library and Fisher Library, University of Toronto," paper presented at the preconference on Canadian library buildings, at the International Federation of Library Associations, Frankfurt-am-Main, 1982. 24pp.

"The Development of Canadian Academic Libraries Since 1947," in *Canadian Contributions to Library and Information Science,* Occasional paper #8, McGill University Graduate School of Library Science, Montreal, 1984. 7–14.

"Accreditation," *Feliciter* (Canadian Library Association), November 1984, 12.

"Origin of the Canadian Historical Review," *Canadian Historical Review,* December 1984, 542–6.

"Winifred Glen Barnstead, 1884–1985," *Focus* (Ontario Library Association), October 1985, 16–17.

"Origins of the University of Toronto Press in the University Library, 1888–1934," in *Readings in Canadian Library History* (Canadian Library Association, 1986), 167–73.

Convocation Address, McGill University, 11 June 1986, *McGill University Libraries Gazette,* Special Issue, June 1986.

Report of a Review of the National Collection, Carried Out for the Canada Institute for Scientific and Technical Information, 19 November 1986.

News release: "National Study of Photocopying in Canadian Libraries," draft for Canadian Association of Research Libraries, 1987. 12p.

"Dewey and Cutter as Building Consultants," *The Library Quarterly*, October 88, 377–84.

"Mackenzie King, William Mulock, James Mavor, and the University of Toronto Students' Revolt of 1895," *Canadian Historical Review* 4 (1988): 490–503.

"Reminiscences," *Library Editions* (University of Alberta Library), Winter 1989, 4–5.

"Crossroads: Five Options as Seen by a Layman," *Fellowship Magazine*, May 1991, 2.

"A New View of Congregational Opinion about Ordaining Homosexuals," *Theological Digest and Outlook*, July 1992, 118–19.

"New Claims for Presbyteries," *Fellowship Magazine*, March 1998, 18–20.

"Things Are Not Always What They Seem, re the M&S Fund," *Concern* (Community of Concern within the United Church of Canada), 18 August 2000, 3–4.

"How Do Trends Affect the Mission and Service Fund?", *Fellowship Magazine*, September 2000, 17.

"Convocation Address," *University of Toronto Library News*, 20 June 2002.

Stories

"Recipe for Pork," *The Atlantic Monthly*, July 1947, 66–9. Also in *The New Trail* (University of Alberta Alumni Association), August 1949, 164–9. Also in *Varsity Graduate* (University of Toronto), May 1950, 31–7. Also in *Prose and Poetry for Canadians—Adventures* (Toronto: Dent, 1951), 527–33.

"Next Year for Sure," *Maclean's Magazine*, February 1949, 16–17, 37–8.

"The Clay Dish," in *Canadian Short Stories*, ed. Robert Weaver and Helen James. Toronto: Oxford University Press, 1952. 28–36 (first read by John Drainie on *CBC Short Story*). Also in *The Eye of the Beholder*, ed. by B. Vance. Toronto: Thomas Nelson, 1970. 107–14.

"Against the Snow: A Story for Christmas," *CBC Times*, December 1953 (first read on *CBC Short Story*, December 1952, and repeated there at least once; read again on *CBC Matinee*, 24 December 1953).

"Between Me and the Dark," *Queen's Quarterly*, Spring 1954, 61–70.

"The Secret," read on *CBC Short Story*.

"The Ancient Alexandrian Library: Part of It May Survive," *Library History* (journal of the Library History Group), March 2003, 23–34.

294 Works by Robert H. Blackburn

Poems

"Hard Times," *Vegreville Observer*, c. 1932.
"Dust," *Gateway Literary Supplement* (University of Alberta Students Union), c. 1940.
"Sonnet," *Alberta Poetry Yearbook, 1940–41* (Canadian Authors Association, Edmonton Branch), 11.
"Moraine Lake," *Canadian Home Journal,* September 1941, 29 (second prize in a national literary contest sponsored by Women's Canadian Club, Toronto). Also in *The New Trail* (University of Alberta Alumni Association), November 1942. Also in *Prose and Poetry for Canadians – Enjoyment.* Toronto: Dent and Sons, 1951, 350. Also in *Panorama: Western Canadian Literature for Youth* (Alberta Education Department, 1979), 142.
"Prayer before Battle," accepted by *The Canadian Forum,* 15 April 1942, but not published.
"Parting," *Canadian Home Journal,* June 1942, 25.
"Leaves," *Canadian Home Journal,* October 1942.
"September," in *Greetings from No. 4 Initial Training School, RCAF* (#4 ITS, Edmonton), 1943.
"Ambition," *Canadian Home Journal,* February 1943, 30.
"Summer Night," *Canadian Home Journal,* July 1944, 32.
"Continuity," *The New Trail* (University of Alberta Alumni Association), January 1946, 20. Also in *Anthology Eighty,* ed. John Chalmers (Canadian Authors Association, Edmonton Branch), 1980.
"Gleaners," *Here and Now,* December 1947, 75.
"Jetplane," *Queen's Quarterly,* Autumn 1954, 365.
The Dying Dragon (verse drama), CBC Wednesday Night, 2 May 1956. 28pp. produced by J. Frank Willis, with Francis Drake played by Barry Morse.
"Leavings," *Queen's Quarterly,* Winter 1983, 971.